Matthew Arnold
THE ETHNOLOGIST

By
FREDERIC E. FAVERTY

NORTHWESTERN UNIVERSITY PRESS
EVANSTON, ILLINOIS
1951

NORTHWESTERN UNIVERSITY STUDIES

VIRGIL B. HELTZEL, *Editor*

Humanities Series Number Twenty-Seven

Open access edition funded by the National Endowment for the Humanities/Andrew W. Mellon Foundation Humanities Open Book Program.

Frederic E. Faverty. Matthew Arnold The Ethnologist.
Evanston, Ill.: Northwestern University Press, 1951.

ISBN 978-0-8101-3838-4 (paper)
ISBN 978-0-8101-3839-1 (ebook)

To

Margaret

Preface

This book deals with some of the maddest of theories and one of the sanest of men—nineteenth-century racial doctrines and Matthew Arnold. It seems strange to associate Arnold with madness in any form, and actually the racial doctrines of his day can be charged only with being erroneous. But the error of one generation too often becomes the madness of the next, so that Spenser's comment on the Knight of the Red Crosse, "God helpe the man so wrapt in Errours endlesse traine," can be applied to nations as well. Little did the philologist dream that in promoting his researches he would unsettle the world. Yet such—because of the identification of language with race—has been the result. Nor did the anthropologists know that by their distinction between long heads and round heads they would revive the Neanderthal in man. Upon the findings of these sciences the extreme nationalists—the chauvinists, the jingoists—seized, bending them to their purpose; the same sciences through whose "gentle ministration" Arnold sought to bring a "message of peace."

The racial and national issues dealt with in the following pages are almost as controversial today as they were in Arnold's time. Even yet, after the Franco-Prussian War and two world-wide conflicts, France and Germany have not composed their differences. England and Ireland have separated seemingly to dispute the more. And the role of Semitic culture in the western world is still a subject of debate. On all these matters I have tried to be impartial. I am, I hope, neither a Celt-lover nor a Celt-hater; neither an Anglophile nor an Anglophobe. If in recording the controversies of the nineteenth century I am at times in spite of my intention betrayed into partisanship, it is because the way of the disinterested critic is hard, so hard, in fact, that Arnold himself failed of complete success.

To three friends who read this work in manuscript and offered suggestions by which I have profited I wish to express my thanks: Professor E. K. Brown, of the University of Chicago; Professor V. B. Heltzel, of Northwestern University; and Professor Leon Howard, of the University of California, Los Angeles.

Evanston, Illinois F. E. F.
October 1, 1950

Contents

Chapter I

Introduction

The history of the controversies among the learned on the vexed problem of racial origins has been written.[1] As yet, however, no attempt has been made to trace the course of these opinions in the literature of the nineteenth century. Although the work of literature is, as Arnold says, one of synthesis and exposition rather than of analysis and discovery, it is not for that reason less important. That it may be received of men, the jargon of the schools and the laboratory must, as a rule, be translated into the "effective and attractive combinations" of literature. Through Shakespeare, Holinshed gains the ear of the world; through Huxley, Darwin finds a public voice, and argues with bishops and a prime minister. Renan's *The Poetry of the Celtic Races* and Arnold's *On the Study of Celtic Literature* have had their due share in the spread of heat as well as light on racial questions.

It must be admitted at the start that Arnold was no systematic racialist. Almost to the end of his life, he delighted in repeating the charge made against him in the 'sixties by Frederic Harrison that he was a writer "without a philosophy, based on inter-dependent, subordinate, and coherent principles." With the men of a school, of a system, the Rabbis, as he called them, in whatever field, he had little sympathy. He was no haunter of Social Science Congresses, and though he dabbled in ethnology, he evidently never thought it worth his while to attend a meeting of The Ethnological Society. Having rescued Wordsworth from the philosophers, he would probably in turn wish to be rescued from the scientists, certainly from the pseudo-scientists. The fact remains, however, that much of his work is based on the anthropological and ethnological theory of his day.

In a sense the chief labor of Arnold's life is ethnology, the study of the "cultures" of human groups. It is natural, therefore, that he should turn to "the pregnant and striking ideas of the ethnologists" for support. In a letter to his mother, where, if anywhere, a mild self-laudation should be permissible, he boasts that his poetry represents "the main movement of mind in the last quarter century," that he has applied such powers as he possesses "to the main line of modern development." The comment serves equally well for his prose. One of the most pervasive of the contemporary intellectual movements was the explanation of national traits on the basis of race. To this theory, which earlier had seduced such eminent historians as Niebuhr, the Brothers Thierry, Carlyle, Michelet, Mommsen, and his own father, Arnold became a convert. As early as 1859, the correspondence reveals him, already half persuaded, at the feet of the eloquent oracle Renan. Thereafter, to the close of his career, none of his major books is free of speculation on the subject. At the beginning, in *The Popular Education of France* (1861), he is inclined to reject the racial explanation of national differences as inadequate. The hypothesis proves too alluring, however, to be dismissed peremptorily and permanently. In *A French Eton* (1864) he again plays tentatively with the idea. By 1867 he has become a full-fledged convert: *On the Study of Celtic Literature* gives the most explicit and fullest expression to the articles of his creed. In *Culture and Anarchy* (1869), the newly-espoused belief is employed as occasion demands. Always, however, he is ready to take issue with his fellows in the Faith when their zeal outruns their discretion, as is shown in *Essays in Criticism* (1865) and *Literature and Dogma* (1873). His own more temperate position is defended in *God and the Bible* (1875). Ten years later, in *The Discourses in America*, he stands still firm in the received tradition.

Few of England's major authors have devoted as much attention as has Arnold to the study of national characteristics. "And we, then, what are we? what is England?" he asks in *On the Study of Celtic Literature*. A formidable question! And the one hundred and thirty-seven pages of the Celtic studies did not suffice for an answer. In fact, much of his prose work in varying degrees is concerned with the problem. Nor did Arnold rest in mere analysis. He addressed himself further to the important task of improving the English race and the national culture. And this end, he says, can be reached only by disinterested study of things "that are outside of ourselves." Hence his concern with other countries, other cultures. At the age of twenty-seven, in a sonnet on the Hungarian struggle for freedom, he presents his first review of the nations.

> Not in sunk Spain's prolong'd death agony;
> Not in rich England, bent but to make pour
> The flood of the world's commerce on her shore;
> Not in that madhouse, France, from whence the cry
> Afflicts grave Heaven with its long senseless roar;
> Not in American vulgarity,
> Nor wordy German imbecility—
> Lies any hope of heroism more.
> Hungarians! Save the world!

His first pamphlet deals with England's part in the Italian question, in 1859 a matter of gravest European importance. His next work is a book on the popular education of France. In the pattern thus set, he continues to the close of his career. For such comparative studies, he was eminently fitted by training and experience. As a boy, he visited the Continent on a number of occasions in the company of his father, himself a diligent student of other peoples and cultures. At Rugby, one of the innovations was the emphasis upon modern languages, particularly French and German, in addition to the customary regimen of Greek and Latin. In 1859 and 1860, 1865 and 1885–6, he spent a great deal of time in Europe as a commissioner investigating continental education. He made two extended visits to the United States. In addition, he had hostages in various parts of the world: one brother in India, another in Tasmania, a brother-in-law who served for several years under Gladstone as chief secretary for Ireland. His daughter, Lucy, married an American and moved to New York; a son, idle at Oxford, he sent to Australia to learn discipline as a clerk in a Melbourne bank. Strong antidotes, all these, to insularity and provincialism.

Because of his habitual use of the comparative method, Arnold's patriotism has often been impugned. The "disinterestedness" which he advocated and practiced has been interpreted as disloyalty to the nation of his birth. His reports on continental education aroused the protests of indignant patriots. The *Edinburgh Review* found the whole tone of *Popular Education in France* (1861) in its praise of the bureaucratic continental spirit "painful and repugnant to the mind of every liberal Englishman."[2] *Schools and Universities on the Continent* (1868) met with a similar reception, Arnold again being arraigned for advocating bureaucracy. "We would rather remain barbarians than purchase civilization at such a price," says the reviewer, who objects further to Arnold's finding everything foreign good and everything English bad.[3] In commenting on the same report, the *Athenaeum* censures Arnold for putting on such airs and despising all English institutions that fall short of an imaginary Franco-Prussian ideal.[4] The *Contemporary Review* is even more hostile. The result of English education, it says, has been an unquestioned moral superiority; the result of French education has been a moral degeneracy equally unquestioned. In scholarship, the English because they think things through thoroughly are superior to the Germans who hasten into print. Arnold in regarding English ignorance as nearly total and absolute does his country scant justice.[5] The *Saturday Review* grants that its love of country is a prejudice, but is certain that such patriotism is everywhere preferred to a cosmopolitanism such as Arnold's, for "the citizen of the world is nowhere a very popular character."[6] It is reviews like these that cause Arnold in 1866 to use the pages of the *Pall Mall Gazette* "to disclaim that positive admiration of things foreign, and that indifference to English freedom, which have often been imputed to me."[7] But the disclaimer had little effect. Seven years later, Herbert Spencer attacks Arnold's "anti-patriotism" as an affectation. In speaking slightingly of what is English, Arnold is trying to give the impression, says Spencer, that he has great knowledge of what is foreign, and to gain a reputation for culture. Furthermore, his unpatriotic statements in *Essays in Criticism* and in *Culture and Anarchy* show that his culture is exclusively literary. Spencer then proceeds to review the sciences—abstract, abstract-concrete, and concrete—in evidence that the English are not, as Arnold charges, deficient in ideas.[8] It is the opinion of *Blackwood's Magazine* in 1873 that Arnold is an amateur theologian who, not content with misrepresenting God, completely misrepresents the British character as well.[9] For recommending lucidity to the British nation in 1882, Arnold is ridiculed by the *Saturday Review*. The term is considered to be simply another of his vagaries. His originality again leads him down un-English paths.[10] And in the same year, the *Saturday Review*, discussing *Irish Essays and Others*, rebels at another lecture on the old theme of Irish urbanity as against English inurbanity. In the reviewer's opinion, the Philistine English merchant is a more urbane individual than the proverbial French journalist or the German professor.[11] Even Swinburne, delighted as he is at the onslaughts against the "dull, dumb" Briton, reproves Arnold for bending the knee in such deferential fashion to the French Dagon.[12] In 1904, the *Edinburgh Review* patriotically defends England's love of the practical and its distrust of theory against Arnold's method, which, it thinks, is theoretic and doctrinaire in the extreme French manner.[13] To the distinguished critic, Sir Walter Raleigh, Arnold is lacking in affection for England. He is "a well-bred, highly cultivated stranger."[14] In *The History of English Patriotism*, Wingfield-Stratford devotes a chapter to "The Waverers." Arnold is first in the list. His culture and his pose as a disinterested spectator are equally displeasing to Wingfield-Stratford, who finds it impossible to approve of a critic who discovers only faults in his fellow-countrymen and only virtues in foreigners. Arnold is accused of seizing every opportunity to glorify some other country at the expense of his own. His sneers at England would have been ungenerous in a foreigner; in an Englishman, they are unpardonable.[15] Discussing the essay on Wordsworth, Lane Cooper, the American critic, takes exception to Arnold's alien standards and witnesses.[16]

On the Continent, critical opinion has been divided between those who commend Arnold on his cosmopolitanism and those who condemn him on his insularity. Among those of the first group is Louis Etienne. He draws a forceful contrast between Hazlitt and Arnold. In their comments on English society both range over the European field for illustrations, but toward what different ends! Hazlitt, always the Englishman, employs foreign contrasts to prove the virtue of things English. Arnold, the cosmopolitan, employs such contrasts to underline the defects of his countrymen. Although Arnold places the current literature of his country below that of France, finds original imperfections in the Anglo-Saxon race, faults in the English language, defects in the constitution and serious inconveniences in the prevailing utilitarian spirit, it does not follow, therefore, that one must consider him an "intelligence qui s'est dénationalisée." He is simply following the practice of other good Englishmen like Carlyle.[17] Etienne's view of Arnold as a cosmopolitan is shared by other critics of the *Revue des deux mondes*, and by Edmond Schérer in *Études sur la littérature contemporaine.* On the other hand, Albert Réville and Maurice Vernes find *Literature and Dogma* an example of English insularity.[18] In Germany, Hermann Levy regards Arnold as a cosmopolitan. No country, says Levy, is so willing as England to satirize itself. But most of the satirists stay within English bounds. Few go for their models outside

England itself. In this, Arnold differs from his fellows and he has paid the price in unpopularity. Like the later satirists, Shaw, Wilde, and Viscount Haldane, he is regarded by his countrymen as un-English.[19] Another German critic, Johannes Renwanz, however, refuses to grant Arnold a place among the cosmopolitans. Rather, he is a nationalist. All his efforts are bent toward raising the cultural level not of Europe, but of England. Renwanz, therefore, calls his chapter on this phase of Arnold's activity "Der nationale Zug in Arnolds Kulturkampf."[20]

In this disputation, the palm need not be awarded to either side. As the following chapters will show, Arnold is always a rather elusive figure, an alien in every group in which he moves, a member, but always with a difference. Just as he is a liberal, but a liberal of the future, a Philistine, but with leanings toward the Barbarians, so he is a lover of France, but with a keen eye for her failings, an admirer of Germany, constantly dismayed at her bourgeois way of life, a defender of the Jews, who would divest their one book of its turbid Rabbinic fancies, a champion of the Irish who praises their Celtic nature and their literature but at the same time denies them political autonomy. Of such a man it is certainly unjust to say that he is blind to the faults of every country except his own. He does indeed, as T. S. Eliot says, "build a bridge across the channel," but he is never under the delusion that Elysium is to be discovered on the other side.

Although Arnold is no nationalist in Kingsley's sense, chanting the virtues of the church, the country, and the crown, there can be no question of his patriotism. His ironic and satiric method has for some observers obscured his patriotic intentions. His talent, like that of Voltaire, "breathes most in ridicule." He does not sing with Roebuck the "fine old English stave about 'self-reliance.'" The iridescent dream of the *Times* "that the fabled life of the Happy Islands is already beginning amongst us" he does not share. Nor with Tennyson will he celebrate "'the great broad-shouldered genial Englishman,'" who by his patience, his devotion to duty, and his respect for law saves Britain from the revolutions "which upset other and less broad-shouldered nations." Arnold's method is different. Nations, like heroes, he says, are what they are, by their limitations as well as by their powers, by what they lack as well as by what they possess. Knowing that there is always a sufficient chorus to celebrate England's powers, he assumes the thankless task of calling attention to her limitations. It is to enable England to run at her best in the international race, that he points out "how many clogs she wears." It is "to enlarge and complete" the being of his countrymen that he praises the qualities of Greek, Latin, and Celtic authors. He takes for granted the relative soundness of the other members of the body politic, and, like a good physician, concentrates upon the national Achilles' heel. The English heart, for example, is "very well off," though English conduct in India and Jamaica, he adds parenthetically, is not the best instance in proof. When the "fumes of patriotism" grow too hot in the heads of his contemporaries, English, French, or American, he is inclined to smile. There are, of course, serious drawbacks involved in the use of the satiric method, as Arnold, later in life, professed to realize. In his lecture, *Numbers*, delivered in America in 1883, he begins "to reflect with tender contrition, that perhaps I have not,—I will not say flattered the patriotism of my own countrymen enough, but regarded it enough. Perhaps that is one reason why I have produced so very little effect upon them. It was a fault of youth and inexperience." In the five years of life that followed, however, he did not reform. He remained unregenerate, confirmed in irony to the end. But to the discerning it is obvious that he is a true patriot. His are the faithful wounds of a friend. In fact, his castigations of England are a higher and subtler form of flattery, for they are made on the assumption that the nation is great enough to be above the need of flattery.

The determination of racial characteristics is, as Arnold himself remarks, a "delicate and inward" matter. Equally difficult is the determination of national characteristics. Indeed, authorities to the present day are not even agreed on what constitutes a nation. Arnold enters resolutely into the subtleties and distinctions involved in these problems. But he enters, and emerges, without a precise definition of basic terms. No word, perhaps, appears more frequently and loosely in his writings than *race*. The term is employed to denote now physiological differences among peoples, again, spiritual and cultural ones. The race and the nation are identified. Thus, the Germans are Teutons, the French are Celts, and the English are a mixture of the two.[21] Against such confusion in the use of words denoting nations and races, Renan, in his illuminating lecture, *What Is a Nation?* (1882), warned the world, though he himself had been guilty of the practice earlier in his career. Arnold, through life a faithful reader of the great Frenchman's works, presumably did not read this lecture. At any rate, he did not follow its precepts. And as a result, he falls, as he had fallen earlier, into many of the errors prophesied by Renan for those who confound the nation with the race, or who, in the case of the British Isles, inquire too closely into the mixture of Celtic and Teutonic blood, "the relative proportions of which it is singularly difficult to define."

As ambassador-at-large in that great intellectual and spiritual confederation which for him was Europe, Arnold is distinguished from many of his contemporaries by his motives. One of his chief aims is conciliation. Even when his facts are wrong, or his premises unsound, or his conclusions questionable, his animating purpose is usually right. He desires not to divide races or nations, but to bring them together. Ignorance and insularity, he believes, accompany each other. He therefore advocates a fuller understanding among nations, and a freer interchange of ideas. These purposes are clearly stated as early as 1861 in the Introduction to *Popular Education in France*.

> It seems to me, then, that one may save one's self from much idle terror at names and shadows if one will be at the pains to remember what different conditions the different character of two nations must necessarily impose on the operation of any principle. That which operates noxiously in one, may operate wholesomely in the other; because the unsound part of the one's character may be yet further inflamed and enlarged by it, the unsound part of the other's may find in it a corrective and an abatement. This is the great use which two unlike characters may find in observing each other. Neither is likely to have the other's faults, so each may safely adopt as much as suits him of the other's qualities. If I were a Frenchman I should never be weary of admiring the independent, individual, local habits of action in England, of directing attention to the evils occasioned in France by the excessive action of the State; for I should be very sure that, say what I might, the part of the State would never be too small in France, nor that of the individual too large. Being an Englishman, I see nothing but good in freely recognizing the coherence, rationality, and effica-

> ciousness which characterise the strong State-action of France, of acknowledging the want of method, reason, and result which attend the feeble State-action of England; because I am very sure that, strengthen the action of the State as one may, it will always find itself sufficiently controlled. But when either the *Constitutionnel* sneers at the do-little talkativeness of parliamentary government, or when the *Morning Star* inveighs against the despotism of a centralized administration, it seems to me that they lose their labour, because they are hardening themselves against dangers to which they are neither of them liable. Both the one and the other, in plain truth,
>
> 'Compound for sins they are inclined to,
> By damning those they have no mind to.'
>
> They should rather exchange doctrines one with the other, and each might thus, perhaps, be profited.[22]

The following chapters will illustrate, it is hoped, that Arnold's mind moves as a rule in charity, even if it does not always turn upon the poles of truth.

Chapter II

The Teutomaniacs

The glorification of the Teutonic race, an outgrowth of the labors of philologists who identified language and race, and of historians animated by pride in their particular nation, was but one aspect of a general cultural phenomenon. A strong pro-German and anti-French sentiment prevailed in England during the second and third quarters of the century. This sentiment is easily explained. First of all, France had long been England's rival. Apprehension concerning French military power persisted long after the battle of Waterloo, fears of a possible French invasion being entertained even so late as the middle of the century. From the petty German states, as yet ununified, no such danger was anticipated. In fact, the German soldier was held in some contempt.[1] Even more, the English feared the spread of French revolutionary ideas. The Celtic demos, to the ruling classes at least, was in very fact a demon. The frequent and violent changes culminating in the rule of the despicable Emperor, Louis Napoleon, were an object-lesson in what to avoid. The Germans were a more stable people. Again, France was largely Catholic, and although only a few Englishmen, perhaps, would have agreed with Browning's childhood pastor, the Reverend Mr. Irons, that a Catholic and a midnight assassin were the same thing, most were disposed to turn a more favorable eye toward the land of Luther. Antiquarian researches also served to establish the sisterhood of the Teutonic nations. And, finally, Victoria had connections with the House of Hanover. These are only a few of the causes of the preference for things and peoples Germanic. Such views moderately held could be defended. Arnold, as will later be shown, did defend some of them. But too often they were carried to absurd extremes, and for "the falsehood of extremes" Arnold had as deep an aversion as Tennyson. It was to do battle with the "Teutomaniacs"[2] that he entered the lists.

For bringing the general public to a recognition of the virtues of the Teutonic race, two stout champions, Carlyle and Kingsley, deserve particular mention. Emerson, with his more temperate views, also played a part. As a historian, Carlyle tried to recall the English to a sense of their racial inheritance, to stimulate in them an emulation of the heroisms of their Teutonic past. Long before the appearance of the Count de Gobineau's famous *Essay on the Inequality of Races* (1854), Carlyle was convinced of the superiority of the Teutons. To the French he grudgingly conceded a few virtues of the less admirable kind, but for the most part they were a light, sceptical, vain-glorious, gesticulating, voluble people. They lacked the deeper, solider qualities to be found in the Germanic folk. After the Franco-Prussian War, he found it reassuring that the presidency of Europe was to be undertaken by "the German race, not the Gaelic." His hero-worship, it has never been sufficiently remarked, was not confined to individuals, but extended to race—the Teutonic race, in which vague classification he included the Scandinavian people, the Germans, the Dutch, the English, the Americans, and the English colonists through the world. He devoted no single complete book to the subject of the hero-race, but his partiality was vehemently expressed in almost all his works. In the most unlikely places, the mere mention of the word Germanic, or Teutonic, or Scandinavian, or Dutch, or Norse was enough to send him into a dithyrambic frenzy. The Teutons, too, he said, as well as the Greeks, have their Heroic Age, "and round the old Valhalla, as their Northern Pantheon, a world of demi-gods and wonders." The *Nibelungen Lied* is the "German Iliad"; the ancient city of Worms, their holy city, is to a right imagination as venerable as any Thebes or Troy. Already in possession, through conquest, of a considerable part of the habitable places of the globe, the Teutons as a race seemed to be entrusted with a divine commission to dominate. As "the marching music of the Teutonic nations" he recommended a hymn by Goethe. One of his earliest enthusiasms was for Norse mythology, and his last book treated with evident gusto of "the horse-eatings, blood-sprinklings, and other sacred rites" of his heroes, Eric Blood-axe, King Blue-tooth, Svein Double-Beard, and Olaf the Thick. Since most of Carlyle's works appeared before the triumph of Aryanism, he was able to employ only the preliminary labors of the philologists. Of the later anthropological wisdom—the use of calipers and the reading of skulls—he was ignorant. He saw "but with divining eyes" the racial virtues which the Nazis since have not lacked "tongues to praise," and the Nazis have paid tribute to his prescience.[3] For his long labors in the Teutonic cause, Carlyle deserves to sleep with his own beloved Friedrich Wilhelm among "the primeval sons of Thor."

Among the great English writers of the century, Carlyle, though the most extreme, was by no means the only propagandist on race. In Charles Kingsley he had an ardent follower, one who reached an even wider or, at any rate, a different public. Kingsley calls the English "the only real Teutons left in the world."[4] In his works, the racial issue became confused with the religious. "The Church of England is wonderfully and mysteriously fitted," he said, "for the souls of a free Norse-Saxon race; for men whose ancestors fought by the side of Odin; over whom a descendant of Odin now rules." Muscular in his nationalism as in his Christianity, he found in the Northmen, "the great male race," the source of the energy which had made England stand out among the nations. He believed firmly in the doctrine of difference and superiority in race, and, therefore, took exception to John Stuart Mill's view that the condition of Ireland—its economic collapse, its inability to govern itself—was not to be accounted for by a "peculiar indolence and *insouciance* in the Celtic race." The conception of the love-match was born among the ancestors of the English while they still lived in the German forests. "What," asked Kingsley, "has produced more of nobleness, more of practical good in the human race than the chivalrous idea of wedlock which our Teutonic race holds and which the Romance or Popish races of Europe have never to this day grasped with any firm hold?" The British constitution was a Teutonic inheritance, brought with them by the English "out of the bogs and moors of Jutland." It had done the English valiant service, and it would continue to do so till they had carried it "right around the world." As he reviewed, in *The Roman and the Teuton*, the remarkable deeds of the Germanic people, he saw that "the welfare of the Teutonic race is the welfare of the world." In their mighty and continuous conquests, the Lord had obviously been their general, and the conclusion was inescapable that "the hosts of our forefathers were the hosts of God." These ideas and others like them were most fully expressed in Kingsley's Cambridge lectures, published in book form as *The Roman and the Teuton*, but they were scattered also through his novels, his public addresses, his sermons, and his correspondence. They also inspired his verse, as, for example, his *Ode to the North-East Wind*:

'Tis the hard grey weather
  Breeds hard English men.
What's the soft South-wester?
  'Tis the ladies' breeze,
Bringing home their true-loves
  Out of all the seas.
But the black North-easter,
  Through the snowstorm hurled,
Drives our English hearts of oak
  Seaward round the world.
Come, as came our fathers,
  Heralded by thee,
Conquering from the eastward,
  Lords by land and sea.
Come; and strong within us
  Stir the Viking's blood;
Bracing brain and sinew;
  Blow, thou wind of God.

With justification, Kingsley has been called "a mid-Victorian Nordic."

On the other side of the Atlantic, Emerson, too, was interested in ethnology. He was familiar with the speculations of Humboldt, Blumenbach, and Charles Pickering on the races of mankind. He had read Robert Knox's *The Races of Men*, which he found rash and unsatisfactory, "but charged with pungent and unforgettable truths." He knew the classic *Germania* of Tacitus. And he was deeply read in Carlyle. With this and other equipment—particularly his own observation—he attempted an analysis of the English. Confused, evidently, by his reading in the ethnologists, but having learned that the English were probably a composite of many strains, he threw science to the winds, and said simply, "We will call them Saxons."[5] And he painted a full-length portrait of them as Saxons. One chapter of *English Traits* was devoted specifically to race, and the whole book was concerned with the question. Thereafter, in his journals, his correspondence, his essays, and his addresses he often discussed national characteristics in the light of racial theory. "Race avails much." It explained why the Jew "for two milleniums under every climate has preserved the same character and employments." For the Negro it was of "appalling importance." Current opinion had it, he said, that all Celts were Catholics and believers in authoritarian government; all Saxons were Protestants and believers in the representative principle. At the same time he was too intelligent, too close an observer not to be aware of forces that limit or even counteract the importance of race. A "few foolish degrees of the thermometer" may account for the difference in national traits. Civilization can and does modify inherited characteristics. Despite such reservations, however, his analysis of the English followed in the main the pattern set by Knox and Carlyle. Although he recognized that the Celts had contributed to the English stock, he gave little attention to them beyond saying that "they have a hidden and precarious genius." In his opinion, "the English come mainly from the Germans," that is the Saxons, though the Norse strain is also strong. The distinction between the Saxon and Norse races is somewhat academic, however, for they are both hewn from the "Teutonic granite." The English retain to this day the tough qualities of their wild, sometimes Berserker ancestors. "Centuries of churching and civilizing" have "not quite effaced these traits of Odin." From Odin's smiths, the English derived their hereditary skill in metal work. By their seafaring activities, they approved their Saxon blood. Saxon also was their love of horsemanship and hunting, and above all their "passion for utility." For "the Saxons are the hands of mankind, they have the taste for toil, a distaste for pleasure or repose." They were the merchants, the "wealth-makers" of the world. Their genius leaned toward liberty and justice. And they shared with "the Teutonic tribes" in general "a national singleness of heart, which contrasts with the Latin races. The German name has a proverbial significance of sincerity and honest meaning." By their very vices, the English were Saxon, by their overaddiction to ale, by their love of cant, which in America as well as in England seemed to be a taint in the Anglo-Saxon blood. Through the vigorous exercise of all these qualities, the Saxons had been "now, for a thousand years, the leading race." And their future seemed assured.

To the belief widely held in his day that the English were a relatively unmixed race of Germanic origin, Arnold did not subscribe. Whether, as many believed, the Celts had been exterminated in a general and conscientious massacre; or, as Carlyle thought, they had been driven by the fiercer Teutonic invaders "into the mountainous nooks of the West, whither they were not worth following," the result was the same: it was Germanic blood that flowed in the veins of the Englishman proper. Such was the view of the Oxford school of historians: E. A. Freeman grudgingly admitted the possibility of some faint admixture of Celtic blood in the English race, but J. R. Green abandoned even this reservation.[6] Into this common error Arnold did not fall. In his opinion, the Englishman was mainly German, "but true Anglo-Saxons, simply and sincerely rooted in the German nature, we are not, and cannot be."[7] From his reading in French history and ethnology, he had had strongly impressed upon him the Celtic elements in the English race. His emphasis upon Celtic traits therefore was motivated partly by the desire to correct the current fallacy. The Normans, too, he thought, had contributed their share in the formation of the English people, but not primarily in a racial sense, since, like those they conquered, they were basically Teutonic. Their contribution was a Latin civilization, the governing point in their history.[8] Racially, then, England in Arnold's view was a mixture of Celts and Teutons. Today, Arnold would be called a fusionist; his fusion, however, is not complex enough. According to anthropologists, philologists, and ethnologists of the twentieth century, the English, in spite of their comparative isolation for the past thousand years, must be considered a people, not a race. The population is now known to be very heterogeneous in its origin. The Cro-Magnon type, the Iberian, and the Celtic-speaking Alpine races must be considered along with the later Teutons. For many centuries, all the main racial elements of Europe have been represented among the British people.[9]

It is to the prose works that one must turn for Arnold's interest in race, but there are even in the poetry a few evidences that anticipate his later concern with the question.

Carleton Stanley considers *Balder Dead* "a valiant attempt to revive our supposed Norse ancestors and make us admire them." In support of this view on the purpose of the poem, he cites Arnold's modest defense of the work to Palgrave: "We have enough Scandinavian in our nature and history to make a short conspectus of the Scandinavian mythology admissible."[10] Had circumstances permitted, Arnold might have employed more extensively than he did materials drawn from Teutonic sources, for in July, 1876, he wrote to his sister, Frances Arnold, that the Bayreuth performance turned his mind longingly to the Nibelungen ring, and Fafnir and Siegfried and Gudrune and Brunhilde, all subjects that he had once hoped to deal with in poetry.[11] To his cosmopolitan practice, begun early in his career and continued through life, of reading French periodicals such as the *Revue des deux mondes* and the *Revue de Paris* can be ascribed, in part, at least, his lively interest in Celtic matters. "Tristram and Iseult," published in 1852 but probably composed a number of years earlier, is his first ambitious use of a Celtic theme. The poem grew out of his reading in the *Revue de Paris* a series of articles by Theodore de la Villemarque on "Les poemes gallois et les romans de la Table-Ronde."[12] His visit to Brittany in 1859, and his discovery of Renan's essay *La poesie des races celtiques* provided the inspiration for "Stanzas from Carnac," probably composed in 1859 though not published until 1867,[13] and "Saint Brandan," published in 1860. At any rate, Arnold by 1859 had reached some definite conclusions about the Celtic strain in the English race. In recommending Renan's essay to Mrs. Forster, he added: "I have long felt that we owe far more, spiritually and artistically, to the Celtic races than the somewhat coarse German intelligence readily perceived, and been increasingly satisfied at our own semi-Celtic origin, which, as I fancy, gives us the power, if we will use it, of comprehending the nature of both races. Renan pushes the glorification of the Celts too far; but there is a great deal of truth in what he says."[14]

To comprehend "the nature of both races,"—herein lay a key to an understanding of much in English life and thought, to say nothing of that of the Continent, where from the beginning of the Christian era the two races supposedly had contended for superiority. It was a fascinating problem, one that from this time on never ceased to have an appeal for Arnold. Whole libraries, of course, had already been written on the subject, largely by blind partisans of one race as against the other, so that to Arnold in 1861 it seemed vain to attempt an explanation of a great modern culture on the basis of race. In view of the fact that six years later he was to devote an entire book to an elaboration of "the pregnant and striking ideas of the ethnologists," his temporary repudiation of the whole theory is difficult to explain. After a long passage devoted to the significance for the future of France of a great national agent like popular education, he closed his report on French schools with a vigorous rejection of the racial hypothesis.

> The two peoples are alike in this, that they are each greater than all others, each unlike to any other. It is in vain that we call the French Celts, and ourselves Teutons: when nations have attained to the greatness of France and England, their peoples can have no profound identity with any people beyond their own borders. Torrents of pedantry have been poured forth on the subject of our Germanic origin; in real truth, we are at the present day no more Germans than we are Frenchmen. By the mixture of our race,

> by the Latinisation of our language, by the isolation of our country, by the independence of our history, we have long since lost all vital connection with that great German stem which sixteen centuries ago threw out a shoot in this island. France is equally dissociated, by her eminence, from her once fellow Celtic or Latin races. It is the same with the greatness of the peoples; each is unique, and has no counterpart but in that of the other. From Messina to Archangel, and from Calais to Moscow, there reigns a universal striving after Parisian civilization; the ideas which move the masses (I do not speak of aristocratic and learned coteries) are, when ideas reach them at all, French ideas. Cross the straits and you are in another world: in a world where French ideas have not a breath of influence.[15]

A saner and more enlightened recognition of the many influences at work in modifying the importance of race in the development of national life one can hardly imagine. But Arnold did not maintain this attitude for long. In spite of his earlier emphasis on the "semi-Celtic origin" and his protest against the pedantry concerning the "Germanic origin" of the English, he probably from the beginning was of the opinion expressed in *A French Eton* (1864) that his countrymen were "mainly of German blood." Having been introduced to the work of Amédée Thierry, probably by Renan or Michelet, both of whom acknowledge his influence, he was struck by that racial historian's distinction between "the Gaulish and Germanic races," the first being "characterized by the instinct of intelligence and mobility, and by the preponderant action of individuals; the second, by the instinct of discipline and order, and by the preponderant action of bodies of men." This general law, Arnold believed, had "a solid basis of truth in it," and he applied it in an analysis of the English middle class, "mainly of German blood," to account for their Philistine hostility to ideas and ideals.[16]

In the beginning, Arnold's charges were general in character, directed against a movement of thought, a common English bent toward Teutonism. From 1864 on, however, he made his accusations specific. It was the *Saturday Review* that he singled out for eminence in such misguided interpretations of history. Later, in *Culture and Anarchy*, when he wished to illustrate the absence in England of literary standards, he chose a company of Nonconformists, who, in their ignorance, placed the *Saturday Review* and the *British Banner* on a plane of equal authority, though the first was "a kind of organ of reason," distinguished for its sanity of judgment and its taste in literary matters, and the second was a newspaper ranking low in these concerns. He referred humorously and half affectionately to the *Saturday Review* as "my old adversary." For a number of years he had carried on a running battle with it, each regarding the other with respect tempered by disagreement.[17] If, then, on the subject of Teutonic origins, even this worthy journal erred, what gross misconceptions could one expect in such a paper as the *Times*?[18] As early as 1859, Fitzjames Stephen, in a *Saturday* article, had taken issue with Arnold on his Gallic sympathies, challenging particularly his opinion that the French masses were more intelligent, more open to ideas, than were the English masses.[19] Five years later, Stephen returned to the charge, his chief objection being that as self-appointed preceptor to the English people, Arnold dwelt chiefly on the national faults, in particular the English inferiority to the French in all intellectual and artistic matters. To such an extreme did Arnold carry his preference that his very writing was in "a dialect as like French as pure English can be."[20] As a natural result of such criticism, Arnold in his thrusts at the *Saturday* looked for evidence of a pro-Teutonic bias, and, looking, found it. As his later works, especially and most explictly *On the Study of Celtic Literature*, reveal, he regarded Philistinism, Teutonism, and Utilitarianism as three aspects of the same regrettable failing in the English. The preface to *Essays in Criticism* gives a picture, in his best satiric vein, of the "Palatine library of the future." There the great Bentham will be found side by side with the editor of the *Saturday Review*. Often in the old days has this editor nipped the Philistines, but now in his old age he is "staunch for Goliath and 'the most logical nation in the whole world.' " Then, on the bookshelves, along with Bentham's *Deontology* "there will be found . . . a monograph by Mr. Lowe on the literature of the ancient Scythians, to revenge them for the iniquitous neglect with which the Greeks treated them."[21] As Arnold explained two years later, the Scythians are not the "obscure, far-separated Mongolian people . . . they used to appear to us," but "are essentially Teutonic and Indo-European."[22] In similar fashion, at the close of *On the Study of Celtic Literature*, Mr. Lowe and Mr. Roebuck, with their panegyrics on English happiness, are linked with Mr. Cobden, who desires that Oxford should teach "a little less about the Ilissus, and a little more about Chicago," a reform which, in Arnold's opinion, would result in an excessive "stimulation of our Anglo-Saxonism."[23] But to return to the *Saturday Review*—Arnold made a frontal attack upon it in "The Literary Influence of Academies."

> I will not speak of the immediate present, but to go a little while back, it had the critic who so disliked the Emperor of the French; it had the critic who so disliked the subject of our present remarks —academies; it had the critic who was so fond of the German ele-

> ment in our nation, and, indeed, everywhere; who ground his teeth if one said *Charlemagne* instead of *Charles the Great*, and, in short, saw all things in Teutonism, as Malebranche saw all things in God. Certainly any one may fairly find faults in the Emperor Napoleon or in academies, and merit in the German element; but it is a note of the provincial spirit not to hold ideas of this kind a little more easily, to be so devoured by them, to suffer them to become crotchets.[24]

A vigorous protest over this usage occurs in a number of *Saturday* articles. The very name "France" is a case of petty larceny, since it applies properly to the Franks in Francia, East of the Rhine, now called Franconia. By identifying itself with old Teutonic Francia, France "contrives to degrade Charles the Great into a Frenchman."[25] Again, "The mythical Charlemagne has led the world to mistake the greatest of Germans for a Frenchman and the mythical Arthur has done not a little to make us forget that in a sense we are Germans too."[26] And "as long as the *Times* mistakes Teutonic Karl for a Frenchman reigning in the Tuileries it cannot possibly understand anything that he did."[27] Since Freeman was notorious in his day for his Germanic preferences, and was besides one of the most prolific of the contributors to the *Saturday* during the first eighteen years of its career, he was probably the critic to whom Arnold referred as seeing "all things in Teutonism."

In his strictures upon the *Saturday Review* for its Germanic leanings, Arnold was not alone. A less urbane contemporary, in an anonymous pamphlet, charged it with being "a most bigoted pro-Teutonic journal."[28] This the *Saturday* denied. It was guiltless of any German conspiracy, it said, but would still have to insist that the basic words in English are "Teutonic to the backbone."[29]

The latest historian of the *Saturday* credits it with some attempt at a cosmopolitan view, though he discovers a Teutonic bias in its historical criticism and a deviation from the objective and temperate norm in reviews of French writers who display Ultramontane or imperialistic tendencies.[30] These are, of course, significant exceptions. And other exceptions can be found without difficulty in other departments, if one deliberately searches for Germanic preferences. Even in the tomb, the distinction between races was maintained. Archaeological investigations in Somersetshire revealed signs of an ancient battle, and when the skeletons were removed from the barrow, it was seen that they were evidently of two different races. In one group, indeed, a man of giant stature had fallen in a hand-to-hand fight with two comparative pigmies: a conquering Teuton beside two conquered Britons.[31] The classification of races on the basis of skull measurements was followed with interest by the *Saturday*, and it was pleased to report that German and English skulls had a greater capacity for knowledge than did French and Spanish ones.[32] When Montalembert, reporting favorably in 1855 on English schools, exhorted the French people to work harder for freedom, the *Saturday* critic suggested that it was "owing to inherent differences of race that an Englishman is free and a Frenchman not."[33] Carlyle's famous contrast of the Gallic fire fit for "roasting eggs" with the Germanic fire needed for "smelting metals" was quoted with approval.[34] The strong hand and fearless heart of the German carried him into every land as a noble or a king.[35] A Frenchman, of course, could not be expected to feel about Norway as an Englishman did, for to an Englishman Norway was the country from which a large proportion of his blood was derived.[36] Collections of Danish ballads, and of Icelandic and Anglo-Saxon sagas, were reviewed with enthusiasm, but ballads and songs of Brittany received the comment that it was hard to awaken interest in anything Celtic.[37] Significantly, it was desirable that the Arthurian legends be traced to their earliest state so that one could the better understand "the marvellously beautiful cycle of romance to which the great Teutonic poets, such as Wolfram von Eschenbach and Alfred Tennyson, have devoted their highest powers."[38] By the end of the sixth century, said the *Saturday*, the early Breton inhabitants had been to a large extent exterminated. At any rate, a venture such as Arnold's to search out the Celtic and Norman elements in the modern Englishman was vain, since the Norman element, like the much smaller Celtic element, had now been almost completely absorbed in the English nation.[39] From such a list of references, scattered though they are, one is justified in concluding that an anti-Gallic and pro-Teutonic note appeared on occasion in the pages of the *Saturday Review*. Arnold had some basis for his charge.

As already indicated, the Teutonism of the Victorian period was, in part at least, an outgrowth of antiquarian research, of the revival of interst in the Middle Ages, and of the study of origins in the period, the limits of which are roughly set by the Venerable Bede and Chaucer. To the discussion of this period, Arnold came with little knowledge and less sympathy. Steeped in the enchantments of the Periclean age, he found even the Elizabethan period, by comparison, somewhat primitive, less adequate, less modern. The enthusiasm for the rude and grotesque displayed by Carlyle and Browning, he never shared.

Oxford itself, "that sweet city with its dreaming spires," might, by moonlight at least, whisper the charms of the Middle Age, but in broad daylight the shouting on the same subject by the Oxford school of historians left him rather cold.[40] This attitude toward the early period of English history and toward "the school of Freeman" was revealed also in the essay on Marcus Aurelius. In attempting to determine the appeal which the Roman emperor had for a modern reader, Arnold singled out his "goodness." For this quality, two other sovereigns, Saint Louis and Alfred, were also noted. The claim of Marcus Aurelius upon our attention was increased, however, in that he lived in an enlightened age, in a society like our own, and thus "becomes for us a man like ourselves," subject to the same temptations. To the medieval Catholicism of Saint Louis, on the other hand, a nineteenth-century man could no longer lend credence. And "Alfred belongs to a state of society (I say it with all deference to the *Saturday Review* critic who keeps such jealous watch over the honour of our Saxon ancestors) half barbarous. Neither Alfred nor Saint Louis can be morally and intellectually as near to us as Marcus Aurelius."[41] The critic again would seem to be Freeman. Arnold was nothing if not persistent: twelve years later he still indulged himself in a bit of raillery at the expense of Freeman's Teutonic obsession. The true martyr of the Great Civil War was Falkland, a man of singular "lucidity of mind and largeness of temper." In these respects he was contrasted with the fanatics of genius who too often prevailed. "So we have the Philistine of genius in religion,—Luther; the Philistine of genius in politics,—Cromwell; the Philistine of genius in literature, —Bunyan. All three of them, let us remark, are Germanic, and two of them are English. Mr. Freeman must be enchanted."[42]

Freeman was obviously, in Arnold's opinion, a Teutomaniac. That Arnold was guilty of no exaggeration in his remarks on Freeman is proved by even the most cursory glance at that author's works. His research on the history of his country led him to conclude that the English nation—its laws, its language, its national being—down to the present day was a Teutonic fabric.[43] Of the Celts he had an exceedingly low opinion: at no time had they played any great part in history except when under Roman or Teutonic influence.[44] It was from the union of Teuton and Roman that modern Europe was born.[45] Ravenna for men of Teutonic blood could claim a special glory, which neither Rome nor Constantinople enjoyed, for it was the center of the first established Teutonic dominion beyond the Alps.[46] In his opinion, Tacitus was the greatest of the Roman historians, and his flattering description of the Germans was no mere dream of a disaffected Roman, but an essentially faithful description of the Teutonic race when it first appeared upon the scene of history.[47] Gradually the Teutons took over the rule of the provinces of the Roman Empire until with the crowning of Charles the Great "The golden crown at last rested on the open brow of the lordly German," and "We might almost say that the world recognized the Teuton as its chosen and natural ruler."[48] As he traced the glorious and continuous history of the Teutonic race in its three great homes, the European mainland, England, and North America, he found that Arminius, "liberator Germaniae," was but the first in a list which ran on to Hampden and to Washington.[49]

Turning to a consideration of England, Freeman maintained that if the Germans are Teutons, then "we are Teutons still more."[50] No nation, not even England, he admitted, could claim purity of blood in any strict physical or genealogical sense,[51] but nonetheless the English were not what the Germans called a *Mischvolk*: "a mere jumble of races in which no one element is predominant."[52] In the early invasions by the Teutonic tribes—the Angles, the Saxons, the Jutes, and the Frisians—the native Britons were either put to the sword or were driven into the western and northern mountains, except for some few, mostly women, who were kept as slaves. "Thus there may doubtless be some little British and Roman blood in us . . . But we may be sure that we have not much of their blood in us, because we have so few of their words in our language."[53] This wholesale extermination combined with the fact that England was an island made the country more Teutonic than Germany itself.[54] Subsequent invasions, the Norman included, only served to strengthen this predominant racial element. The Norman, contrary to the opinion of some historians, "was a Dane, who, in his sojourn in Gaul, had put on a slight French varnish, and who came into England to be washed clean again. . . . The blood of the true Norman . . . differs hardly at all from the blood of the inhabitants of the North and East of England."[55] In his zeal, Freeman discovered a Teutonic character in the very landscape, and in the animals of Normandy. "In every part of Normandy, as compared with France or Aquitaine, the Englishman feels at home, but in the district of Bayeux he seems hardly to have left his own country. . . . The land is decidedly not French; men, beasts, everything, are distinctively of a grander and better type than their fellows in the mere French district;

the general aspect of the land, its fields, its hedges, all have an English look. And no contrast can be greater than that which may be often seen between the tall, vigorous-looking Norman yeoman, out of whose mouth we instinctively feel that the common mother tongue ought to issue, and that French soldier, whose stature, whose color, whose every feature proclaims him to be a man of another race, and whose presence proclaims no less unmistakably that the glory of Normandy has passed away."[56]

The English language was without question Teutonic, differing from its cousin the High-Dutch, and its brother the Low-Dutch, only in those modifications which naturally result during a separation of fourteen hundred years. In spite of the foreign words, chiefly Latin and French, that had poured into the language, it could still be said that English speech when most natural and least artificial was most purely Teutonic. On its highest as well as its lowest levels the language could divest itself almost wholly of Romance words. On the other hand, it was almost impossible to speak English which should consist of Romance words alone. After all changes, the English language remained, as it had been ten centuries earlier, in all essential respects a Teutonic speech.[57] Although Freeman was sufficiently versed in the science of ethnology to know that language is no absolute proof of race, or even of nationality, he insisted that, evidence to the contrary being lacking, he was justified in assuming a Teutonic race on the basis of language.[58]

The political institutions of England also attested its Teutonic origin. On the Continent, Teutonic kingships progressed and flourished, while Greek and Italian kingships for the most part died out. But only in England had the old idea of kingship—and other Teutonic institutions—a chance to grow and improve undisturbed by the influence of Rome until feudal and ecclesiastical developments began.[59] More than Denmark, more than Germany, England had had the advantage of an unbroken political life. As a result, said Freeman, it was not upon the Continent, but in their second home, England, that the Angle and the Saxon had preserved, if not always the form, at any rate the spirit, of the ancient institutions of the Teutonic race.[60]

Freeman's racial bias was carried to such an extreme that even his friend and disciple, J. R. Green, recognized in his works "What Mr. Matthew Arnold would call an overpowering Teutonism."[61]

Whether or not Arnold was aware of the fact, vigorous support was being lent him in other quarters in the battle against Freeman and the Teutomaniacs. Throughout the decade of the 'sixties, the question of the racial origin of the English people was debated by English anthropologists and ethnologists. And in these debates, the Celts were by no means without their champions. In the pages of the *Anthropological Review and Journal*, the extirpation of the ancient Britons by the Saxons was regarded as a romantic theory no longer tenable. The Saxon and other Teutonic invaders had been the conquerors, not the extirpators, of the nation.[62] The belief of the majority of Englishmen that they were Saxons, or Anglo-Normans, rather than Celts, was called a popular fallacy which anthropology condemned. By "those who have mastered the science of man" it was numbered with the prejudices of a bygone age.[63] The conclusion arrived at by a number of investigators was that "the ethnic results of the Teutonic invasion were purely baptismal."[64] Hector MacLean, a prolific writer on ethnological subjects, took vehement issue with Freeman and contended that the English were basically a Celtic people.[65] A similar view was taken in a satiric article entitled "Mr. Freeman's Dutchmen."[66] From 1865 to 1868, when Arnold's interest in the subject was at its height, the Welsh National Eisteddfod annually offered a prize of one hundred guineas for the best work on "The origin of the English nation with reference more especially to the question 'How far they are descended from the ancient Britons?' " The judge was Arnold's friend, Lord Strangford, who supplied the philological notes for *On the Study of Celtic Literature*.[67] One of the contenders for the prize, Owen Luke Pike, published his researches in 1866 in book form: *The English and Their Origin: A Prologue to Authentic English History*. By four methods of investigation: the historical, the philological, the anatomical, and the psychological, Pike attempted to prove that the English were descended not from the Teutonic conquerors of South Britain, but from the Cymric division of the Celts. In his opinion it was impossible to account for the physical and psychological characteristics of the modern Englishman on the assumption that his forbears were German or even half-German.[68] By other writers, the invaders of England were regarded not as Teutons at all, but as Celts, the Angles and Saxons being not Gothic or German, but Scandinavians occupying the south shores of the Baltic. And the Scandinavians were a branch or off-shoot of the Celts.[69] It was the Norman invasion, however, that aroused the most heated controversy. The arguments of the defenders of the Celts may be summarized as follows. The region from which the Normans came was inhabited in Caesar's time by the Galli, a Celtic people.

The successive invasions by Romans, Franks, and Norsemen, left the population substantially Celtic, for the invaders came in small numbers and without wives. Thus, although William the Conqueror and his knights may have been Teutons, the army which invaded England must have been largely Celtic since it was made up mostly of natives.[70] Such, in brief, was the reply of the ethnologists to Freeman's statement that the Normans were Danes, who in their sojourn in Gaul "had put on a slight French varnish, and who came into England to be washed clean again," and to Carlyle who said flatly that "the Normans were Saxons who had learned to speak French." Paradoxically, therefore, the Celtic element in the population of Britain was increased rather than decreased by the so-called Teutonic invasions.

Had he known of them, Arnold would have found these English authorities useful to his purpose, particularly since many of them based their conclusions on the evidences of philology and physiology, the two sciences to which he turned for support of his view that the English were semi-Celtic in origin. It was as a layman that he entered these specialized fields. In such matters his care was not to part and prove. It was enough that investigations thus far conducted tended to confirm his thesis. In philology the tests, Arnold confessed, were as yet incomplete. Conclusions were tentative, and would have to be accepted with caution. But if it were true that some "of our raciest, most idiomatic, popular words—for example, *bam*, *kick*, *whop*, *twaddle*, *fudge*, *hitch*, *muggy*,—are Celtic," there was reason to believe that the Celtic race had not been completely exterminated at the time of the Saxon invasion, that it had intermingled with the conquerors and had added its part in the formation of the modern Englishman.

Toward such a conclusion, said Arnold, the evidence in physiology also seemed to point. On the Continent, W. F. Edwards, a versatile French physician, author of *Recherches sur les langues Celtiques* and a member of the Société ethnologique de Paris, had opened up a new world of speculation in his attempt to verify history by the tests of physiology. Earlier, Amédée Thierry had based his *Histoire des Gaulois* on the assumption that the traits of the ancient Gauls had been preserved into modern times, and that the distinction between the two great branches of the Gallic race, the Gaels and the Cymris, could still be observed in France. This theory Dr. Edwards put to physiological proof. More interested, evidently, in measuring his patients than in curing them, he collected a great deal of evidence, particularly on the proportions of the head. Two distinct races he found still dwelt side by side on French soil—the long heads, or Cymri, and the round heads, or Gaels.[71] The Hun was also a round-head, according to Edwards, but could be distinguished from the Gael by certain marked features: slant eyes, snub nose, projecting lips, thick neck, and scanty beard. Seeing one such in Venice, he was moved to cry out, "Voilà un Hun!"[72] Carrying his researches to England, he discovered abundant evidence that the long-headed Cymric type still existed in the British population. This physiological evidence was enough, he thought, to disprove the contention of most historians that the Celts had been completely exterminated by the invading Saxons. And there were other arguments that confirmed him in his opinion. What reason would the Saxons have for expelling or exterminating the Britons entirely? Conquest is made to bring greater ease of life. It was an epoch when slaves constituted a considerable part of wealth. Did the Britons have so great a love of liberty and so profound a contempt for life that they preferred death to slavery? Their earlier conduct under the Romans showed that they did not. A small number doubtless were killed by the Saxons, but not the whole people.[73]

All this, of course, was grist for Arnold's mill. Edwards' book achieved a considerable fame on the Continent. It helped to introduce to the world the dolichocephalic-brachycephalic controversy which later in the century was to rise to such a furious pitch. At the very start, it was recognized as an important work by such writers as Michelet, Henri Martin, and Gobineau, who used it as a basis for some of their own theories. But Arnold was probably led to Edwards by Amédée Thierry, who in his ethnological introduction to *The History of the Gauls* paid tribute to his scientific supporter.[74] In thus drawing anthropology into the service of his political, social, and literary studies, Arnold followed French guides. He need not have crossed the channel, however, for a precedent. In 1863, just four years before the publication of *On the Study of Celtic Literature*, James Hunt, finding the work of the Ethnological Society of London too limited, had founded the Anthropological Society of London with the express purpose of widening its scope to include curent political and social problems, particularly those dealing with the Irish and the Negro.[75] For Arnold, the conclusion of the whole matter was that "As there are for physiology physical marks, such as the square head of the German, the round head of the Gael, the oval head of the Cymri, which determine the type of a people, so for criticism there are spiritual marks which determine the type, and make us speak of the Greek genius, the Teutonic genius, the Celtic genius, and so on."[76] At such spiritual tests he proposed to try his hand. The nature of these tests and the manner in which he applied them will be discussed in later chapters.

Opposed though Arnold was to Freeman's extreme views, he was not, on the other hand, prepared to follow Renan, who held that England was everyday becoming more Celtic and less Germanic through the operation of a general law by which the primitive race of an invaded country eventually conquers its conquerors. In English policy and public opinion in the second half of the nineteenth century Renan detected the *esprit celtique*, *plus doux*, *plus sympathetique*, *plus humain*. Of such developments, Arnold saw no sign. He felt sure that the Irish Catholics, who had suffered so long at the hands of the Dissenters and Philistines and still had to endure their cant, would not agree that the Germanic element in England was being superseded by the *doux esprit celtique*.[77] Some Englishmen contemporary with Arnold did believe, however, that "the primitive race" was getting the upper hand. On the basis of his own observations and those of other ethnologists, Grant Allen took violent issue with Freeman and his Germanic thesis. The objection to students like Freeman and J. R. Green, said Allen, was that their conception of the Englishman was based almost entirely on their researches in the Middle Ages, the period in which, as everyone admitted, the Teutons had everything their own way. But since the time of Elizabeth, the subjugated race had been reasserting itself until today "most true British people are not 'Anglo-Saxons,' but Celts." It was a little-known fact, said Allen, that one of every fifteen inhabitants of the British Isles still spoke "some form of the old British tongue." Of the thirty-two million people in England, Scotland, and Ireland, seven million were undeniably Celtic in blood, and still dwelt in countries "absolutely untouched by Teutonic colonisation." In England proper, the Celtic element, though more difficult to determine, was unquestionably very strong. Only the rural sections could any longer claim to be purely Teutonic. Everywhere else the Welsh, the Irish, and the Highland Scots had penetrated, had intermarried, had been Anglicized, and in many cases no longer knew their true racial origins. The great industrial centers—London, Birmingham, Manchester, Liverpool—were flooded with Celtic workers, many of them emigrants from the virgin Celtic countries. Furthermore, most of England's power and influence had shited in the past few centuries from the eastern half of the country, which was agricultural and Teutonic, to the western half, which was industrial and Celtic. And finally, Allen regarded the genius of the Anglo-Saxon race in colonization as a myth. It was the Celtic sections of the British Isles that had contributed colonists in the greatest numbers. Even in England itself colonists went rather from the Celtic western half than from the Teutonic east. As a result, by far the largest number of Canadians were of Irish, Highland Scotch, Welsh, or Breton extraction. And the same was true of Australia and New Zealand.[78]

Among those impressed by Grant Allen's arguments was George Meredith, who, to be sure, had been from the beginning sympathetic with the Celtic cause. In a letter to his son, Meredith recommended Allen as a writer of some distinction upon the English race. "He thinks," said Meredith, "that Celtic blood preponderates. I do not, though I see it flooding."[79] By 1885, such views had come to prevail rather generally, if one can accept the testimony of John Beddoe, the ethnologist: "It is not very long since educated opinion considered the English and Lowland Scots an almost purely Teutonic people. Now the current runs so much the other way that I have had to take up the attitude of an apologist of the 'Saxon' view."[80] In this shift of popular opinion from the Teutonic to the Celtic extreme, Arnold's Celtic studies were at least a contributing factor though he himself approved as little of one extreme as of the other.

Chapter III

The Saxon Philistine

From the material presented in the preceding chapter, it is evident that Arnold waged intermittent war against Teutonism in general and against its advocates. Much of the evidence however, may seem to be peripheral, comment incidental to or illustrative of other subjects in which he was more vitally interested. That the racial theme is more central in his work can be shown, however, when one turns to his presiding interest: Philistinism. For the Saxon is usually a Philistine wherever he may dwell: in North Germany, in England and her colonies, or in America. Lord Strangford, reviewing the first of Arnold's papers on Celtic literature, pointed out with keen critical discernment that anyone familiar with Arnold's previous writings could without cutting the pages of the work under review construct its argument: "the contrast between the Celtic children of light and the Saxon Philistine."[1] Twenty-two years later, in "Milton," a public address delivered two months before his death, Arnold was still concerned with the defects of the Saxon Philistine. In opening the address, he paid to another prophet a tribute, which, though he did not know it, was to apply with ironic force to himself: "The most eloquent voice of our century uttered, shortly before leaving the world, a warning cry against 'the Anglo-Saxon contagion.' "[2] There was a real danger, Arnold thought, that the commonness and vulgarity of the Anglo-Saxon race might overspread the world. In a word, Philistinism.

As Arnold advanced upon the enemy, Goliath, he gathered, like David before him, some smooth pebbles as ammunition. The first, a new term charged with opprobrium: Philistine, he took from Heine; the second, a racial explanation of the deficiencies of the Philistine, he adapted from Amédée Thierry; the third, a slurring epigram upon the foe: "For dulness, the creeping Saxons," he borrowed from MacFirbis, the seventeenth-century Irish genealogist. A disaffected German Jew; a French historian of the Gauls, who bases his study on ethnological principles; and an ardent chronicler of the glories of Ireland: alien witnesses all! But it was the truth that Arnold sought, and he found it oftener, he thought, in the unkind remarks of foreigners than in the compliments, however well-intended, of friends.

In a study such as this, perhaps in any study since the term has entered into common currency, Philistine does not need to be defined. Arnold defined it again and again, taking evident delight each time in adding some new unflattering epithet. Heine, he said, applied the name to "the poor German Hodge," on the wrong side of the Rhine, "the Jordan which divides the consecrated land of freedom from the land of the Philistines." Arnold gave it a more general application. Philistinism was "that plant of essentially Germanic growth, flourishing with its genuine marks only in the German fatherland, Great Britain and her colonies, and the United States of America."[3] Because of its mixed nature—Celtic and Norman elements entering into the composition—the English race was saved from some of the blighting effects of Philistinism. The German nature, in contrast, was "all of a piece."[4] This conception of the German people as an unmixed race, frequently and vigorously expressed by German authors for obvious reasons, was widely accepted even in France and in England, though Gobineau, the most notorious of the advocates of Aryanism, in his book on the inequality of races regarded the modern German as no longer pure and unmixed racially. Caryle saw in the Germans "a separate unmixed people . . . one of the two grand stem-tribes, from which all modern European countries derive their population and speech," a great people "growing up distinct . . . following its own course," as it advanced "through fifteen centuries of culture."[5] Meredith alluded satirically to the belief: "No doubt the German is the race the least mixed in Europe; it might challenge aboriginals for that. Oddly, it has invented the Cyclopedia for knowledge, the sausage for nutrition! How would you explain it?"[6] It was, in any case, among the North Germans that Arnold found the purest examples of Philistinism; upon them "*das Gemeine, die Gemeinheit*, that curse of Germany" lay most heavily. On his travels through Germany, it was not until he came to Austria that he saw "grace, light movements, and attractive faces" again, "but then here there is evidently a strong infusion of a lighter and more mercurial blood."[7]

According to Amédée Thierry, the Germanic race lacked the intelligence, mobility, and individualism of the Gauls; was characterized, in contrast, by a love of discipline and order and by herd instinct.[8] Since the English were chiefly of German blood, Arnold found Thierry's law valuable in explaining their national traits. For his typical Englishman, he went not to the aristocracy, in whom the racial traits had been modified and etherealized, nor to the masses, who as yet were not solidified into a national type, but to the middle classes. In their indifference to new ideas and ideals, in their militant defense of the *status quo*, in their disposition to rest content with the limited aims and acts of men of their own kind, Arnold saw Thierry's analysis exemplified.[9] And all these were the marks of the Philistine.

That the Saxon was a dull fellow, distinguished neither for the vivacity of his manner nor for the arresting nature of his conversation; that he was slow of movement and remained by preference near the ground, Arnold probably discovered from his French authorities. This view of the Germanic nature was fostered by Gallic historians. Tacitus supplied the precedent. In his account, the German who in the field of battle displayed great energy and courage, became in time of peace a listless sluggard, leaving to women and the infirm the management of house and lands. Following this Latin tradition, Michelet emphasized the second characteristic. In his ebullient youth, the German might perhaps display a degree of impulsiveness and enthusiasm, but his fundamental trait was "impersonality": a massive brute strength coupled with indecisiveness. The ox and the elephant were his animal parallels.[10] Henri Martin delighted in the contrast between the lively Celt and the sluggish, sedentary German.[11] Among English anthropologists and ethnologists, whom Arnold evidently did not consult, similar pictures of the Saxon can be found. His slowness of perception, lack of analytical power, and absence of ambition were emphasized.[12] William Maccall, an ethnologist undeterred by the general Victorian reticence on subjects anatomical, employed a striking metaphor: "A man cannot sit without a wherewith; but the wherewith, though indispensable, is not deemed the divinest part of the human frame. The Anglo-Saxon is

England's sitting part."[13] Even Carlyle, the Saxon apologist, confessed that before the coming of the Normans—Saxons, too, under the skin—the Anglo-Saxons had shown a tendency toward "pot-bellied equanimity." By Carlyle's standards, however, stolidity was not a defect but a virtue. If the Englishman lacked the Frenchman's exuberance and wit, it was because he put his faith in acts, not words; if he moved one foot slowly after the other, it was because he desired that they be planted on the solid rock. The Irish, of course, would hardly employ so flattering a rationalization. The old Irish poem which Arnold quoted with such telling effect said simply: "For dulness, the creeping Saxons."[14] MacFirbis regarded the poem as an excellent illustration of his thesis that the races "all have some one peculiar characteristic by which they are known."[15]

Having established the fundamental qualities of the Saxon, or Teutonic, Philistine on the foundation supplied by these not altogether unimpeachable authorities, Arnold proceeded to a closer definition. "On the side of beauty and taste, vulgarity; on the side of morals and feeling coarseness; on the side of mind and spirit, unintelligence,—this is Philistinism."[16] Illustrations in support of this triple charge are supplied in profusion through the body of Arnold's works from 1867 to the close of his career. Vulgarity, coarseness, unintelligence, these three, and the greatest of these was unintelligence.

For the first of these unlovely traits, vulgarity, Arnold found in North Germany the most appalling examples. Everywhere a "blank commonness," a "universal dead-level of plainness and homeliness," a "lack of all beauty and distinction in form and feature" prevailed in this, "the most *bourgeois* of nations."[17] With approval, he quoted a passage from Amiel on the deficiencies of Germany:

> 'It is in the novel that the average vulgarity of German society, and its inferiority to the societies of France and England are most clearly visible. The notion of a thing's *jarring on the taste* is wanting to German æsthetics. Their elegance knows nothing of grace; they have no sense of the enormous distance between distinction (gentlemanly, ladylike) and their stiff *Vornehmlichkeit.* Their imagination lacks style, training, education, and knowledge of the world; it is stamped with an ill-bred air even in its Sunday clothes. The race is practical and intelligent, but common and ill-mannered. Ease, amiability, manners, wit, animation, dignity, charm, are qualities which belong to others.'[18]

Even in Berlin, as he explained to his friend, Fontanès, Arnold discovered society to be "plus borné, plus sec, et beaucoup moins intéressant que le monde de Londres et de Paris."[19] The language was "hideous," "rough guttural," as contrasted with the civilized speech of the Italians.[20] German poetry was deficient in style in the highest sense.[21] The very greatest writers weighed in the balance of style were found wanting: Luther for all his powers of expression lacked "dignity and distinction";[22] Goethe's prose, though it was free from all affectation and allowed the real Goethe to reach the reader, was "loose, ill-knit, diffuse."[23] Not inheriting, as the English did, the Norman gift for rhetoric, the Germans in their public addresses were capable only of "half talk,—heavy talk,—and half effusion."[24] In the very nature of the language, both in syntax and vocabulary, there was "something heavy and trailing."[25] Although Arnold acknowledged that these qualities might be in part the result of a deficient civilization, the lack of a long and distinguished national tradition and training such as England and France possessed, he attributed them also to "the steady humdrum habit of the creeping Saxon"; they were a natural outgrowth of "the Saxon's phlegm."[26] In Germany as in Holland it was *élan* that one searched for in vain, an *élan* that England, thanks to her Norman ancestors, had, that had "kept her from getting stupid and humdrum too, as the pure Germanic nations tend to become for want of a little effervescing salt with their magnesia."[27] Further, the North German was "a very gross feeder." To the German as contrasted with the Frenchman, nature had assigned, said the physiologists, a larger volume of intestines.[28] For this arresting fancy, which Arnold said, "sets one's spirits in a glow," and which he therefore used twice, he was evidently indebted to the vehement champion of the Celtic strain in the French race and in French history, Henri Martin. Having listed some of the physical traits of the Germans and Scandinavians, Martin added,

> Ajoutons à ces traits extérieurs que, dans ses savantes études d'anthropologie comparée, M. Serres constate chez les Français un plus grand devéloppement de l'appareil respiratoire et un moindre volume d'intestins que chez l'Allemand, caractère qu'il faut certainement reporter aux Gaulois et aux Germains.[29]

This physiological difference between the nations was employed by Martin and Arnold simply as an interesting discovery of science. It remained for a twentieth-century French physician to put it to practical use. One Dr. Edgar Berrillon gave to the world through the *Bulletin of the Society of Medicine of Paris* (June 25, 1915) and the reports of the French Association for the Advancement of Science (February 4, 1917) his discovery that the large intestine of people of the German race was some nine feet longer than it was in other races. Along with this abnormality went polychesia (excessive defecation) and bromidrosis (body odor), diseases resulting from intemperance and leading to unnatural crimes. By means of such tests, Dr. Berillon was able to detect German spies during the world war.[30] Arnold's experience as a layman confirmed the findings of the physiologists. If proof was needed, he said, one had only to observe any German at a table-d'hôte.[31] As a result of his observations at first hand in the country of their habitation, he concluded, "Never surely was there a people of so many millions so unattractive."[32]

With Germanism enough to make them Philistines[33] the English were, of course, not exempt from that vulgarity which came of want of delicacy of perception in matters of taste and beauty. The aristocracy, though materialized, still retained vestiges of its heritage in manners and civilized taste; the populace, brutalized as it was, had not yet risen to a comprehension of these subtle distinctions; it was, therefore, the middle classes, the true Philistines, who displayed this Teutonic incapacity in its most flamboyant dress. In Trafalgar Square, "the finest site in Europe," they had built as their noblest monument a Truss Manufactory of which the Irish Celt was incapable of seeing the symbolic force.[34] Again, "what a touch of grossness in our race, what an original shortcoming in the more delicate spiritual perceptions, is shown by the natural growth amongst us of such hideous names,—Higginbottom, Stiggins, Bugg!" And as a corrective to Sir Charles Adderley's exuberant praise of the superior Anglo-Saxon race, Arnold murmured to himself "*Wragg is in custody*," the concluding lines of a newspaper clipping about a girl who had murdered her illegitimate child. "*Wragg is in custody.*

The sex lost in the confusion of our unrivalled happiness; or (shall I say?) the superfluous Christian name lopped off by the straightforward vigour of our old Anglo-Saxon breed!"[35] From Llandudno he wrote to his sister, Fan, that he was quite overpowered by the poetry of Celtic place-names.[36] He was haunted by the "penetrating, lofty beauty" of such names as "Velindra, Tyntagel, Caernarvon."[37] Quite different, however, was his reaction in the Philistine, and in his opinion, Anglo-Saxon United States. There the grotesque nomenclature reminded him of *Tristram Shandy*. A "congenital" lack of "artist-sense," he believed, accounted for the hideous names with *ville* endings—Briggsville, Higginsville, Jacksonville, etc.—found from Maine to Florida.[38] His ears stopped by the wax of Philistinism, he was never lured, as Coleridge and Southey were, by the siren call of Susquehanna. In his comment on the United States, however, Arnold never descended to the level of rudeness reached by Oscar Wilde, who, on his trip across the western plains, if one may believe his report, received a telegram from Griggsville, Kansas, asking him to deliver a lecture on aesthetics, and replied that the people should first prove their interest in the subject by changing the name of the town.

The second of the failings of the Philistine, coarseness in morals and feeling, was evident both in Germany and England. Among the Germans it manifested itself in the form of arrogance; among their cousins, the English, in the form of hardness. Arminius, in *Friendship's Garland*, with his "coarse Prussian sneers," and his "harsh, arrogant, Prussian way of turning up his nose at things and laying down the law about them" was an example.[39] In 1871, at the close of the Fanco-Prussian war, Arnold found in Switzerland many Germans, who had come to show themselves after their victories.[40] A sufficient commentary on the German character was provided in the spectacle of Strasbourg, a city of German race and language, going "mad for joy at a victory gained by the French over Germans."[41] In the asperities of organized research in Germany, he discovered further proof of coarseness: Dr. Volkmar on Tischendorf; Tischendorf on Dr. Volkmar; Professor Steinthal on a rival. "And only the other day the newspapers brought us an address of Dr. Mommsen, in which the new Rector of the University of Berlin, with a charming crudity, gravely congratulated his countrymen on not being modest, and adjured them never to fall into that sad fault."[42] In his objections to the Germans on the ground of bad taste in general and coarseness in particular, Arnold, whether knowingly or not, was continuing a long English tradition. Half a century earlier, Carlyle, the staff of whose spear was like a weaver's beam, had dealt stout blows in their defense on these very charges.[43]

What in the Germans became coarseness, in the English became "hardness and insolence," qualities derived from the Normans, who were basically of Teutonic race, even though their genius was determined chiefly by their Latin civilization.[44] This defect of the Philistine middle classes was to Arnold a matter of vital concern in his *Irish Essays*, for it was in Ireland that its most alarming effects were to be observed. Repeatedly, he commented on the attractive nature of the French, by means of which Alsace, though German and Protestant, was held in bonds of strongest allegiance to Catholic and Celtic France, while Protestant and Germanic Great Britain, on the other hand, failed so humiliatingly in its relationship with Ireland.[45] No longer could England hope by belated material concessions to conciliate the Irish. The middle-class Englishman—the only class with which the Irish came into contact—must be born anew, he must be transformed. Healing measures must be employed. "The Irish quick-wittedness, sentiment, keen feeling for social life and manners, demand something which this hard and imperfect civilization cannot give."[46] For centuries the English had treated the native Irish with contempt and tyranny, "a disposition to hardness" being "perhaps the special fault and danger of our English race in general, going along with our merits of energy and honesty."[47] The uncompromising Mr. Murdstone, of the *History of David Copperfield*, served as an example, with his firmness, his austerity, his lack of courtesy, and his inability to enter into other people's feelings. People of this kind led a dull and dismal life; they possessed none of the "irresistible magnetism" of the Irish. No wonder, therefore, that many an English conqueror had been won over to the point of forgetting his own nature, foregoing his own nation, and becoming a convert to Popery.[48] Amiability was the only bond that would hold together the seemingly incompatible English and Irish, but unfortunately the English regarded the amiable man as weak and the hard man as strong.[49] How deeply Arnold felt the want of this desirable quality in his countrymen is indicated in the fact that he devoted an entire essay to the phenomenon of one Englishman, Falkland, who was amiable. As a text for the essay, he used an observation by a Frenchman on the English rule in India: "The English are just, but not amiable."[50] In one of his last letters, written a month before he died, Arnold commented on a picture of himself which his wife thought very weak-looking; for his own part, he was well enough pleased to be made to look amiable.[51] That the Englishman is a person of difficult and unbending temperament, what redeeming qualities he may possess being vitiated by his haughty and contemptuous manner, whereas the Frenchman is a person of indescribable amiability and charm, is, of course, a differentiation enthusiastically accepted in France.[52] Upon justice as an English trait one would expect to find less Gallic agreement. But even for this quality there is the distinguished authority of Taine,[53] though in the eyes of some his report must be discounted, since, as has been charged, he spent most of his life vainly regretting that France was not England.

The main outlines of Arnold's distinction between the Irish and the English were repeated in Meredith's novels. A favorite device with Meredith was to join the two in marriage, and within the confines of this close union to study the interplay of their racial characteristics, as in the case of Diana and her first English husband, in *Diana of the Crossways,* or that of the genial Captain Con O'Donnell and his hard, unamiable English wife, in *Celt and Saxon.*[54] Like Arnold, Meredith was alarmed at the growing alienation between England and Ireland, and he proposed essentially the same remedies. Both men in their advocacy of conciliatory measures on the part of the English would fall into that group to whom Carlyle referred contemptuously as desiring to rule Ireland through the gentle agency of love.

However much Arnold might stress the national and racial inadequacies of the Philistine on the side of beauty and taste and on the side of morals and feeling, and from the preceding pages it is evident that he stressed them to the point of strain in many of his prose works, it was on the side of mind and spirit that he placed his chief emphasis. Vulgarity and coarseness were the outward manifestations of a chronic and deep-seated inner ailment, unintelligence. Though present in its most virulent form in the Philistines, the virus had infected the whole Teutonic race, all the northern peoples. First, however, unintelligence must be defined, for Arnold did not use it in its current and accepted sense. Often during his career he was chided on his penchant for vague generalization, as in the case of his famous phrase "the grand style," which he confessed he could define best by example. He cultivated by preference an "easy, sinuous, unpolemical" style. But for once he has been at some pains to explain his term exactly.

> '*Der Engländer ist eigentlich ohne Intelligenz*,' said Goethe; by which he meant, not that the Englishman was stupid, but that he occupied himself little with the *rationale* of things. He meant that an Englishman held and uttered any given opinion as something isolated, without perceiving its relation to other ideas, or its due place in the general world of thought; without, therefore, having any notion of its absolute value. He meant, in short, that he was uncritical.[55]

An uncritical habit of mind, then, was the prevailing characteristic of the English people. Heretofore, particularly in the first two quarters of the century, another dominant English trait, energy, had sufficed to preserve the nation. But now, in the third quarter, England in her customary reliance on energy alone was falling to the rear in the march of European progress. For England, the time was out of joint, and Arnold seemed born to set it right.

Unlike Hamlet, he did not curse his fate, but cheerfully embraced it. He conceived his function in England to be that of Renan in France: preceptor to the nation. As Renan, in France, had made it his major endeavor to inculcate morals, so Arnold, in England, would make it his major endeavor to inculcate intelligence, always, he added, in a high sense of the word.[56] And for many years this was the public role that he assumed, though he also espoused the cause of morals, particularly after 1870, Renan having proved to be a renegade in this latter worthy cause.

Goethe's indictment of the Englishman, in itself of sufficient weight to carry conviction, was made doubly authoritative by the similar view of French historians. From Amédée Thierry's ethnological introduction to the famous *History of the Gauls*, Arnold learned to look upon the French, that is the Celts or Gauls, as being "eminently intelligent," and upon the Teutons as being undistinguished in this respect.[57] Michelet, of whom Arnold was early enamored, whom later he met in person, and whose works he read at intervals through life, was in the first chapters of *The History of France* a disciple of Thierry and, like his predecessor, was prone to make broad and often baseless distinctions among the races. Later, in the Preface of 1869, Michelet had come to the opinion that all the races of the world have contributed in the formation of the modern Frenchman, and he, therefore, repudiated Thierry and his hypothesis of the continuance of racial traits unchanged from ancient to modern times.[58] It is from Michelet the racialist, the Michelet of 1848, however, that Arnold took a remark which he applied frequently thereafter to the Americans and the English. Writing to his friend Clough, who had spent his early boyhood in Charleston, South Carolina, Arnold said: "Have you seen Michelet's characterization (superb) of your brothers—'La dure inintelligence des Anglo-Américains.' "[59] And as a final authority, Renan was cited on the lack of general intelligence among the people of the United States.[60]

For Arnold, the two determining factors in the possession of intelligence, or the lack of it, by a people were culture and race. French intelligence he was inclined to attribute to the influence of Latin civilization; Teutonic unintelligence, on the other hand, was most frequently explained on the basis of race. Against the patriotic objections of many of his contemporaries, he consistently maintained that among modern nations France stood out preëminently in intelligence, a quality to which he referred at other times and in other places as Hellenism, lucidity, and *eutrapelia* or flexibility. Its beneficent and luminous effects were to be seen among all the French classes, the lower as well as the middle and upper. Yet, "I suppose that this intelligence is a thing not altogether peculiar and innate in the people of France."[61] In his report on French education, he listed school legislation as one of the influences at work in the imparting of this attitude of mind. French law was also an influence, by its form as well as its spirit: the Code Napoléon was the essence of clarity and intelligibility as contrasted with the bewildering text of an English Act of Parliament. If the French mind had not itself craved lucidity, the language would almost have compelled it.[62] But in the German mind these attributes "seem to be even by nature somewhat wanting. In the German mind, as in the German language, there does seem to be something *splay*, something blunt-edged, unhandy and infelicitous." This deficiency he ascribed definitely to race in *On the Study of Celtic Literature*,[63] an explanation which he did not abandon even later when he considered the lack of "a long practical conversance with great affairs" as another possible cause.[64]

Though Arnold in his poetry strove to achieve the sequence, the right placing of relative parts, the unity resulting from the wise disposition of materials, that he so much admired in the Greeks, he recognized his comparative failure. *Sohrab and Rustum* possesses feeling, fire, and eloquence, he believes, but is weak in composition in the painter's sense. As in painting, so in poetry, "is it not to be expected that in this same article of *composition* the awkward incorrect Northern nature should show itself?"[65] Grandeur is achieved by the great northern poets as well as by the Greeks, but the grandeur of Shakespeare and of Goethe is "mixed and turbid," whereas that of Homer is pure and clear, perfect and lovely, without sacrificing energy and power characteristic of the poetry of the ruder northern climates.[66] There are two kinds of serenity: that of the Greeks, which comes from the ordering and harmonising of ideas, and that of Teutonic aristocracies which "appears to come from their never having had any ideas to trouble them."[67] And as for *eutrapelia*, the happy and gracious flexibility in which the Athenians were eminent, "that quality, as we all know, is not a characteristic quality of the Germanic nations, to which we ourselves belong."[68] The Northern peoples, it is evident, are *eigentlich ohne Intelligenz*. In a word, they are uncritical. All this is obviously a continuation of the debate, familiar to students of the seventeenth and eighteenth centuries, on the respective merits of the Classical and Gothic styles. In the nineteenth-century defense of Gothic, Arnold was not a participant. Of the author whose central book is based on the text, "*Estote ergo vos perfecti!* Be ye therefore perfect!" it is hardly to be expected that he will greet with the delirious enthusiasm of a Browning the "nowise polished," or that he will believe "What's come to perfection perishes." Nor would he agree with Carlyle that elegance is "more admirable for men-milliners than for critics and philosophers." Arnold is never rapt away, as is Ruskin, into an ecstasy of panegyric on the savageness of Gothic architecture.

The failure in critical power, that is, in intelligence, was abundantly manifest among the Germans in their literature and in their scholarly criticism. It was T. H. Huxley's view that the Germans, at least in the scientific field, had no notion of style and were wont to compose their books with a pitchfork. Arnold's comment upon them was much the same, though expressed in language somewhat less picturesque. Style in the highest sense did not exist by nature in the German genius and literature. Of this Goethe was aware. Regarded not as a European, but solely as a German, he was noteworthy chiefly as the author who did most to supply this deficiency. Half his effort was spent in the attempt to create a German style, a labor which he would have been saved had he been born a Frenchman.[69] Even so, his prose fell short in this respect. By their want of style, the Germans succeeded in marring the *Nibelungen* story, which potentially was a magnificant theme. That the Norse versions of the same story did display power of style and a certain technical development was perhaps to be explained by a Celtic leaven which the Germans proper did not have.[70] Dead to style themselves, the Germans naturally tended to depreciate it in others, witness the ungracious reception in Germany of the stylistically brilliant work of Renan.[71] In a field where giants, such as Luther and Goethe, contended without full success, the average man, the Philistine, would, of course, succumb ignominiously. In the popular literary field of hymnology, the Germans—and with them their English cousins—discovered to the world their racial weakness. "Only the German race, with its want of quick instinctive tact, of delicate, sure perception, could have invented the hymn as the Germans have it; and our non-German turn for style,—style, of which the very essence is a certain happy fineness and truth of poetical perception,—could not but desert us when our German nature carried us into a kind of composition which can please only when the perception is somewhat blunt."[72] It is perhaps consoling to know that Arnold's own German nature did not desert him at the last. A few hours before his death, he was heard singing softly to himself the hymn, "When I Survey the Wondrous Cross."[73] But his animus against English hymns was displayed throughout his works. In the brick-and-mortar chapel at Hawley Square, Miss Emma Tatham chanting with Protestant fervor

> My Jesus to know, and feel His blood flow,
> 'Tis life everlasting, 'tis heaven below,

served as a case study.[74] Shakespeare had done more to moralize and ennoble English statesmen than Dr. Watts with his six hundred hymns.[75] And though Arnold rejected the anthropomorphic God of received Christianity in favor of an Eternal Power, not ourselves, which made for righteousness, he was certain that this vaguely defined cosmic force must be displeased on its æsthetic and intellectual side by such doggerel hymns as: *Sing glory, glory, glory to the great God Triune!* and, *Out of my stony griefs Bethels I'll raise!*[76] All this was a matter of taste, to be sure, but it was an indication, also, of that "something *splay*," which Arnold detected in the German mind. This quality, which he regarded now as a cultural, and again as a racial, defect, was apparent not merely in the manner of expression but in the thought itself, as was evident in the field of Biblical criticism. Diligent beyond all others in the amassing of facts—an indispensable and highly honorable service—the Germans too frequently were unable to draw the right conclusions from them. For this latter part of the mental process, critical power and discernment were demanded. Critical tact, the quick and sure perception of the true relationship of things—this the Germans did not have. In this vital matter, whether by reason of race or long cultural tradition, the Italians, the French, and even the English were superior to the Germans.[77]

Though the Germans were deficient in critical power, they were not without ideas. After all, said Arnold, Germany was the home of science and philosophy. In fact, as Heine had pointed out, the nation suffered from a surfeit of ideas, which unfortunately it did not know how to apply. The case of the English was more to be deplored, for they lacked both critical power and ideas. Unintelligence with them was a dominant trait, and it was to be observed not only among the Philistines, where it was seen in its most repulsive aspects, but among the aristocracy and the populace as well. To provide both ideas and a critical habit of mind, or at least to show that they were needed and to indicate in what manner they might be achieved, was for a number of years Arnold's chief concern.

As Professor of Poetry at Oxford, he chose for his inaugural lecture to define the modern element in literature. The age of the most advanced civilization was the most modern age, and by this standard, Greece of the age of Pericles was more modern than England of the Elizabethan age, and by implication more modern than contemporary England. In the culminating epoch of Greece, society had arrived at a state of peace, in which repose, confidence, and free activity were possible. Along with these characteristics went a tolerant spirit, the development of the conveniences of life, and the formation of taste. "And this leads us to the supreme characteristic of all: the intellectual maturity of man himself; the tendency to observe facts with a critical spirit; to search for their law, now to wander among them at random; to judge by the rule of reason, not by the impulse of prejudice or caprice."[78] As Arnold in subsequent works turned his gaze upon the English of his own era, it was just in these essentials—the critical spirit and the rule of reason—that he found them most wanting. The pamphlet *England and the Italian Question* (1859) discussed the inadequacy of the English aristocracy in the current crisis. Aristocracies by their very nature were not amenable to ideas. Profiting more than do any other groups by the *status quo,* they desired no change, no new ideas. Their last great work was the treaty of Vienna, by which the future of Europe for the following fifty years had been determined. Force, the customary weapon of aristocracies, was the means employed. Now, as democracy on the Continent, and even in England, gathered strength, reason was demanded. Everywhere the masses were open to ideas in their struggle to improve their conditions, though in England this was far less true than in France. Intelligence was not a characteristic of the

English lower classes, as it was of the French. Neither had there been the same provocation to revolt, the English aristocracy always having tempered its domination with more justice than had been the case in France. This arraignment of the English aristocracy and masses Arnold developed on much the same basis in the essay, *Democracy* (1861) and in sections of *Culture and Anarchy* (1869). His slur upon the intelligence of the English masses did not go uncontested at the time. To Fitzjames Stephen, the contrast between the English and French groups seemed unfounded. In Stephen's opinion, Arnold had been rendered blind to the real virtues of the English by his excessive zeal for all things French.[79] Actually, though Arnold was unaware of the fact, the working class during this period was animated in the conduct of its affairs by a number of large and even generous concepts. Furthermore, it was carrying some of them into effect. In its frequent, if ineffective, petitions to Parliament for the redress of industrial evils and in its support of the government in the Crimean War on the theory that England in international affairs should take a determined stand against despotism, the populace was showing a conception of the state as a strong centralized power which agreed with Arnold's own conception. Alone among the English classes, it displayed some sense of *Europeanism*. Against their own interests, the cotton operatives supported the North in the American Civil War, whereas the upper classes sympathized with the South. And all through these years the trade unions were being organized and developed.[80]

Intelligence, the critical habit of mind, is a dominant theme in *Essays in Criticism, First Series* (1865). The most famous chapters of *Culture and Anarchy* (1869) are "Sweetness and Light," and "Hebraism and Hellenism," the very titles indicating the relevance to intelligence and criticism. In *Friendship's Garland* (1871), the opening letter is called "I introduce Arminius and 'Geist' to the British Public," Geist being, as Arnold explained, that quality which the English and French knew as intelligence, the idea that "is at the bottom of democrary, the victory of reason and intelligence over blind custom and prejudice."[81] And the volume closes, in "My Countrymen," with an attack upon the middle class, which because of its lack of intelligence did not know the way the world was going. What intelligence it had was without plan or zeal, and led nowhere; was ineffectual. It exercised no influence whatever upon the mind of Europe.[82] For his "A Speech at Eton" (1879), Arnold traced the history of the word *eutrapelia*, the quality of flexibility of mind. "Lucidity of thought, clearness and propriety of language, freedom from prejudice and from stiffness, openness of mind, amiability of manners —all these seem to go along with a certain happy flexibility of nature, and to depend upon it." And all these the Germanic nations seemed to be without.[83] Finally, "A Liverpool Address" (1882), is devoted to an exposition on lucidity for which the French had a natural turn, and the English, seemingly, a natural abhorrence. As a result, England had become the scene of such violent and barbaric orgies as those of the Salvation Army, and of such fantastic rituals and absurd doctrines as those of the Oxford Movement. A little lucidity would have been fatal to both.

"At once so resolute and so unintelligent"[84]—this was Arnold's dictum on the English, a pronouncement amply supported by evidence from whatever field of thought or action he chose for illustration: politics, religion, education, and literature. Believers in action, in immediate crude reforms, rather than in the slow, long-range, but eventually more fruitful schemes which grow out of the cultivation of a critical, intelligent frame of mind, the English were confronted internally with anarchy, and internationally with a rapidly-waning influence. Arnold was deeply apprehensive about England's future, was convinced that the nation was in imminent danger of "declining into a sort of greater Holland" because of its hostility to ideas and its failure to see the trend of world developments.[85] Though not, like Carlyle, a clamorous advocate of empire, with visions of vast savannas about the world awaiting tillage by men of right Teutsch, that is, English, stock, neither was Arnold, like Edward Fitzgerald and many others, a Little Englander, grown weary with world hegemony, and sighing plaintively, "Once more I say, would we were a little, peaceful, unambitious, trading nation like—the Dutch." According to Arnold, it was Burke's peculiar distinction that he lived in a world of ideas, a world into which neither the Tories nor the Liberals were likely to enter. Arnold's sympathies lay rather with the Liberals than with the Tories, yet even to the Liberals he could not give full allegiance. They also were given too much to settling things first and understanding them afterwards, if at all; they too were slaves to party catchwords and party habits. If, therefore, Arnold was to be of the party, it had to be with qualifications: he desired to be a Liberal of the future.

If England had ordered its political activities badly, it had ordered its religion even worse. Heterodoxy and nonconformity were rife, each "hole-and-corner" sect wasting its energies in the defense of its narrow, stunted creed;

whereas right reason and the intelligible law of things should have dictated a few establishments, say the Anglican, the Presbyterian, the Catholic, and the Jewish, tolerant enough so that among them they would include the whole nation as communicants. Arnold was deaf to Mill's argument that in division there is strength, that in an establishment the spirit dies because it is never contested and the letter alone giveth a semblance of life. And though on Arnold's bookshelf Thomas à Kempis occupied a position of honor at one end and Voltaire an equally honorable position at the other, there is no evidence that Arnold knew Voltaire's comment that the English dwelt together in amity because of their many sects; that had there been but two, they would in their religious zeal have slit each other's throats. To Arnold, the unintelligence of the English was nowhere more evident than in their many and misguided interpretations of the Bible. He, therefore, set aside some ten years of his life to a rational interpretation of the Scriptures. His avowed and noble aim was to rescue the Sacred Book from the miracles imposed upon it by the superstitious disciples, after all men of their age and subject to its errors, from the "turbid fancies" of the Rabbis, from the metaphysical glosses of the Church Fathers and the Anglican Bishops, and from the narrow exegesis of the Non-conformists. How low the English had sunk in such matters was indicated by the notorious reception given to Colenso's *The Pentateuch and Book of Joshua Critically Examined.* "Occasionally, the uncritical spirit of our race determines to perform a great public act of self-humiliation. Such an act it has recently accomplished. It has just sent forth as its scapegoat into the wilderness amidst a titter from educated Europe, the

Bishop of Natal."[86] The effect of the book on the religious world was to be seen in a newspaper called *Public Opinion*: "There, week after week, the critical genius of our nation discovers itself in captivating nudity."[87] As a man of light and leading in the surrounding critical darkness, Arnold did not in this particular instance shine with his accustomed brightness, for he swelled the chorus in condemnation of the book on the ground that it would unsettle the faith of the masses, a charge that could with equal justice be brought against his own labors in the religious field. In view of his repeated insistence on the unintelligence of the English masses as compared with the French, his desire in this case to limit the exercise of what intelligence they have seems at the very least contradictory. His argument is less open to question when he says that compared with the investigations of such continental scholars as Strauss and Renan, Colenso's work was the veriest primer. It is assuredly a reflection, he says, on the intelligence of the English that they accept with any seriousness such a childish venture in a subject where adult and mature treatises are available.

The relationship between intelligence, or the critical habit of mind, and culture was, of course, obvious, and the chief instrument for the spread of both was education —his own profession, on which he spoke, therefore, with the voice of authority. One of the strongest agencies in the promotion of the vaunted French intelligence was their enlightened school legislation. Even Germany and Holland had much to teach the English in the conduct of their schools, both higher and secondary. The English middle class could never hope to rise out of its circumscribed existence, "with a defective type of religion, a narrow range of intellect and knowledge, a stunted sense of beauty, a low standard of manners,"[88] until it saw the necessity of better schools for its children. This was Arnold's one nostrum, to use his own word, and he recommended it in and out of season, as the only certain cure for all the ailments—political, religious, social, and literary—of the body politic.

A schoolman by necessity, a literary man by choice, Arnold could harldy fail to apply his theory of unintelligence to the literature of his countrymen. As one reviews the whole body of his commentary on English literature, one is startled by the severity of his judgment.[89] Of Shakespeare he could say, "Others abide our question. Thou art free." But Shakespeare, too, had his fault, one foot, at least, of clay. For all his God-like qualities, he lacked the crowning gift of simplicity. He was too often led astray by his wonderful faculty of expression "into a fondness for curiosity of expression, into an irritability of fancy, which seems to make it impossible for him to say a thing plainly, even when the press of the action demands the very directest language, or its level character the very simplest." As a model in "clearness of arrangement, rigour of development, simplicity of style" Shakespeare remained inferior to the ancients.[90] All these qualities, as Arnold explained in "The Literary Influence of Academies," were the affair of intelligence, that is of critical judgment, as contrasted with genius. Shakespeare possessed genius in superb abundance; he was not so splendidly endowed with critical judgment. England's one grand master of style, Milton, failed in amiability; in his Puritan disputations he was capable of saying of an opponent, "I mean not to dispute philosophy with this pork, who never had any."[91] Chaucer was deficient in high seriousness. No English author received Arnold's unqualified approbation. And as of individuals, so of epochs. The Elizabethan age with its love of the excessive, the fantastic in language, style, and dress showed vestiges of its barbaric origin. It was not yet completely civilized, had not yet fully attained "the manifestation of a critical spirit, the endeavour after a rational arrangement and appreciation of facts."[92] A spiritual east wind blew through the eighteenth century, leaving a "touch of frost" upon "the imaginative life of the soul" so far as poetry is concerned. And as for the prose of the century, though it was the best that England had achieved, though it was Attic in style—with Arnold the highest of compliments—it yet fell short in Addison, one of the ablest and most representative men, in adequate ideas. Turning to the Romantic period, with Goethe for his guide, Arnold found Byron intellectually a child – "*Sobald er reflectirt ist er ein Kind.*"[93] Though Byron in this respect ranked lowest among the Romantic writers, all of them in varying degrees displayed the same weakness. All were strong in the quality which was the chief strength of the English—energy; all, in varying degrees, were weak in the quality which was the chief weakness of the English—critical power. Deprived of a current of "animating and nourishing ideas," indispensable to any truly great creative effort, they simply "did not know enough." In consequence, Byron was "so empty of matter, Shelley so incoherent, Wordsworth even, profound as he is, yet so wanting in completeness and variety."[94] On much the same basis, Arnold disparaged his own era. Because of his failure in intellectual power, Tennyson was not "a great and powerful spirit in any line."[95] Browning did indeed possess a vigorous mind, but he had not that critical intelligence which supplies "an Idea of the world" to centralize and unify impressions. He achieved "but a confused multitudinousness."[96] In similar vein, Arnold commented on Alexander Smith and the Spasmodic poets, much in vogue in the middle years of the century. Overcome by the multiplicity of the world, they lost themselves, like Browning.[97] As their name, the Spasmodics, indicated, they were deficient in *architectonicè*, that is in form and construction over which the intelligence presides. Their defect was the characteristic defect of English poetry, a preference for single passages of brilliance and beauty over the total grand impression produced by a work of art.[98] They were "young gentlemen with really wonderful powers of perception and expression, but to whom there is wholly wanting a 'bedeutendes Individuum'—so that their productions are most unedifying and unsatisfactory."[99] Accused by his sister of becoming as dogmatic as Ruskin, Arnold replied that there was a difference: Ruskin was "dogmatic and wrong."[100] For the "Carlylean strain" all "clear-headed" men had come to feel an "utter contempt."[101] In "preaching earnestness to a nation which had plenty of it by nature, but was less abundantly supplied with several other useful things," Carlyle was carrying coals to Newcastle.[102] Among these "other useful things," as Arnold for years had been pointing out, intelligence was chief.

So ended the long catalogue on the Englishman's prime defect. Arnold made his diagnosis, read

> each weakness clear;
> And struck his finger on the place,
> And said: *Thou ailest here, and here!*

Once determined on the cause, he was persistent in calling attention to the ailment, ingenious in discovering evidences of its effects. It is clear that the unintelligence of the English was with Arnold a central doctrine; around it as a nucleus he built to a considerable extent the structure of his criticism of English life and thought. In this analysis of the fundamental English weakness, one German commentator, with an understandable national bias, since he seemed unaware that the same criticism was applied to his own countrymen, saw the real worth of Arnold's life work.[103]

That the English are lovers of action rather than of thought, of ideas, was one of Arnold's most often repeated observations. And his criticism was borne out, he believed, by the traditional emphasis in the great public schools—Eton, Harrow, Winchester, Rugby—and in Oxford and Cambridge upon the training of the gentleman and man of action who would become a leader of men in the community and in the state. It was this limitation of their function that caused Arnold to speak of the great English universities as "hauts lycées," finishing schools for young gentlemen.[104] Whether deliberately or not, he took issue with Newman's concept of the ideal university as a training ground for gentlemen. Without denying the merits of the training that the older universities did provide, he would have added as an equally important service the "spread of mental activity," the "love for things of the mind," the cultivation of "the higher studies of Europe."[105] Although by no means alone in his championship of intelligence—for the valiant labors in the same cause by such men as John Stuart Mill cannot be ignored—Arnold was unquestionably in the minority. The traditional English view, the view of the majority, was better expressed by Carlyle in his praise of intuition as against logic, that meagre rushlight by which such peoples as the French are content to be guided, of action as against mere theorizing and word-spinning, in his praise of "the deep fathomless domain of the Unconscious," whereon the conscious rests and has its meaning.

Secure in its position as one of the leading nations of the world, and at times the leading nation, England has good-naturedly tolerated the remarks of Arnold and others on its incapacities in the field of the intelligence, has even half agreed. What matter by what means, whether by energy, by character, or by intelligence, so long as one arrives at the goal? Perhaps as a nation it has stumbled upon achievement, blundered upon success. No matter. The solid accomplishment is there, and the world's acclaim is testimony to the fact. Thus on Dec. 23, 1872, the *Times* conceded, "There is truth, however, in the assertion that we are backward in appreciating and pursuing abstract knowledge."[106] The *Edinburgh Review* granted that there was no root for ideas among the English, and that Arnold was correct in ascribing this to "the want of flexibility in our race."[107] And Stanley Baldwin, as Prime Minister, admitted that the criticism "often made of us is not without an element of truth . . . .that as a nation we are less open to the intellectual sense that the Latin races," though he balanced this admission with an emphatic statement that no nation on earth had the same knack of producing geniuses.[108] To such general, if somewhat qualified, agreements there were, however, exceptions. Fitzjames Stephen's objection to Arnold's contrast between the English and French intelligence has already been cited.[109] Herbert Spencer flatly denied the validity of Arnold's thesis, and attempted by a lengthy survey of English contributions in the abstract and concrete sciences to prove that the English were by no means deficient in intelligence.[110] Further exception was taken by the *Edinburgh Review*. The English because of their practical, untheoretic nature are able to range freely among ideas in every department. Arnold's method, said the reviewer, is too restrictive, too theoretic, too French, too doctrinaire. It attempts to apply ideas without sufficient consideration of race, personality, climate and inheritance. And the method is weak particularly in its failure to bring the imagination into play. Had Arnold taken race sufficiently into account, he would have realized that the English mind adapts itself less easily to French *esprit* than to German *geist*. With *esprit* are associated quickness of wit, clarity of intellect, an intelligence equipped for making distinctions. *Geist* is soulfulness of mind; it is charity allied with clarity; it is, as Goethe said, *esprit* with *âme* added. In its teaching, *esprit* is too direct, not imaginative enough, too prone to consider individuals always as part of a movement of thought or current of ideas. A right analysis reveals that human beings are not, as Arnold and the French seem to believe, primarily intellectual; they are far more the creatures of their senses, their feelings, their moods.[111] In this series of distinctions the anonymous *Edinburgh* reviewer unwittingly fell into the errors of the school against which he inveighed: he was himself too theoretic, too restrictive, too doctrinaire. A more sympathetic, if not a more thorough, reading of the very works on which the review was based—*Irish Essays and Others*, *Culture and Anarchy*, *Essays in Criticism*, *Letters of Mat-*

thew Arnold (*1848–1888*), *Friendship's Garland*—would have revealed that if there is any tendency which to Arnold is anathema it is the tendency toward the preponderance of any single element in the life of the individual or the nation. Culture is defined repeatedly as the harmonious development of all the powers, more specifically: the power of conduct, the power of intellect and knowledge, the power of beauty, the power of social life and manners. If any one of these powers in Arnold's formula is given too much weight, it is that of conduct, not that of intellect, for he assigns to conduct three-fourths of life, leaving only one-fourth for the intellectual and aesthetic disciplines to divide between them.[112] From the charge of over-intellectualism he is further absolved by his insistence throughout his works on the importance of the 'imaginative reason' in the life of the modern spirit. It is only when the imagination and the rational faculty work together in harmony that the greatest works are produced in any field: politics, religion, education, literature. It is because of the fusion of these powers that Spinoza must be ranked higher than Locke, Homer higher than Voltaire.[113] All this one can say in Arnold's defense. Nontheless, there is a real basis for the criticism by the *Edinburgh* reviewer. As this present chapter has shown, Arnold for a considerable period in his career did place chief emphasis on intelligence, the crying want of the English race. And the emphasis told upon his contemporaries. As early as 1865, he was accused of "a deficiency in sympathies lying beyond the intellectual sphere,"[114] and as late as 1898, he was reproached for "preferring an intellectual standard to a moral standard for fear of displeasing one of his French friends."[115] It is also true that Arnold dearly loved a generalization. He was apt at cataloguing, industrious in classification. And seldom, as E. K. Brown has pointed out, was he satisfied in the discussion of a limited subject until he had related it to some eternal principle, until he had elevated it to the plane of some wide movement of ideas, some significant current of thought. Hence, in his pages, the frequency of references to epochs and eras: the Periclean, the Augustan, the Elizabethan, the Romantic. And around such movements as the Reformation, the Renaissance, and the French Revolution a large part of his argument revolved.

As a conclusion to the foregoing analysis of Arnold's full-length picture of the Saxon as a Philistine, it should be noted that he was anticipated in some of his indictments by the English physician and ethnologist Robert Knox in *The Races of Men: A Fragment*, which appeared in 1850 and was republished in 1862 under the title, *The Races of Men, A Philosophical Inquiry into the Influence of Race over the Destinies of Nations*. Emerson, in *English Traits*, was influenced by Knox's theories, and acknowledged his indebtedness. Nowhere in Arnold's works thus far published, however, is there any mention of Knox. This is not, of course, conclusive proof that Arnold was unfamiliar with the ethnologist's book. And even if he had not read *The Races of Men*, he could have come into contact with Knox's ideas, for in the introduction to the 1850 edition Knox says that the substance of the work had been delivered as lectures in such cities as Manchester and Birmingham, where the press had reported his theories. And in London, he adds, the great newspapers had stolen his ideas and used them without acknowledgement in leading articles. Though he does not call the Saxon a

Philistine, he attributes to him many of the qualities which Arnold employs in defining the type.

> I may probably, then commence with the Physiological history of the Saxon, tracing the moral and physical characteristics which distinguish him from all other races of men—his religious formulas, his literature, his contempt for art, his abhorrence for theory—that is, for science and scientific men, his acquisitive and applicative genius, tracing all to the eternal, unalterable qualities of race.
>
> Thoughtful, plodding, industrious beyond all other races, a lover of labour for labour's sake; he cares not its amount if it be but profitable; large handed, mechanical, a lover of order, of punctuality in business, of neatness and cleanliness. In these qualities no race approaches him; the wealthy with him is the sole respectable, the respectable the sole good; the word comfort is never out of his mouth—it is the beau ideal of the Saxon.
>
> His genius is wholly applicative, for he invents nothing. In the fine arts, and in music, taste cannot go lower. . . . Accumulative beyond all others, the wealth of the world collects in their hands.
>
> No race perhaps exceeds them in an abstract sense of justice, and a love of fair play; *but only to Saxons*. This of course they do not extend to other races.
>
> He is a man of circumstances, of expediency without method; 'try all things, but do not theorize.' Give me 'constants,' a book of constants; this is his cry. Hence his contempt for men of science.[116]

As the first of these excerpts indicates, Knox is no reformer. He regards himself as a scientist, whose function it is to discover and classify racial traits, not to change them; in fact, they cannot be changed, for the qualities of race are "eternal, unalterable." In this respect he is distinguished from Arnold, whose labors were all directed to the one great end of changing the English race, of bettering it. Such change can be affected at will, evidently, by giving greater prominence to one or another of the three racial strains that make up the English blend: the German, the Celtic, the Norman. The underlying confusion in Arnold's argument is that at one and the same time he regards racial qualities as constant and yet alterable. The modern Englishman is what he is because the three strains have retained their individual characteristics. Now, to meet the requirements of this latter day, Arnold would alter the balance—a little less weight on the German side, a little more on the Celtic. By taking thought, he seems to say, one can literally add a cubit to one's stature, change the nature of one's blood. By laying stress on the virtues of Celtic authors, he hopes to lessen the preponderance of the Teutonic element in the English. More and more he sees evidences of success in this direction, for "the English people are improvable, I hope. Slowly this powerful race works its way out of its confining ruts and its clouded vision of things, to the manifestation of those great qualities which it has at bottom,—piety, integrity, good-nature, and good-humour."[117] What rut more confining than that of Philistinism; what vision more clouded than that of the materialistic Saxon?

Chapter IV

The Teuton Redeemed

Coiner of phrases as he was, Arnold must have appreciated Swinburne's description of him as "David the son of Goliath." In regard to the Teutonism of the two Arnolds, the phrase is strikingly apt, though Swinburne did not give it that application. Thomas Arnold was a fervent admirer of the Germanic races, the most moral that the world had known; he was a disciple of Niebuhr, the historian, and an intimate friend of Bunsen, the German ambassador to England; he came to be known as "that Teuton of Teutons, the Celt-hating Dr. Arnold." Matthew Arnold was, and is still, regarded as the champion of the Celts, the sympathetic friend of France, and the arch-enemy of Philistinism, that evil flower, sprung from Teutonic soil. No one, of course, can deny that many of his most significant essays are devoted to praise of the Celtic and French elements in modern civilization. But a consideration of his work as a whole shows that he placed his deepest trust in the "serious Germanic races." Theirs were the sterling virtues, theirs the solid, if also unhappily the stolid, qualities which the world must fall back on at last. It is because he knows them to be strong that he speaks chiefly of their weaknesses. By pointing out their defects, he will enable them to become stronger still. If the Germanic race, freed of its deficiencies, can be brought to add the best that the Celtic genius has to offer, it may rise to a culture higher than any thus far recorded. Like the Lord, Arnold loveth whom he chasteneth. He is, after all, the legitimate son of Thomas Arnold.

From the preceding chapters, it might reasonably be inferred that Arnold looked always upon the Teutons and their characteristics with jaundiced eyes, that he spoke of them only when moved by the spirit of detraction. Such a view is, of course, incorrect. He spoke also in their praise, less often, to be sure, but emphatically, since the traits which he singled out for approval are those without which no people can hope to achieve any great place in the world. From their many and grievous faults the Teutons were at least partially redeemed by their energy, their honesty, and their morality.

If unintelligence is the leading defect of the English, energy is their "strong point and favourable characteristic."[1] Neither of these two ideas is original with Arnold. On the unintelligence of the English, as was shown in the last chapter, writers, both native and foreign, had commented before Arnold's time, and continue to comment to the present day. On energy as a distinguishing trait there is an even more imposing array of witnesses. Most analysts agree that the English are a vigorous people; they are of different opinions only as to the cause. Montesquieu in the *Esprit des Lois* is convinced of the importance of climatic influence. As a hot and dry climate produces lethargy and indolence, so a cold and damp one, such as that of England, produces energy. Another French commentator, Émile Boutmy, in *The Political Psychology of the English People*, ascribes the energetic nature of the English to the difficulties of life in the early history of England. Without unceasing struggle against the forces of nature, the race would have died.

Forced upon them in the early period, energy has since become a national trait. In addition, they are driven into physical activity to counteract the effects of the excessive humidity. Variation in temperature, according to Ellsworth Huntington, in *Civilization and Climate*, stimulates energy, and England is blessed with a sufficient but not excessive range—sixty-four degrees in summer to thirty-eight degrees in winter. It is the opinion of Wilhelm Dibelius, a German historian, in *England*, that the essential English traits, of which energy is one, are derived from the Saxon founders of the nation. To Ernest Barker, in *National Character*, a compromise seems necessary: the national characteristic of energy is partly derived from the predominant Germanic racial strain, partly developed by the influence of climate. Arnold's speculations on the subject are confusing. The influence of "an eager and a nipping air" he leaves entirely out of account, for what he considers good and sufficient reasons. "Modes of life, institutions, government, climate, and so forth,—let me say it once for all,—will further or hinder the development of an aptitude, but they will not by themselves create the aptitude or explain it. On the other hand, a people's habit and complexion of nature go far to determine its modes of life, institutions, and government, and even to prescribe the limits within which the influences of climate shall tell upon it."[2] With him, race is the determining factor. Strangely, he believes that energy comes to the English "in part from Celtic and Roman sources."[3] Yet the argument of "The Literary Influence of Academies" is based on the contrast between English energy and French intelligence, France being made up chiefly, according to Arnold's own explanation, of Celtic and Roman elements. Again, steadiness, a form of energy, is the main basis of the Germanic genius. In developing this distinction between English energy and German steadiness, Arnold is forced to confess that "It is evident how nearly the two characterizations approach one another."[4] In theory, then, he derives English energy partly from Celtic and Roman sources, but in practice regards it mainly as a Germanic trait.

The high opinion which the English have of their own energy Arnold believes is just. It has brought them prosperity, has given them "the comforts and conveniences of life." Material well-being is worth striving for. Arnold is no lean ascetic, scorning the delights of the world. He too prefers that doors should open, windows shut, locks turn, razors shave, coats wear, and watches go. He refuses to grant, however, that in these things lies final blessedness. And even in the bounded utilitarian sphere, England can no longer feel secure. Continental countries such as Germany, Switzerland, and France, perhaps with less energy, certainly with less capital, but with more intelligence, are entering the field of commerce and threaten England's supremacy. The lead in international affairs,—the determination of policies, political, economic, and cutural—which England, relying on energy alone, held in the early years of the century, it is now losing to the nations moved by intelligence, by ideas: France, the United States, perhaps even Prussia. Energy, "the driving at practice," is still, and will continue to be a powerful, and indispensable force, but in the future it must be supplemented with intelligence, the "driving at those ideas which are, after all, the basis of right practice."[5]

On all sides of English life, this dominant and favorable characteristic energy works its effects. It lies at the basis of the successes and also the comparative failures of the Philistine and the Aristocrat, the industrialist and the statesman. It explains also the nature of English literature, so strong in poetry, so weak in prose. "The Literary Influence of Academies," in which the relationship between energy and literature is most fully discussed, is a revealing example of Arnold's own strength and weakness: on the one hand, the intuitive grasp of essential national characteristics and the deft selection of instances to show them in operation; the provocative nature of the argument—one of the functions of criticism, by Arnold's definition; the urbane, persuasive style; on the other hand, the debatable major premise; the broad and sometimes questionable generalizations of which he accused his opponent and critic, Sidgwick, and evidently believed himself innocent; the occasional inconsistencies. The first step in the argument is taken with a statement which Arnold believes no one will seriously dispute: the chief spiritual characteristic of France is a quick and flexible intelligence; that of England is energy. Then follows a syllogism, of the "vigorous and rigorous" type for which in his later religious writings he takes the mechanical German critics to task: "Genius is mainly an affair of energy, and poetry is mainly an affair of genius; therefore, a nation whose spirit is characterised by energy may well be eminent in poetry;—and we have Shakespeare. Again, the highest reach of science is, one may say, an inventive power, a faculty of divination, akin to the highest power exercised in poetry; therefore, a nation whose spirit is characterised by energy may well be eminent in science;—and we have Newton."[6] Having settled in this airy fashion the age-old enigma of genius, he is ready to proceed with his theme. Of science and Newton he has little more to say. Indeed, he does not really believe that England is eminent in science. First place in this field the Germans have won through their steadiness. With enough of this same steadiness in their nature to achieve great efficiency in practical matters, the English fall short of science, partly perhaps because of their Celticism, which is impatient with ideas.[7] It is with literature that the essay is chiefly concerned, and Arnold thinks he has paid sufficient tribute to the English in granting their pre-eminence in poetry. Rather than dwell on their merits, he will, for the good of their souls, fix upon some of the shortcomings attendant upon their genius or energy. "And what that energy, which is the life of genius, above everything demands and insists upon, is freedom; entire independence of all authority, prescription, and routine,—the fullest room to expand as it will."[8] Here is the crux of the matter. Along with this flower, energy, he finds the nettle, anarchy—his constant subject in other works as he surveys English government, religion, and education. Something of French discipline and order, he feels, is necessary to check the extravagances into which the English are carried by their energy. Hence his advocacy of the more centralized state and of religious establishment. English literature, because energy is subjected to too few restraints, is not sufficiently subordinated to intelligence, falls short "in form, method, precision, proportions, arrangement."[9] In poetry—mainly an affair of genius—the lack of these qualities, though deplorable, is not fatal. It is in prose—mainly an affair of the intelligence—that these requisites are absolutely essential, and in English prose they are wanting. With no academy—organ of the intelligence—to set standards and act as a guide, English prose runs off into eccentricity, provinciality, and violence. Of eccentricity, a frequent object of his attack in other works, he finds examples in the "orthographical antics" of the *Times*, and in the ludicrous books of Mr. Charles Forster: *Mohametanism Unveiled! An Inquiry*....2 vols. (1829), and *The One Primeval Language Traced Experimentally through Ancient Inscriptions*....(1851). The provincial note he detects in the style of such gifted writers as Jeremy Taylor and Burke, to whom simplicity and measure are unknown; and in the ideas of such a worthy stylist as Addison. The violence of English prose is to be seen in the eruptive manner of such critics as F. T. Palgrave of *Golden Treasury* fame, of such historians as A. W. Kinglake, whose *Invasion of the Crimea*, done in the Corinthian style, was acclaimed in the 'sixties; and in the aggressive manner of most English newspapers which seem "to aim rather at an effect upon the blood and senses than upon the spirit and intellect." All these examples are adduced not to prove that English prose is wholly without merit; it has, Arnold recognizes, its own peculiar excellences. These excellences are, however, the same as those to be found in English poetry. Over both, genius, or energy, presides, and Arnold, for his part, desires that intelligence be given some share in the dominion.

A second syllogism follows as supplement to the first, both being fundamental in the argument of the essay: prose is mainly an affair of the intelligence; the dominant characteristic of the French is intelligence; therefore, "the power of French literature is in its prose-writers....

Nay, many of the celebrated French poets depend wholly for their fame upon the qualities of intelligence which they exhibit,—qualities which are the distinctive support of prose."[10] Arnold's purpose in the present essay being to use the French as a contrast to the English in the writing of prose, he is content with merely noting that their poetry also is ruled by intelligence. Their inadequacies in poetry, resulting from their devotion to "form, method, precision, proportions, arrangement"—all matters of intelligence, he treats more fully and damningly in the essay on Heine, and in "The French Play in London." In denying the highest excellence to English prose, he probably expected to meet with contradiction, and he was not disappointed in the expectation;[11] in denying the highest excellence to French poetry, he perhaps did not expect to meet with a similar contradiction from the French. Yet in the judgement of Émile Legouis, he has done irreparable damage to the reputation of French poetry among English-speaking peoples by his insensitiveness and his unfair selection of unrepresentative passages for illustration.[12] With this French estimate, Lionel Trilling agrees. He finds it difficult to forgive Arnold for his insistence that French poetry "always failed of greatness."[13] E. K. Brown sees in this imperviousness the same blindness which prevented Arnold from recognizing the merits of eighteenth-century English poetry.[14] There is another explanation, however, that is worth considering. It is possible to see in Arnold's severity another instance of his having passed, as Sainte-Beuve said, through French "life and literature by a deep inner line, which confers initiation," for there is a fairly long French critical tradition in support of his view, and with that tradition he may have been familiar. Diderot's comment on the French language is in point: "La langue française est plus propre aux sciences et à la philosophie, moins à la poésie et à l'éloquence que le grec, le latin, l'italien ou l'anglais. C'est la langue de l'esprit ou du bon sens; les autres sont la langue de l'imagination et des passions." So also is Madame de Staël's remark on French poets: "nos seuls grands poètes peut-être sont nos grands prosateurs, Bossuet, Pascal, Fénelon." P. J. Proudhon defines French *esprit* as "un esprit de clarté, de finesse, de précision, d'élégance, très peu poétique en lui-même." Alfred de Vigny writes in his *Journal*: "Les Français n'aiment ni la lecture, ni la musique, ni la poésie, mais la société, les salons, l'esprit, la prose." Baudelaire speaks of "l'horreur de la France pour la poésie."[15] And Renan believes that "Le génie français n'est pas de tous ceux qui se partagent le monde le plus philosophique, le plus poétique surtout; mais c'est certainement le plus complet, le plus mesuré, le plus propre à créer une forme de culture intellectuelle qui s'impose à tous."[16] In the same year, 1864, in which "The Literary Influence of Academies" appeared in the *Cornhill Magazine*, Arnold declined Taine's request that he review the *Histoire de la littérature anglaise*, at the same time thanking him for the treatment accorded Dr. Thomas Arnold. In reading this work, Arnold could have found a precedent for his own opinion of French poetry, or at any rate a corroboration of his opinion. The Frenchman, says Taine, possesses a nimble intelligence. "At once and without effort he seizes upon his idea. But he seizes that alone." There are no half-visions, vast depths, or far perspectives. The French are moved only superficially. "That is why no race in

Europe is less poetical."[17] And even today, some French critics share Arnold's view. John Charpentier believes that the preservation of the aristocratic classical tradition in French poetry has prevented the development of individual originality. Poetry is allied with "les bonnes manières et le bon ton"; it does not emanate, as it does in England, from the soul. "Intelligents, délicats, appliqués, modérés, prudents, plus habiles à choisir qu'à inventer, nous n'avons pendant deux siècles et demi que le rôle ingrat de préserver la tradition. On s'instruit chez nous; nous sommes l'université du monde, mais, en poésie, toute notre ingéniosité se confine dans le perfectionnement de la technique." Charpentier adopts Arnold's distinction between energy and intelligence, and attributes to the latter the fact that the French have fallen to the inglorious level of becoming the policemen of taste.[18]

English energy and German steadiness, in Arnold's opinion, are closely related, and thin partitions do the bounds divide. "Take away some of the energy which comes to us, as I believe, in part from Celtic and Roman sources; instead of energy, say rather *steadiness*; and you have the Germanic genius: *steadiness with honesty*. It is evident how nearly the two characterizations approach one another."[19] But it is the differences between the two that he wishes to stress, since their greater steadiness gives to the Germans certain qualities which the English are the worse for being without. First of all, a patient fidelity to nature, which enables the unmixed Germanic races to arrive at considerable eminence in the plastic arts and in music. The English fail of an equal success because of the undisciplinable, emotional Celtic element in their nature, what success they do attain being attributable to the Germanic element.[20] Chiefly, however, it is to science that the German steadiness leads. By science as applied to Germany, Arnold usually means the systematic and impartial pursuit of knowledge in any field.[21] Thus, he is impressed by the mind of Goethe, which is impartial and aspires "after the science, not of men only, but of universal nature."[22] For a thorough searching-out of the facts and an impartial exhibition of them, particularly in the field of Biblical learning, Germany deserves honor above all other nations,[23] even though the conclusions drawn from the facts are not always sound or penetrating. "German practice is governed by the notion that what is to be done should be done *scientifically*, as they say; that is, according to the reason of the thing, under the direction of experts, and without suffering ignorance and prejudice to intrude."[24] By following this practice, the Germans have managed to set up a school-system superior in all its stages—primary, secondary, and higher—to that of the English. The Crown patronage schools of Prussia serve as an example. Founded and endowed by the Sovereign, who by reason of his position is raised above local, and party, and class prejudices; administered by experts such as Wilhelm von Humboldt and Schleiermacher, the schools provide the best that the national culture has to offer. The English in contrast have no such centralized and systematized educational administration. Each class founds and administers schools for its own children, and the instruction is limited to the ideas and ideals of that particular class. In the case of the great public schools for the upper classes, the result is not disappointing; but these schools are few. The vast majority of the schools for the middle classes are of the type represented by the institutions for the education of the children of the Licensed Victuallers or the Commercial Travellers.[25] By establishing his practice on reasonable principles, by consulting authorities, and by refusing to allow religious prejudice to intrude, Bismarck has solved the vexing problem of university education for the German Catholics: they are to have their own universities, staffed by their own priests, but these priests must be trained in the national universities, not in their own seminaries. In their treatment of the Irish Catholics, the English are guided by no such reasonable principles. Protestant prejudice excludes the Catholics entirely from the national life.[26] It is in "*Wissenschaft*, science, knowledge systematically pursued and prized in and for itself" that the German universities are strong and the English universities are weak.[27] The Germans demand a thorough and systematic training in their professional men; the English, with their disbelief in science, proceed by rule of thumb. An English engineer learns his business through practice: that is, he builds three bad bridges that tumble down, and thus learns to build a good one that will stand—a wasteful and expensive method, which only a wealthy nation like England could allow.[28] Thus, as all these illustrations go to prove, the steady-going German habit, which on one side leads to all the repulsive characteristics of Philistinism and *Gemeinheit*,[29] can lead on its better side "to the comprehension and interpretation," perhaps even the mastery of the world.[30]

With English energy and German steadiness, Arnold almost invariably associates honesty. He evidently regards the trait as Teutonic, for he credits no other race with it—not the Greeks whom he so much admired; never the Celts, of whom in some other respects he speaks so highly. Further, the trait at least in the case of the English is a dominant one: it is the second of their great spiritual characteristics, energy being the first.[31] For energy a profusion of examples is supplied throughout Arnold's works; for honesty, very few, perhaps because he felt that no one would question the trait as fundamentally English, possibly because it leads to no extravagances on which he could admonish his countrymen. The ascription of honesty to the English is probably a continuation of the tradition, dating from the time of Tacitus, that the Teutons are above all else a moral race. In the transactions of the ethnological and anthropological societies of London in the 'sixties, a frequent theme is the contrast between the untruthfulness of the Celt and the opposite quality in the Saxon.[32] Carlyle lauds the veracity of the English, and condemns the mendacity of the Irish.[33] And Emerson records that "the German name has a proverbial significance of sincerity and honest meaning.[34] Even J. S. Mill, though he denies the English the general moral pre-eminence with which they compliment themselves, grants that they do possess a love of truth—the higher classes do not lie, and the lower, though guilty, are ashamed of lying.[35] There is even a Spanish proverb for truth: on the word of an Englishman.[36] Yet staunch as the English are in their defense of honesty as a British trait, they realize that beyond the national boundaries the reputation is not suffered to go unchallenged. When a nation like England leads the world in wealth and power, its enemies and even its friends are loth to grant it in addition the seven cardinal virtues. Quite naturally, therefore, in many quarters on the Continent, England is regarded as a Machiavelli among the nations, employing duplicity and even perfidy in furthering her ends. Indeed, J. Bodin, in *De Republica*, would have it, citing the notorious case of Odysseus of Ithaca, that all islanders are by nature untrustworthy. And the taunt *perfide Albion* is to a considerable extent, perhaps, justified by the shifting international policy which England has for centuries pursued, partly because of the necessity of maintaining a balance of power on the Continent, partly because of changes in party government at home, with the consequent alteration of foreign alliances, both political and commercial. And England's general opportunism in the conduct of practical affairs has also contributed to the reputation for inconstancy.[37] In France and Germany, it is sometimes granted that the English are honest in business, since trustworthiness is a condition of trade, but their superior truthfulness in other areas of conduct and endeavor is denied.[38]

Of all the Teutonic characteristics, however, morality, in Arnold's eyes, is the most important; to it he devotes the most consideration. First of all, he believes firmly that conduct, or righteousness, or morality—the terms are used interchangeably—is three-fourths of human life. He believes, also, that of all the races, the Teutonic is the most moral. It follows, therefore, that the stability, the well-being, the promise of a nation will bear a direct relationship to the proportion of the Teutonic element in the national mixture. Tested by this formula, France is almost damned; the United States seems destined to be saved. Each step in this argument demands a separate treatment.

After his appearance before the public for a decade or more as the champion of intelligence, or Hellenism, as against morality, or Hebraism, Arnold's change of front in the 'seventies must have seemed apostacy to many of his contemporaries. He himself wonders whether he might not be "reproached with inconstancy." Perhaps a *palinode* is necessary. Yet, he says, he is guilty of no inconsistency. In his frequent praises of Hellenism, he has never denied that conduct, or morality, is three-fourths of life.[39] "A Liverpool Address" (1882) states most clearly the position which he felt he had held throughout his career. In this address, he contrasts Voltaire with Luther, the differences being those which he sees also between their respective nations. Voltaire represents lucidity, but with it want of seriousness, want of reverence. Luther represents conduct. And "a man who works for conduct . . . works for more than a man who works for intelligence."[40] Since much of Arnold's work before 1870 had been for intelligence, this statement at first glance seems like a repudiation of his former labors, a recantation of his former views. Yet, at the very time he was making his most eloquent plea for Hellenism, he had granted that "the priority naturally belongs to that discipline which braces all man's moral powers, and founds for him an indispensable basis of character."[41]

As with individuals, so with races and nations: those which work for conduct, work for more than those which work for intelligence. In England the stress has always been on conduct, on morality, as it has been also in Germany. The United States can be complimented, therefore, on its ancestry.

> You are fifty millions mainly sprung, as we in England are mainly sprung, from that German stock which has faults indeed,—faults which have diminished the extent of its influence, diminished its power of attraction and the interest of its history, and

> which seems moreover just now, from all I can see and hear, to be passing through a not very happy moment, morally, in Germany proper. Yet of the German stock it is, I think, true, as my father said more than fifty years ago, that it has been a stock 'of the most moral races of men that the world has yet seen, with the soundest laws, the least violent passions, the fairest domestic and civil virtues.' You come, therefore, of about the best parentage which a modern nation can have.[42]

The people of the United States, then, are predominantly of German stock, but a distinction must be made. Three years earlier, in "A Word about America" (1882), he had written: "The ethnology of that American diplomatist, who the other day assured a Berlin audience that the great admixture of Germans had now made the people of the United States as much German as English, has not yet prevailed with me. I adhere to my old persuasion, the Americans of the United States are English people on the other side of the Atlantic. I learned it from Burke."[43] What he learned from Burke, he could have derived from many another source, for it was the prevailing view through most of the nineteenth century both in England and in the United States. Carlyle, writing to Emerson in 1839, suggests that the two Saxon countries, Mother and Daughter, arrange for an annual meeting-place of All-Saxondom. At present, he says, London is the most convenient center, but Boston or New York will have their turn later.[44] The closing two stanzas of Tennyson's "Hands All Round," as it appeared in the London *Examiner* (1852), stress the mother-and-daughter relationship and the oneness of blood.

> Gigantic daughter of the West
> We drink to thee across the flood,
> We know thee most, we love thee best,
> For art thou not of British blood?

Should war's mad blast again be blown,
Permit not thou the tyrant powers
To fight thy mother here alone,
But let thy broadsides roar with ours.
Hands all round!
God the tyrant's cause confound!
To our great kinsmen of the West, my friends,
And the great name of England, round and round.

E. A. Freeman asserted that "Americans are English for the most part, but will rarely admit it."[45] On the birthday of George Washington, February 22, 1886, Freeman gave emphatic expression to the idea in an address at Oxford entitled "George Washington, the Expander of England." "What is England? The old Teutonic name speaks for itself; it is the name of the English, the land of the English wherever they may dwell. . . . In our onward march we passed from the European mainland to the European island and from the European island to the American mainland. In each case there was a making of England, an expansion of England."[46] In the United States much the same view was held. In a speech delivered before the St. George's Society of Montreal, Quebec, on April 23, 1852, Emerson could say: "But you know that we Americans feel our relation to England to be so strict—we have kept our pedigree so pure—that we praise very willingly England, as a son praises his mother."[47] The pride of Americans in their Anglo-Saxon origin and in the Teutonic source of their political institutions was further stimulated by historians like Herbert B. Adams of the Johns Hopkins University, and John Fiske, the latter of whom in "Our Aryan Forefathers" (1885) develops the doctrine of Teutonic and particularly English racial superiority. Further fuel for the fire was added by such political scientists as Francis Lieber and

John W. Burgess. Most of these men had been trained in Germany and therefore continued the tradition of Tacitus.[48] James Bryce, writing in the 'eighties as Arnold does, is better informed and therefore takes into sufficient account the Irish and German immigrations. The people of the United States, he realizes, are not what fifty years before they may have been for the most part, simply "English people on the other side of the Atlantic." Yet, even in the 'eighties, Bryce thought that the ratio borne by the Celtic elements to the Teutonic elements in the population of the United States did not differ much from the ratio between the two elements in the population of England. In fact, he saw being repeated on the Western continent the mixture of Celtic and Germanic races which a thousand years before had formed Britain.[49] In spite of the heterogeneous immigrations of the close of the nineteenth century and of the early years of the twentieth century, the Anglo-Saxon tradition continues to the present day, and is one of the many paradoxes noted by Chesterton in 1922.[50]

So much, then, for Arnold's ideas on the race of the people of the United States, ideas which accord, as has been shown, with the prevailing opinion of the day. A closer study would have proved to Arnold in 1885 that he was wrong in considering the United States a nation made up almost wholly of transplanted Englishmen. He was more correct, however, in his statement that the population was sprung mainly from Germanic stock. Before considering the relationship between morality and race—the chief problem of this chapter—it will be necessary to take up Arnold's view on the proportion among the racial strains in France, for the whole question of comparative national and racial morality arose in Arnold's mind out of the condition of defeated France in the 'seventies.

For the decline of France in the nineteenth century, Arnold has a very neat and ingenious explanation. It is a racial one. The fall of France can be laid to the dying out of the Germanic element in the national life. In fact, the whole history of France from the Middle Ages on is a record of this gradual decline. The Middle Ages, when the Germanic element was strongest, is, in Arnold's opinion, "the soundest and most attractive stage, perhaps, in all French history." In showing how France has come to the present-day worship of the great goddess Lubricity, with such fatal consequences, Arnold says:

> First, there was the original Gaul, the basis of the French nation; the Gaul, gay, sociable, quick of sentiment, quick of perception; apt, however, very apt, to be presumptuous and puffed up. Then came the Roman conquest, and from this we get a new personage, the Gallo-Latin; with the Gaulish qualities for a basis, but with Latin order, reason, lucidity, added, and also Latin sensuality. Finally, we have the Frankish conquest and the Frenchman. The Frenchman proper is the Gallo-Latin, with Frankish or Germanic qualities added and infused. No mixture could be better. The Germans have plenty of faults, but in this combination they seem not to have taken hold; the Germans seem to have given of their seriousness and honesty to the conquered Gallo-Latin, and not of their brutality. And mediaeval France, which exhibits the combination and balance, under the influence then exercised by Catholicism, of Gaulish quickness and gaiety with Latin rationality and German seriousness, offers to our view the soundest and the most attractive stage, perhaps, in all French history.[51]

But the balance among the races was not maintained. By her refusal to accept the Reformation, a creation of the Germanic races, France placed a check upon the

Germanic side of her nature. Through the seventeenth and eighteenth centuries, the Gaulish and Latin sides of the French nature prevailed more and more. In the French Revolution and its long aftermath, the Germanic construction of Old France had been swept away.[52] Of the modern Frenchman, therefore, it may be said that "the German in him has nearly died out, and the Gallo-Latin has quite got the upper hand. For us, however, this means that the chief source of seriousness and of moral ideas is failing and drying up in him, and that what remains are the sources of Gaulish salt, and quickness, and sentiment, and sociability, and sensuality, and rationality."[53]

Arnold's description of the French population as being made up historically of three races: the Gaul, the Roman, and the Frank, is, of course, an over-simplification. Among authorities today in history, anthropology, and ethnology it is generally agreed that the French ethnological blend is one of the most complex in Europe. Even in 1869, Michelet in the "Preface" to his *History of France* had come to the conclusion that all the races of the world had contributed to the glory that was France. But the division into three races was commonly accepted in the nineteenth century among the French themselves, and each race had its zealous advocates. The Nordic, or Germanic, or Frankish tradition established by Boulainvilliers and Montesquieu was accepted and given general currency in the first half of the century. Of this tradition, Gobineau, with his eulogy of the Aryan, is the extreme development. But by the middle of the century, a patriotic reaction toward Gallic and Roman origins developed, a reaction which was of course strengthened by the Franco-

Prussian War.[54] The Gallic, or Celtic, revival—with Renan as its leading figure—enlisted, perhaps, the largest number of historians, statesmen and literary men under its banner. Of the arguments employed by those who believed in the preponderance of the Roman blood and the Roman tradition, the following excerpt from Charles Maurras is an extreme example:

> *I am Roman*, because Rome as early as the Consul Marius and the divine Julius up to the dying Thedosius hewed out the first outline of my France. *I am Roman*, because Rome, the Rome of the priests and popes, has given eternal solidity of sentiment, of customs, of language, of religion, to the political work of the generals, of the administrators and of the Roman judges. *I am Roman*, because, if my fathers had not been Roman, as I am, the first barbarian invansion between the fifth and tenth centuries would have made me to-day a sort of German or Norwegian. *I am Roman*, because, if it had not been for my tutelary Romanity, the second barbarian invasion which took place in the sixteenth century, the Protestant invasion, would have converted me into a sort of Swiss. *I am Roman*, since I am full to overflowing with my historical, intellectual, and moral being. *I am Roman*, because, if I were not, I would have almost nothing else French.[55]

France may be regarded, as Anatole France in *Le Génie Latin* regards it, as a modern fulfillment of the ancient prophecy that Rome should have an empire without end. Accordingly, he begins *Le Génie Latin* with an appropriate quotation from Frédéric Plessis,

> Car nulle fleur ne fait pâlir tes violettes,
> Ville de Périclès! Et ce n'est pas en vain
> Que par la bouche d'or du plus doux des poètes
> Le dieu promit à Rome un empire sans fin.

In France, as in most other countries, the racial issue lent itself readily to contemporary political uses, the Germanists being generally of the royalist camp, the Gallo-Roman, of the republican.

In explaining the decline of France as the result of the dying out of the Teutonic element in the population, Arnold is following the belief widely current in the nineteenth century that the most virile, the most regenerative ingredient in modern western civilization was the Teutonic. E. A. Freeman's vehement espousal of this idea has already been commented on.[56] Carlyle believed that whatever of the masculine and the durable there might be in the Spaniards, the Italians, and the French could be attributed to the intermixture with the Germans.[57] Thomas Arnold was deeply impressed by the qualities of the Teutonic race and the effect of those qualities upon modern civilization. In his opinion, the intermixture of the Teutonic stock with the Celtic and Roman races changed the entire nature of Europe. In the Roman Empire at the end of the fourth century, A.D., he found Christianity, plus all the intellectual contributions of Greece, and all the social and political contributions of Rome. What was not there was the German race and the peculiar quality that characterized it. This one addition was so powerful that it changed the nature of the whole mass. The peculiar stamp of the Middle Ages was undoubtedly German. In the last three centuries, this element had been less prominent, but it still preserved its force, he thought, and was felt for good or evil in almost every country in the west of Europe.[58] According to the later racialists, Gobineau, Vacher de Lapouge, Houston-Stewart Chamberlain, and in the twentieth century, Madison Grant, the amount of Nordic or Germanic blood in a European nation determines that nation's standing in war and in civilization. Madison Grant's view of France is much like Arnold's: the Nordic element in France declined, and with it the vigor of the nation.[59] Spain's decline, says Grant, is to be explained on similar grounds, and even England and the United States are in danger as the Teutonic element diminishes.

On the basis of these ethnological analyses, Arnold applies his theories on morality to the nations of modern Europe and to the United States. In his discussion of morality, he is influenced, whether consciously or not, by two powerful currents of thought: the Nordic-Latin antagonism, and the Protestant-Catholic controversy. First, however, it is necessary to indicate what his ideas were.

As we have already seen, Arnold, like his father before him, considered the Teutonic stock to be a stock "of the most moral races of men that the world has yet seen."[60] He was, therefore, prepared to see in Germany, in England, and in the United States evidences of this quality, and in France and in the southern nations generally, a lack of it.

The contrast between Voltaire, representing lucidity, and Luther, representing morality—with the conclusion that the man or nation working for conduct works for more than the man or nation working for intelligence—has already been cited. Even as early as the lectures on Celtic literature in which Arnold spent much of his effort in ridiculing the limitations of the German genius, he conceded that in the main business of modern poetry—moral interpretation—only Germany had been very successful. The task of the modern poet was to supply a new spiritual basis for human life, and for this task the "scientific, serious German spirit . . . . has peculiar aptitudes."[61]

On England, as on Germany, Arnold's strictures were many, but the English, too, possessed the saving grace of morality. "No people in the world have done more and struggled more to obtain this relative moral perfection than our English race has. For no people in the world has the command to *resist the devil*, to *overcome the wicked one*, in the nearest and most obvious sense of those words, had such a pressing force and reality. And we have had our reward, not only in the great worldly prosperity which our obedience to this command has brought us, but, also, and far more, in great inward peace and satisfaction."[62] This is Hebraism with a vengeance in the very work noted chiefly for its advocacy of Hellenism. Years later, in recommending lucidity to the English, a quality which in France is accompanied with dangers, chief of which is laxity of morals, Arnold is sure that in England it will carry with it no such disadvantages, for English influences will join with it.[63] And in spite of his repeated attacks upon Puritanism, the prison into which the English voluntarily entered "and had the key turned upon their spirit there for two hundred years," in spite of his shivering at the hideousness and "immense ennui" which it spread everywhere in English life, in spite of his objection to the hole-and-corner sects, and the "dissidence of dissent" in which it had resulted, he nonetheless granted that "The impulse of the English race towards moral development and self-conquest has nowhere so powerfully manifested itself as in Puritanism."[64] It was needed to develop the moral fibre of the English race.[65] Though it did not give the

English culture, it did give them character, for want of which in France at least, as his esteemed Lacordaire had pointed out, "our age is the age of miscarriages."[66] The United States is doubly fortunate, therefore, in its Germanic stock and in its severe Puritan discipline.[67]

In resisting the devil and overcoming the wicked one, particularly when the wicked one takes form as "the strange woman," France, because of the diminution in the Germanic part of her nature, is not very successful.

> Moral conscience, self-control, seriousness, steadfastness, are not the whole of human life certainly, but they are by far the greatest part of it; without them—and this is the very burden of the Hebrew prophets and a fact of experience as old as the world—nations cannot stand. France does not enough see their importance; and the worst of it is that no man can make another see their importance unless he sees it naturally. For these things, just as for the more brilliant things of art and science, there is a bent, a turn. 'He showed his ways unto Moses, his works unto the children of Israel,'—to them and to the heavy Germanic nations whom they have moulded; not, apparently, to the children of Gomer and to Vercingetorix. But this opens a troubled prospect for the children of Gomer.[68]

The vice lubricity goes hand in hand with the virtue lucidity. The French have lusted after the strange Goddess Aselgeia, and heavy indeed is the retribution. The French type is *l'homme sensuel moyen*, "And from her ideal of the average sensual man France has deduced her famous gospel of the Rights of Man."[69] Out of this gospel grew the French Revolution, out of which, in turn, arose the turbulent political conditions of the nineteenth century, culminating in the abasement of the Franco-Prussian War, from which Arnold for a time thought it impossible that France could ever again arise to take a place among the great nations. The linking of these national disasters with sex, as Trilling has recently indicated, seems strange until one remembers that in Arnold's system of fractions morality is three-quarters of life, and of morality, sex is one-half.[70]

By his use of the phrase "the children of Gomer," in the essay on Renan, Arnold seems to be denying morality to the Celts. And indeed he does regard the French as Celts; but the phrase is employed probably because Renan had so definitely identified himself with the cause of the Celts. Actually, Arnold thought the sensuality of the French a Latin, not a Celtic characteristic. He distinguishes between the pure Celt, or the Irishman, who is chaste, and the Latinized Celt, who is something altogether different.

> Au fond, le Français est un Irlandais; soit, mais un Irlandais *latinisé*, et, avec cela, on établit contre les deux hommes une difference profonde. Pour ne toucher qu'à un seul point, mais un point bien important—la chasteté. Le Celte pur, l'Irlandais, est chaste; le Celte latinisé, le Français, est tout autre chose. Selon Ste. Beuve, Proudhon disait que 'la France était tournée toute entière vers la fornication'; et c'est là, en effet, votre plaie; or, à cet égard, l'Irlande offre aux autres pays un exemple vraiment admirable, ses fautes sont ailleurs.[71]

Earlier, in *Obermann Once More*, Arnold had traced the Latin degeneracy,

> On that hard pagan world disgust
> And secret loathing fell.
> Deep weariness and sated lust
> Made human life a hell.
>
> In his cool hall, with haggard eyes,
> The Roman noble lay;
> He drove abroad, in furious guise,
> Along the Appian way.

> He made a feast, drank fierce and fast,
> And crowned his hair with flowers—
> No easier nor no quicker passed
> The impracticable hours.

The fall of France is due to the same cause as that of the fall of the Graeco-Latin nations: Greece, Rome, and the brilliant Renaissance Italy.[72] The curse of Italy has always been "a relaxed moral fibre."[73] And Greece has indeed entered on her latter days when in a religious ceremony, the courtesan Phryne, representing *Venus Anadyomene*, enters the sea at Eleusis.[74]

In discussing morality among the races and the nations, Arnold is led naturally to a distinction between Protestantism and Catholicism. Nowhere more than in this matter are those qualities evidenced on which Arnold prides himself: his "inexhaustible indulgence," his sanity, his sense of fairness. These qualities shine the brighter when set against the narrowness and bigotry of some of his eminent contemporaries. Carlyle, for example, speaks of the "false Romish" superstitions; of the "poisened gingerbread" of Catholicism; and of Catholic worship as a "scenic phantasmagory of wax-candles, organ-blasts, Gregorian chants, mass-brayings, purple monsignori." And the anti-popery of Charles Kingsley is notorious. Toward England, he says, the Holy Father has always been "a Holy Step-Father."[75] Like his character, Mark Armsworth, Kingsley "can't see what people want, running into foreign parts to look at those poor idolaters, and their Punch and Judy plays."[76] Jesuit and liar are with him synonymous. Only in the "free air of Protestant countries" do the natural sciences grow and thrive.[77] Popery is alien to the English, but "The Church of England is wonderfully and mysteriously fitted for the souls of a free Norse-Saxon race; for men whose ancestors fought by the side of Odin; over whom a descendant of Odin now rules."[78] Fielding's parson in his mingling of patriotism and Protestantism might well speak for Kingsley: "When I say religion, I mean the Christian religion; and when I say the Christian religion, I mean the Protestant religion; and when I say the Protestant religion, I mean the Church of England." In the violent language of Carlyle and in the chauvinism of Kingsley, Arnold would see more than a touch of fatuity, a lack of good sense and good taste. Like Carlyle and Kingsley, he is on the side of Protestantism, but he is not blind to the virtues of Catholicism. In his opinion, it is to the "healing waters" of Christianity that attention should be directed, not to the particular conduit through which these waters pass. Both faiths have this curative power.[79] Intellectually, there is not much choice between Protestantism with its implicit faith in the divine Book, and Catholicism with its implicit faith in the divine Church; between Protestantism which hears Balaam's ass speak, and Catholicism which sees a wooden Madonna wink.[80] The strength of Catholicism lies in its antiquity, in "its pretensions to universality," in its "widespread prevalence," in its sensuousness,[81] even more in its beauty, richness, poetry, and infinite charm for the imagination. Through these last it has its claim upon the future. Arnold cannot help thinking that the form of future Christianity will be the form of Catholicism—a Catholicism purged, of course, of its grosser elements: miracle-mongering, Mariolatry, and outworn dogma.[82] Protestantism, though it lacks poetry, has in compensation "a prospect of growth in alliance with the vital movement of modern society," whereas Catholicism seems to be losing itself in its miracles and dogmas.[83] Thus Catholicism and Protestantism are held in a kind of balance—except for one particular of the very highest importance. Religion in Arnold's definition is "morality touched with emotion." "The Church exists, not for the sake of opinions, but for the sake of moral practice."[84] And the strength of Protestantism lies in its pursuit of morality. In a reaction against immorality it had its origin, for "the Reformation was a moral rather than an intellectual event."[85] Furthermore, the Reformation was brought about by "the serious Germanic races" who loved Christianity enough to desire to rescue it from the immorality and clericalism of Rome. The Latin nations, on the other hand, did not break with Rome, not because they were blind to the evils of clericalism and tradition, but because they were not seriously interested in Christianity.[86] Herein lies the explanation of France's failure. "France did not go with the Reformation; the Germanic qualities in her were not strong enough to make her go with it. 'France did not want a reformation which was a moral one,' is Michelet's account of the matter: *La France ne voulait pas de réforme morale*."[87] And to this day France pays the penalty.[88] Arnold is, therefore, sympathetic with de Laveleye, who, along with Michelet, Quinet, and Renouvier, desired that France should become Protestant. "M. de Laveleye is struck, as any judicious Catholic may well be struck, with the superior freedom, order, stability, and even religious earnestness, of the Protestant nations as compared with the Catholic." But the secret of Protestantism, Arnold warns, is not to be found in its theological severance from Rome (with the theology of Protestantism Arnold was himself at war); it is to be found in "its signal return to the individual conscience." If France will make this return, it too may hope to achieve some of the blessings of the Germanic, Protestant nations.[89]

Linked with the Protestant-Catholic controversy is the Teutonic conviction of its superior morality, its revulsion at the dissolute life of the southern races, for, as many a northern commentator pointed out, Protestantism is confined to the nations of Teutonic blood.[90] The pattern for the contrast—moral North, immoral South—is set by Tacitus, "the last of the Romans," as Carlyle called him, "born in a most unRoman time, and great by contradicting it." And Tacitus is confirmed by the profligacies of the Italian Renaissance, when Ascham saw in Venice "more libertie to sinne in IX dayes than ever I heard tell of in our noble Citie of London in IX yeare"; when Luther found the villainies, infamies, and atrocious crimes of Rome incredible.

In like manner, Carlyle speaks of the Germans and Huns sweeping away the Roman sensualists.[91] The modern descendants of these Germans are represented by the Prussian Host at Saara: twenty-five thousand pious soldiers "of right Teutsch stuff, tender though stout", advancing through the hollow night singing "a known Church-hymn of the homely *Te Deum* kind."[92] Paris, on the other hand, is a symbol of the French character in its lack of solid and substantial morality.[93] And as for modern Italy, he says in a conversation with Browning, its bondage is a direct judgment from God, who sends the Germans in to possess the nation. For any true Northman, therefore, Iceland, Carlyle thinks, is the one foreign country worth visiting. To which Browning, lover of Italy though he is, can answer only, "Perhaps!" for because of the same conviction, he himself had spoken on at least one occasion against the southern spirit.[94] By his own acknowledgment, Arnold found in his father's works a precedent for his belief in the morality of the Teutonic race. In the same works he could have found, and perhaps did find, an anticipation of his views on the immorality of the southern races. Thomas Arnold censures the Roman nation on moral grounds. In the Roman slave market, in the practice of infanticide, in Augustus the seducer and adulterer, and in Scylla the profligate, he sees proof of the degraded state of Roman morals.[95] Toward "papa's way of feeling about the Italians" Arnold felt drawn more and more.[96] What that feeling was is indicated in Thomas Arnold's description of the Italians as a lying people who "stink in one's moral nose all day long."[97] And like his son, he attributes the warlike spirit of France to the awful moral state of the nation.[98] It was left to Charles Kingsley, however, in his capacity as Professor of History at Cambridge University to carry the well-worn contrast between the moral Teuton and the immoral Roman to its last absurdity. In the first lecture of the series *The Roman and the Teuton*, entitled "The Forest Children," he develops a lengthy comparison of the Teutonic tribes with innocent children of nature attracted to a walled Troll-garden, which is Rome.

> Inside the Trolls dwell, cunning and wicked, watching their fairy treasures, working at their magic forges, making and making always—things rare and strange; and outside, the forest is full of children; such children as the world had never seen before, but children still; children in frankness, and purity, and affectionateness, and tenderness of conscience, and devout awe of the unseen.[99]

Lured into the garden, the Teutonic children are tempted "too often, to sins which have no name." But eventually they destroy the garden and the Trolls, and are themselves saved by Christianity from the corruption with which they have been brought into contact. In his novel, *Hypatia*, Kinsgley credits the Teutons with saving the civilization of the Western world from the collapse with which it was threatened because of the corruption and profligacy of Rome.[100] In answering the accusation that American slavery was as bad as, or even worse than, that of Rome, he declared, "God forbid! Whatsoever may have been the sins of the Southern gentleman, he is at least a Teuton, and not a Roman; a whole moral heaven above the effeminate wretch, who in the 4th and 5th centuries called himself a senator and a clarissimus."[101] Kingsley's friend Max Müller regards Germany and England—the two pillars of the Reformation, the two nations of one blood, who owe allegiance to the same sovereign, the Voice of Conscience—as the logical candidates for the rulership of Europe in the immediate future.[102] The historian W. E. H. Lecky believed that Prussia's victory in the Franco-Prussian War would raise the moral level of civilization, the character of the French people being corroded at the heart.[103] To the Frenchman Taine, it also seems that the distinguishing trait of the Germanic genius is morality. Gross and heavy though the Germans are, and given to gluttony and drunkenness, in them the manly and moral instincts prevail. Hence, their civilization, though slower, is sounder than that of the southern nations. In fact, all southern civilizations, ancient and modern, bear in their bosom a fatal vice, "a bad and false conception of man," which the Germans of the fourth and of the sixteenth century rightly judged.[104] English civilization, therefore, is the product, not, as French culture is, of society, but of the moral sense.[105]

From these numerous citations, one is justified in inferring that Arnold's censure of the French would have met with agreement in many quarters. In many, but not in all. The French free-thinker J. M. Guyau devotes fourteen pages of his popular and influential *L'Irreligion de l'Avenir* to a point-by-point refutation of Arnold's thesis against France, as presented in *Literature and Dogma.* It is impossible, Guyau believes, to prove that the morality of Protestant people is superior to that of Catholics. Arnold's explanation of complex historical events, such as the French defeat in 1870, on the basis of a single cause, and that a debatable one, seems to him naive. Germany won not because of superior morality, but because of superior science. It therefore behooves France to continue in the Hellenistic pursuit of science and the arts, the role assigned her by Arnold himself. According to Guyau, the cult preached by Arnold has flourished always in the most unenlightened times; it has indeed made those nations which followed it strong, but it has also made them intolerant, fanatic, and savage. And the fact that the nobler, more civilized nation is easily vanquished in war, can hardly be construed as an argument for the savage state as the ideal of humanity. Furthermore, Arnold's theory that immorality naturally accompanies Hellenism is deserving of nothing more than raillery. Even if the theory were sound, Hellenism would carry its own cure in the moderation and measure which are among its chief tenets. And finally, says Guyau, Arnold goes completely astray in his conception of the gospel of the rights of man as the ideal of the average, sensual man only. There is no connection between this gospel and sensuality. Nor can the French Revolution be linked with sensuality. Rather, it is a revolt in the name of reason; it has also its metaphysical or religious side, and Arnold as a professed man of religion ought to admire, not condemn it.[106]

The temptation to attribute a nation's decline or fall to moral turpitude is always strong, and to it many twentieth-century critics have succumbed in explaining the collapse of France's armies and government in World War II. As might have been expected, Arnold's name has been invoked to lend weight to the accusation. In the pages of *The Hibbert Journal*, Hamilton Fyfe calls attention to Arnold's diagnosis that lubricity is the dangerous and perhaps fatal disease that is eating at the vitals of France, and also to Arnold's prophecy, "If the disease goes on and increases, then things will go from bad to worse with her. She will more and more lose her powers of soul and spirit, her intellectual productiveness, her skill in counsel, her formidableness as a foe, her value as an ally." All these predictions, Fyfe thinks, have been tragically fulfilled, and he reviews the history of France since Arnold's time to show the diminution in vital force in the minority who lead the nation. This decline in vital force is the natural result of the national lewdness: the too-early, too-frequent, and too-long-continued indulgence in sexual relations. Arnold's suggestion that the growing lewdness results from the dying out of the serious Germanic strain in the French, and the consequent dominance of the Gaulish and Latin elements, he does not accept. Rather, it seems to him, the Latin stock is today exhausted, not only in France, but in Spain, in Rumania, and especially in Italy.[107] To this diatribe, Sir John Pollock, a friend of France, makes a reply. The arraignments by Arnold and Fyfe are merely reiterations, he says, "of the hoary charge of moral decadence made against the French time out of mind by Puritans and Teutons who cloak far worse sins under a show of stern fibre." France's fall he cannot and does not deny, but he attributes it to deep-seated political blunders, not to lubricity.[108]

Arnold's attempt to explain differences in ethical outlook among the nations on the basis of race, a practice widely accepted, as has been shown, in the nineteenth century and earlier, stands discredited today. In so far as such matters lend themselves to experimental and statistical treatment, it would seem that specific differences can be traced to non-racial influences.[109] As it turns out, the ideas of the ethnologists which Arnold thought so "pregnant and striking" were pregnant chiefly with error, as he, were he alive today, would be among the first to admit. He would today be less ready to grant a monopoly in morality to any one race; at any rate, he would hardly, in the light of recent events, assign that role to the Teutons. The best final comment on this phase of Arnold's activity is his own, though he made it with no thought of application to himself: "Morals are often treated in a narrow and false fashion; they are bound up with systems of thought and belief which have had their day."[110]

Chapter V

The Celt

By a kind of ethnological justice, if one may use the phrase, Arnold the crusader against the Teutomaniacs himself acquired the title Gallomaniac for his Celtic sympathies.[1] As a crusader, however, Arnold seems to have a reprehensible habit of changing sides. For all the vigor and promise of his initial onslaught, he is discovered in the final stages of the battle, as the preceding pages have shown, to be on the side of the Teuton. Émile Legouis, discussing Arnold in his *Défense de la poésie française à l'usage des lecteurs anglais*, believes himself justified in questioning the services of a French ally who on so many counts turns out to be an adversary, the more to be feared because of his reputation as an ally. A similar case could be made by any thorough-going Celtomaniac against Arnold as an ally of the Celts. He has a reputation, and it is deserved, as their friend and defender; he became, at the close of the century, a patron saint of the Celtic Renaissance; partly through his influence, university chairs in Celtic have been established in England and America. Yet he is a Celtophile, as he is a liberal, only with reservations. In short, he is no maniac. As a follower of Sophocles, he tries always to see things steadily and to see them whole. It is only to the casual or hurried reader that he seems to change sides, for from the very beginning his stand in Celtic matters is qualified.

On the Study of Celtic Literature, delivered first as a

series of four lectures from the Oxford Chair of Poetry, 1865–66, published next as four separate articles in the *Cornhill*, 1866, and appearing finally in book form, 1867, has had a more varied reception, perhaps, than any other of Arnold's works. At the conclusion of the Celtic lectures, "The old Head of Jesus said audibly. . ., 'The Angel ended.' "[2] An auspicious beginning! Some later critics, however, had they regarded Arnold as an angel, would have placed him among the fallen ones, who, according to Milton, builded Pandemonium. The *Saturday Review* bluntly stated that he knew nothing about the subject he discussed.[3] By the *Times* and the *Daily Telegraph* his "arrant nonsense" was made the subject of "inhuman attacks."[4] Saintsbury, linking *On Translating Homer* with *On the Study of Celtic Literature*, remarks that "no two more valuable books, in their subject, to their country and time, have ever been issued from the press," yet in both books he finds on almost every page opportunity for disagreement.[5] Herbert W. Paul discovers a parallel for Arnold in Gladstone, who knowing not a word of Hebrew, wrote an entire book on the Bible. Arnold's charming study is similarly invalidated by his complete ignorance of Gaelic, Erse, and Cymry. The solidest part of the book is that devoted to Lord Strangford's philological annotations, "and they are comically like a tutor's corrections of his pupil's exercises."[6] In the opinion of Andrew Lang, the Celtic Renaissance is indebted for its form, its ideas, and its aims to two men, Renan, the Moses of the movement, and Arnold, "the eloquent Aaron." Though Arnold's information is wider than Renan's, he is guilty of equally fallacious argument, and his "Celtic theory, if not demonstrably untrue, is, at least, unproved and superfluous."[7] John Munro links Arnold with the phrenologist and the palmist as a purveyor of pseudo-science.[8] Wyndham Lewis regards Arnold's book as ethnologically worthless.[9] And Roland Smith says that "Ever since Matthew Arnold seventy-five years ago divided the world of Celtic scholarship into the two races of Celt-lovers and Celt-haters, the Celtophils and the Celtophobes have been waging war on each other."[10] Carleton Stanley views the work chiefly as an ironical political sermon, England's mistakes in governing Ireland being the theme.[11] By Lionel Trilling the book is discussed as a text on the failure of the middle class.[12] And to Stuart P. Sherman the chief value lies in the stimulus to intellectual curiosity.[13]

Arnold himself was at first dubious as to the appeal the work would have. The attendance at the Oxford lectures was not very gratifying. At the conclusion of a later performance on "Culture and its Enemies" an admirer, Mrs. Drummond, presented him with a keg of whiskey. On the success of the Celtic lectures there was no such material evidence. The subject, Arnold thought, was unsuited for show-lectures, and a bit too scientific for a magazine like the *Cornhill* of general circulation.[14] He was delighted that the publishers, Smith and Elder, were willing to bring out the book at their own risk, since, as George Smith had told him, it was hardly the kind of work that would be bought at a railway station by a British parent for his Jemima.[15] Yet the event showed his fears to be groundless. To his great delight, the book was received enthusiastically all through Wales, a result which at least in this particular instance he preferred to being thought by some two hundred wealthy and literary people to be a clever and interesting writer.[16] This popularity in Wales continued into the twentieth century: Alfred Nutt, the Celtic scholar, recorded in 1910, that in judging Eisteddfod essays dealing with the Celtic influence on English literature, he found most of the papers to be a mere elaboration of Arnold's ideas.[17] Arnold's abandonment of the fit audience though few was only temporary, however; subsequent works reduced him again to the status of "an unpopular author"—the title which in 1870 before the Income Tax Commissioners he assumed, with a touch of humor and more than a touch of profit, since he succeeded thereby in reducing the assessment on his literary earnings from £1,000 to £200 a year. To what was the wider popularity of the Celtic studies due? Arnold believed that it could be laid to his method of presentation, for he could hardly imagine a more hopeless subject with which to approach the British public.[18] In this analysis he is only partly correct. The work, to be sure, is written with his customary vivacity, in the "easy, sinuous, unpolemical style" on which he prided himself, a style which robs comparative philology of its terrors, anthropology and ethnology of their difficulties; it is interpolated, also, with humorous and ironic passages, with brilliant phrases, and with pages of great poetic charm. But as much can be said for any of Arnold's other major works, always excepting, of course, *God and the Bible*, where the style takes on the rigorous and disputatious tone which theologians must assume in order to rise to the height of their great argument. The subject, on the other hand, is far from being the hopeless one that Arnold imagined it. The strife between the Celt and the Saxon was, is, and, it would seem, always shall be of interest, in spite of, or perhaps because of, the fact that scientists have difficulty in determining which is which; are, indeed, convinced that in most modern cases each is partly the other. The connection with the Irish problem is obvious, "The same old sore" that "breaks out from age to age," but was in the last half of the nineteenth century of peculiar virulence and therefore commanded the attention of the whole British public. In the time of the making of nations, the very heyday of nationalism, Arnold's theme is the special characteristics which distinguish one modern state from another, always a controversial and therefore an exciting and interesting topic. At this time, too, comparative philology has just come into its own, and Arnold capitalizes on the current enthusiasm. Antiquarian interests are drawn upon in the consideration of the *Book of Ballymote*, the *Red Book of Hergest*, and the *Book of the Dun Cow*. The work is also a continuation of his battle against the Philistine, to which he had by this time succeeded in drawing wide attention. And finally, lest one forget the most important fact of all, the book is a literary study, a fascinating, if as some think, an impossible, attempt to disengage and bring into full view the strands that make up the complex which is English poetry. These are matters, then, of interest all compact, on which all have views though few have knowledge—just the field for a brilliant and persuasive and, one adds with regret, partly specious disquisition such as Arnold's.

For the fullest understanding of *On the Study of Celtic Literature* a knowledge of the origins of Arnold's interest in the Celts is required. This interest began as a romantic attachment to a lost cause, and "a beaten race," as became a son of Oxford, the "home of lost causes, and forsaken beliefs, and unpopular names, and impossible loyalties." Writing to Lady Rothschild in 1864, he records his first impressions of the Scottish Highlands, with their "sense of vastness," their desolation, "miles and miles and miles of mere heather and peat and rocks, and not a soul. And then the sea comes up into the land on the west coast, and the mountain forms are there quite magnificent." And significantly, he adds, "Then also I have a great *penchant* for the Celtic races, with their melancholy and unprogressiveness."[19] Visiting in Brittany in 1859, he is made aware of the possible Celtic strain in his own blood. He writes to his mother that with the Cranics and Trevenecs all about him, he cannot help thinking of her. And the "peasantry with their expressive, rather mournful faces, long noses, and dark eyes," remind him continually of his brother Tom and his uncle Trevenen.[20] Of this Celtic ancestry Mrs. Humphry Ward, Arnold's niece, makes a great deal, unwittingly illustrating in the process the snares and delusions into which Arnold's ethnological methods may lead. In her own father she saw the ineffectualness in practical life which Arnold ascribes to the Celts; in Arnold himself she could, of course, find no ineffectualness—in fact, quite the contrary. Yet both possessed qualities lacking in their father, and these qualities, she thinks, were derived from a remoter ancestry—perhaps through their mother, a descendant of the Penroses and Trevenens of Cornwall. At other times she is inclined to derive the Celtic traces, the "cradle gifts" of the Celtic race, which, in her opinion, Arnold unquestionably possessed, from his paternal grandmother, though Dr. Arnold possessed none of them. This grandmother was supposedly of Irish blood, of the line of the Fitzgeralds and the Dillons. In Ireland, says Mrs. Ward, the "faces full of power, and humour, and softness" remind her of her uncle.[21]

In his championship of the Celts, Arnold is prompted by the desire, which he indulged so often in other fields, to take the unpopular side. Justin McCarthy, speaking of Anglo-Irish relationships in the third quarter of the century, says that among writers and political speakers, five out of every six accused the Irish peasant of lawlessness and incurable idleness.[22] Dr. Thomas Arnold belonged earlier to this majority. Matthew, the son, remembers being taught in his youth to regard the Celt as being separated from the Teuton "by an impassable gulf." His father, he says, was more insistent on this separation than on that between the Teutons and any other of the world's races.[23] To this criticism of the famous historian, Arnold's mother evidently objected, for he writes to her in 1866 that he does not believe his father ever regarded the Saxon and Celt as "mutually needing to be complemented by each other"; quite the opposite, he felt, was true, for Dr. Arnold so abhorred the Celtic lack of steadiness and truthfulness that he could see no good at all in the race.[24] This friendly family dispute can be settled by turning to Dr. Arnold's account of the early activities of the Gauls:

> The Kelts or Gauls broke through the thin screen which had hitherto concealed them from sight, and began for the first time to take their part in the great drama of the nations. For nearly two hundred years they continued to fill Europe and Asia with the terror of their name; but it was a passing tempest, and if it was useful at all, it was useful only to destroy. The Gauls could communicate no essential points of human character in which the other races might be deficient; they could neither improve the intellectual state of mankind, nor its social and political

> relations. When therefore, they had done their appointed work of havoc, they were doomed to be themselves extirpated, or to be lost amidst nations of greater creative and constructive power, nor is there any race which has left fewer traces of itself in the character and institutions of modern civilization.[25]

His letters show that he regarded the modern Irish as barbarians, leading the life of animals, multiplying in idleness, beggary, and brutality.[26] The *London Quarterly Review*, at any rate, would have agreed with the son as against the wife, for it speaks of "that Teuton of Teutons, the Celt-hating Dr. Arnold."[27]

As a further cause of estrangement between England and Ireland, Arnold cites Lord Lyndhurst's notorious phrase on the Irish: "aliens in speech, in religion, in blood."[28] On the essential difference between the two peoples, Arnold could also have cited Carlyle's lurid contrast between Ireland "in chronic atrophy these five centuries," and "nobler England." Ireland's condition, Carlyle admits, is caused in large part by English misgovernment. The fact remains, however, that the Irish are "immethodic, headlong, violent, mendacious." Driven by famine, they have emigrated in alarming numbers to England where they threaten to drag the population to their own wretched level. To such a state, however, the Saxon British will never allow themselves to fall. Fortunately, the British possess all the qualities the Irish lack—method, insight, perseverance, rationality, veracity, and a deep-seated Berseker rage. By these qualities, says Carlyle, the English will be saved.[29]

That Arnold's sympathetic view of the Celtic cause was not universally held is further shown—if further proof is needed—by the furious attack which Swinburne makes upon the main thesis of the Celtic lectures: "The Celt we have always with us, and never notice him; neither as a poet nor as a critic can a Macpherson, a Moore, a Mangan, and a Maginn be taken into serious account by the countrymen of Chaucer and Shakespeare, of Milton and Wordsworth, of Coleridge and Landor. The 'brutal Saxon'—or Northman—is apt to set his 'bloody hoof' on their pretensions with a quiet and good-humoured smile; if he be not disposed rather to pass them by with a silent wave of his bloody hand and a kindly nod of his brutal head. But the amateur or would-be Celt, brutal if not bloody and Saxon if not sane, who pretends to discover a visible vein of Celtic fancy, a tangible thread of Celtic influence, in the masterworks of English inspiration, is almost too absurd a figure to pass underided and unnoticed among the ranks in which he has enlisted or shown himself fain to enlist as a volunteer."[30] In his comments on Blake, Swinburne distinguishes between the Celtic and the English spirit: "Now that we know him for a Celt by descent we understand whence he derived his amazing capacity for gabble and babble and drivel: his English capacity for occasionally exquisite and noble workmanship we may rationally attribute to his English birth and breeding." Swinburne feels that he may at times have failed to grasp Blake's meaning "for the excellent reason that, being a Celt, he now and then too probably had none worth the labour of deciphering—or at least worth the serious attention of a student belonging to a race in which reason and imagination are the possibly preferable substitute for fever and fancy."[31] Froude says that the modern Irish are of no race, blended as they are of Celt and Dane, Saxon and Norman, Scot and Frenchman; nevertheless, throughout his History he treats them as a distinct race with ingrained characteristics. "If they possess some real virtues"—in his opinion, those of secondary importance: lightheartedness, humor, and imagination, "they possess the counterfeits of a hundred more." There is an incompleteness of character conspicuous in all they do and have done, in their history, their practical habits, their arts and literature. Passion dominates them in all that they think and do; yet "they are without the manliness which will give strength and solidity to the sentimental part of their disposition." The idleness of the Irish peasant "is in the granules of his blood." And "the perceptions of taste which belong to the higher orders of understanding are as completely absent as truthfulness of spirit is absent, or cleanliness of person and habit. The Irish are the spendthrift sister of the Arian race."[32]

Arnold's defense of Celtic studies is motivated also by a romantic preference for picturesque diversity over monotonous uniformity. His brother Saxons, he says, have a terrible habit of improving "everything but themselves off the face of the earth." He, on the contrary, prefers not to find his own visage everywhere; he likes variety, and therefore "would not for the world have the lineaments of the Celtic genius lost."[33] For the same reason he hoped in 1861 that the Southern states would secede from the American Union. Diversity in climate and in race is salutary. A Europe completely Anglicized, or completely Gallicized, would be frightfully dull. Furthermore, nations need to be checked and taught, he thinks, by other nations unlike themselves.[34]

The direct inspiration for Arnold's work was probably supplied by Renan's *La poésie des races celtiques* and by his *L'Instruction supérieure en France, son histoire et son avenir*. In a letter, cited earlier,[35] to his sister in 1859, Arnold indicates that there "is a great deal of truth" in Renan's characterization of the Celtic spirit, though "the glorification of the Celts is carried too far." Arnold leans much more heavily upon his predecessor in the field than the single reference in the text implies.[36] First of all, one of his purposes in delivering the four lectures on Celtic literature is the establishment of a Celtic chair at Oxford.[37] In the last of the lectures, he makes an extended plea for such a chair. The arguments employed would seem to be derived from Renan, who two years earlier, in 1864, in *L'Instruction supérieure en France, son histoire et son avenir*, had advocated the founding of a *chaire de langues et de littératures celtiques* at the College of France.[38] The ineffectualness of the Celts in politics; their turn for sentiment, for melancholy, for natural magic; their intimate feeling for nature, their striving after the infinite; the Celtic element in chivalry; the feminine nature of the race; the tendency toward shyness and embarrassment—all these are dealt with at greater or less extent by Renan in *La poésie des races celtiques*. Arnold also uses a couplet by Crétien de Troies and a passage from *The Mabinogion*, both of which he found in Renan. There is, finally, a marked similarity between the poetic description of Wales with which Arnold's work opens and the description of Brittany with which Renan begins his essay.[39] Yet Arnold is no mere echo of Renan. As his numerous references indicate, he read widely, if not deeply, in philology, ethnology, history, and literature for the preparation of the lectures. In view of his careful and cautious citation of authorities, a practice followed to the same extent nowhere else except in some of his religious works, it is ironic that the Celtic study has been judged the most unsound of his books. Arnold's is the more ambitious essay. Like Renan's, it attempts a delineation of the Celtic spirit and an analysis of Celtic literature, but it goes further: there are political and social implications of great significance, and there is a specific application to English poetry. Arnold's idea of what constitutes the Celtic race is also wider than Renan's, and in consequence more vague. Renan limits his definition:

> To avoid all misunderstanding, I ought to point out that by the word *Celtic* I designate here, not the whole of the great race which, at a remote period, formed the population of nearly the whole of Western Europe, but simply the four groups which, in our days, still merit this name, as opposed to the Teutons and to the Neo-Latin peoples. These four groups are: (1) The inhabitants of Wales and Cambria, and the peninsula of Cornwall, bearing even now the ancient name of *Cymry*; (2) the *Bretons bretonnants*, or dwellers in French Brittany speaking Bas-Breton, who represent an emigration of the Cymry from Wales; (3) the Gaels of the North of Scotland speaking Gaelic; (4) the Irish, although a very profound line of demarcation separates Ireland from the rest of the Celtic family.[40]

Arnold in his definition includes these same four peoples, but, following Amédée Thierry and Henri Martin, adds the French as predominantly Celtic, and, following W. F. Edwards, regards the English as semi-Celtic.

It has been generally assumed among commentators that Arnold's interest in the Celts and his information about them were derived largely from Renan. This influence alone, therefore, has been given any adequate scholarly consideration. Aside from this dependence on Renan, it is further assumed, Arnold proceeded chiefly by divination and intuition. His descriptions of the various original types, it has been pointed out, seem not to have been based on any thorough study of original documents or historical facts.[41] Strictly speaking, such a view has, of course, some validity. Throughout his study, Arnold confesses his lack of the learning required for the use of original documents. He does not for that reason, however, proceed by intuition and divination. In secondary sources —mainly the French historians—he found authority for the racial types, and in the case of the Celts at least, for all the traits of the type.

The contrast between the Teuton and the Celt, of which Arnold makes so much, is only hinted at by Renan.[42] Amédée Thierry, Michelet, and Henri Martin—all of whom Arnold had read—employ it as the dominant theme in the opening chapters of their respective histories of France. Thierry's basic distinction between the two races, and Arnold's use of it have already been commented upon.[43] According to Martin, "l'un a les défauts d'une activité déréglée; l'autre a des défauts paresseux et sédentaires."[44] What is this but Arnold's primary contrast: the lively, but unruly Celt as against the heavy, phlegmatic German. In supporting his literary study with the most recent discoveries in philology and anthropology, Arnold found no model in Renan. It may well be that in this procedure he took his cue from Amédée Thierry, whose *History of the Gauls* is introduced by one hundred and eighteen pages of comment on ethnological investigations.

It is to the incorrigible Celticist, Henri Martin, however, that Arnold is most fully indebted for his analysis of the Celtic race: "Monsieur Henri Martin, whose chapters on the Celts, in his *Histoire de France*," Arnold says, "are full of information and interest."[45] How much of Arnold's own information is derived from this source remains to be shown.

In Arnold's view, the French are Celtic in blood, though Latin in their civilization. In spite of the fact that the laws, manners, and language of the Roman conqueror triumphed, the old race did not become extinct; the people of Gaul remained essentially Celtic. In this resistance to the conqueror, Gaul was unlike Britain, which became mainly German even in blood through the Teutonic invasions.[46] And France remains in this respect Celtic to the present day. Through contact with the stronger civilization of Rome, Gaul did become a Latin country, but "without changing the basis of her blood." Although Latinism triumphed over Celticism, as well as over the Germanism brought in by the later invasions, "Celticism," Arnold maintains, "is everywhere manifest still in the French nation."[47] Even the Celtic language, he adds, lingered on among the lower classes for centuries after the Roman conquest.[48] In all these opinions, Arnold seems to be drawing, with some reservation, upon Martin, who begins the first chapter of his *History of France* with the theme. "Les premiers hommes qui peuplèrent le centre et l'ouest de l'Europe furent les Gaulois (dans leur langue, Gahel ou Gaidhel; par contraction Gaël ou Gâl), nos véritables ancêtres; car leur sang prédomine de beaucoup dans ce mélange successif de peuples divers qui a formé notre nation, et leur esprit est toujours en nous. Leurs vertues et leurs vices, conservés au coeur du peuple français, et les traits essentiels de leur type physique, reconnaissable sous la dégénération amenée par le changement des moeurs et par le croisement des populations, attestent encore cette antique origine."[49] So thoroughly persuaded of the Celtic nature of the French is Martin that he finds "les tendances propres à l'esprit celtique, modifié, tempéré, mais non pas dénaturé par l'education romaine, dans le progrès et dans les manifestations les plus essentielles de l'esprit français."[50] The lingering on of the Celtic language among the common people Martin explains as part of a general reaction to conquest. Loyalty to the old nationality seeks refuge in the heart of the people, always more faithful than the upper classes to instincts of patriotism, and more ready to rebel against the innovations imported by the stranger. Thus, "Le peuple ne parla jamais latin. Il garda sa langue presque intacte pendant plusieurs siècles; puis il se forma peu à peu un grand patois, une langue rustique, mêlée de latin et de celtique, où le vocabularie latin finit par dominer, mais où subsistèrent quelques-unes des formes gauloises et où ne régna jamais le syntaxe latin."[51]

The Celtic nature of the French is emphasized at the very start of Arnold's study in the charming picture which he draws of the blood relationship between the French and Welsh. Walking along the coast at Llandudno, he feels himself almost an alien: the land is strange, the speech, as he hears it from the traffickers about him, unfamiliar. Through the welter of these undecipherable sounds there comes presently, however, a familiar strain, the speech of a French nursery-maid among her charges. "Profoundly ignorant of her relationship, this Gaulish Celt moved among her British cousins, speaking her polite neo-Latin tongue, and full of compassionate contempt, probably, for the Welsh barbarians and their jargon. What a revolution was here! How had the star of this daughter of Gomer waxed, while the star of these Cymry, his sons, had waned! What a difference of fortune in the two, since the days when, speaking the same language, they left their common dwelling-place in the heart of Asia; since the Cimmerians of the Euxine came in upon their western kinsmen, the sons of the giant Galates; since the sisters, Gaul and Britain, cut the mistletoe in their forests, and saw the coming of Caesar!"[52] This passage, in which Biblical genealogy, mistaken philology, and an anthropological theory, then current, but since exploded, are confusedly joined, is a brilliant example of the dangers of being an ethnologist. Even in 1866, it caused "a pang of dreadful misgiving" in the philological breast of Lord Strangford, one of the first reviewers of Arnold's Celtic studies. The Biblical paternity he eyes askance. By what proof, he asks, can the French maid be shown to be the daughter of Gomer, and the Welsh to be his sons. He desires more information on "the common dwelling-place in the heart of Asia." And he is puzzled by the Cimmerians of the Euxine.[53] For an answer to all these queries, Arnold could have referred his reviewer to Henri Martin.

> Dans l'ethnographie biblique, on fait descendre les Gaulois d'Askhenaz, un des fils de Gomer, fils de Japhet.[54] Les Gaëls, à l'origine des temps, lorsqu'ils avaient quitté l'Asie, avaient laissé derrière eux des frères, qui s'étaient avancés à leur tour en Europe. Les traditions des âges mythologiques de la Grèce nous font entrevoir au delà du Pont-Euxin, dans les régions ténébreuses où Homère place l'entrée du royaume des ombres, un peuple redoutable qui porte un caractère tout à la fois sacré et infernal. Là des prêtresses homicides immolent les étrangers sur les autels de dieux inconnus; de là des guerriers

irrésistibles, enfants de la nuit, s'élancent au midi du Caucase et de l'Euxin, et promènent partout l'épouvante (vers le onzième siècle avant J.-C.). Les Grècs appelaient ce peuple Cimmériens (κιμμερίοι, κίμμερι); les Romains le nommèrent Cimbres (Cimbri), légère altération de son nom national, *Kimri*. Les Kimris étaient la seconde branche de la race gauloise, et cette race avait été marquée d'une si forte empreinte à son origine qu'une séparation de bien des siècles n'avait point altéré les affinités essentielles de ses deux rameaux.[55]

The hypothesis, since discredited, that Central Asia was the cradle of the Aryan, or Indo-European race, was first advanced in 1820 by J. G. Rhode, and in the following half-century came to be accepted by almost all the leading philologists and anthropologists of Europe. In England, the Oxford orientalist and philologist, Max Müller, whom Arnold knew, was its most eloquent advocate.[56] The theory appealed to Arnold's imagination, as it did to that of most of his contemporaries. Having employed it in his Celtic studies, he recurred to it in his Note Book for 1868: "The *consciousness of the divine*, which, according to universal tradition, the Greeks brought with them as a common inheritance from the seat of the Aryan races to Greece."[57] Seven years later in his battle with the metaphysicians, he finds it necessary to determine exactly the meaning and history of the word *being*. "With a proper respect for our Aryan forefathers," he goes first to the Sanskrit dictionaries for information.[58]

Arnold was not the first English writer to hold this view. Of all the Victorian authors, Charles Kinsgley presents the fullest and most fanciful picture of the great migration of the Aryans out of Asia. Driven by an irresistible impulse from Heaven; fully equipped with bullock-wagons, stone axes and horn bows; accompanied by their wives and children, and by great herds of cattle, horses and sheep, the great Aryan tribe, "the children of Japhet," as Kingsley calls them, left the holy mountain, Hindoo-Koh, and the Valley of the Oxus, to pursue their European destiny.[59]

From the Middle Ages to the middle of the nineteenth century a legend persisted, enrolling among its perpetuators many a notable English writer, that Odin with a band of followers had migrated from some district in Asia to settle eventually in Scandinavia.[60] Carlyle traces the history of the account, only to reject as legendary the migration and the definite date, 70 B.C.[61]

It is evident, then, that Henri Martin, and after him, Matthew Arnold, were continuing a well-established tradition. Neither were they alone in regarding the French as basically Celtic. As indicated in an earlier chapter, the belief was, and is still, widely held by patriotic Frenchmen. In speaking of the French Revolution, Tennyson says that "Celtic Demos rose a Demon, shriek'd and slaked the world with blood." Carlyle regards the race as Gaelic. Some of the worst of the blunders into which Arnold fell, as will hereafter be shown, resulted from this identification of the French with the Celts.

In his Celtic lectures, Arnold mentions Renan only to disagree with the picture which he gives of the race. Renan's *douce petite race naturellement chrétienne*, the *race fière et timide, à l'extérieur gauche et embarrassée* does not accord with Arnold's own observation of the typical Irishman at Donnybrook fair. Nor does Renan's *infinie délicatesse de sentiment qui caractérise la race Celtique* seem to fit "the popular conception of an Irishman who wants to borrow money." For a truer delineation of the Celts

Arnold goes to Martin. Sentiment, says Arnold, is the best single term to describe the Celtic nature. By sentiment he means "An organization quick to feel impressions, and feeling them strongly; a lively personality therefore, keenly sensitive to joy and to sorrow." Because of this temperament, the Celt may indeed in times of trouble seem "shy and wounded," be capable of a "wistful regret," a "passionate, penetrating melancholy," but the essence of his nature "is to aspire ardently after life, light, and emotion, to be expansive, adventurous, and gay . . . the head in the air, snuffing and snorting."[62] In this list of the essential attributes, Arnold echoes Martin, who describes "Les Gaulois," as "blancs et blonds, colorés de visage, portant haut la tête, dégagés de poitrine et respirant largement, ardents, mobiles, expansifs." The Gauls "aiment tout ce que est vif et brillant, tout ce que réjouit l'œil et l'imagination."[63] The very word *gay*, Martin and Arnold derive from the Celtic *gair*, to laugh, an etymology which Lord Strangford in a note emphatically rejects. To this description Arnold appends the contrast between the German, distinguished for his "larger volume of intestines," and the French with the "more developed organs of respiration," a physiological differentiation which, as shown earlier,[64] he drew from Martin. To combat in himself a natural turn toward lowness of spirit, Arnold deliberately cultivated gaiety. In looking over his *Notebooks*, he must have felt somewhat confirmed in his belief that there was something especially Celtic in this quality, for most of his quotations on the subject are drawn from French authors.[65]

The lively, expansive nature of the Celt expresses itself, according to Arnold, in a desire "to be sociable, hospitable, eloquent, admired, figuring away brilliantly."[66] In Martin a strong contrast is drawn between the Gaul with his love of society and sociability and the German with his "aversion pour la vie en commun."[67] In his discourse, the Gaul ranges from an enigmatic brevity to "une éloquence impétueuse et intarissable en figures hardies."[68] And as for being admired, "Éblouir ses amis et faire trembler ses ennemis est la grande ambition du Gaulois."[69] Not only in his study of Celtic literature, but throughout his works Arnold emphasizes the sociability of the Irish and "their French kinsmen."[70] In the *Irish Essays* the incompatibility of the Irish and the English is shown to be due largely to "The Irish quick-wittedness, sentiment, keen feeling for social life and manners," which demand something that the "hard and imperfect civilization" of England cannot provide. If a fusion is ever to be brought about, Arnold feels that the "dull and dismal" English middle-class must adopt something of the lightness and gaiety and "keen feeling for social life of the Irish."[71] In the essay "Equality," Arnold makes an observation which he repeats again and again in other places: "Certain races and nations, as we know, are on certain lines pre-eminent and representative."[72] Thus the Italians are pre-eminent "in feeling the power of beauty," the Germans, "the power of knowledge." The French possess a "congenital sense for the power of social intercourse and manners." The great contribution of the age of Louis the Fourteenth, when French civilization reached its highest, was "*L'esprit de société*, the spirit of society, the social spirit." In bringing men together, making them more dependent on one another, more considerate and understanding of one another, this spirit promotes equality. Hence the French

Revolution. The English, on the other hand, have never cultivated the social spirit, or its corollary, equality. As a result, inequality prevails everywhere in classes and property, and has materialized the upper classes, vulgarized the middle classes, and brutalized the lower classes.[73]

The distinction between the solitary Teuton and the gregarious Celt has been made repeatedly from the time of Tacitus. According to the Roman historian, the Teuton dwelt by preference apart from his fellows, was not a lover of cities. Robert Knox, the Victorian ethnologist, in his discussion of the Saxons presents a photograph of a manor house, set in extensive grounds, which he calls "A Saxon House; standing always apart, if possible, from all others."[74] What Martin and Arnold call Celtic expansiveness and sociability Carlyle chooses to call "Gallic-Ethnic excitability and effervescence."[75] He cites Julius Caesar who nineteen hundred years before had noted these qualities in the Gauls, how in their insatiable curiosity about the activities of others, they were wont to waylay travellers, by force if necessary, for information. And France today retains the traits of this "old Gaulish and Gaelic Celthood," for "on the whole, are not Nations astonishingly true to their National character; which indeed runs in the blood?"[76]

The unsociability of the English: their reserve, their silence, is a trait which others besides Arnold—notably Montesquieu, Volney, Carlyle, J. S. Mill, Emerson and Boutmy—have singled out for censure or praise. Montesquieu comments disapprovingly on the self-sufficiency of the average Englishman who cares little for society, limiting his desires to "a good dinner, a woman, and the comforts of life." Emerson is of the opinion that "every one of these islanders is an island himself, safe, tranquil, incommunicable. In a company of strangers you would think him deaf; his eyes never wander from his table and newspaper. He is never betrayed into any curiosity or unbecoming emotion. . . . He does not give his hand. He does not let you meet his eye. . . . In mixed or in select companies they do not introduce persons . . . his bearing, on being introduced, is cold."[77] J. S. Mill during his residence in France is struck by the warmth and expansiveness of social relationships. He deplores the fact that the English lack the courage of their emotions, that they stifle any display of the human affections and sympathies.[78] With all these commentators, English unsociability is obviously a defect. In the eyes of another school, however, it has its redeeming side. Volney attributes the success of the English in colonization to their willingness to endure the solitude of far and remote places. The Frenchman, in contrast, is lost without his neighbor, must have someone with whom to converse. He does not by preference set his dwelling place in the desert or the forest. It is the silence of the English, says Volney, that accounts also for their eminence in agriculture, commerce and industry. By their silence they achieve greater concentration in thought, greater clearness in expression, greater assurance of manner. In all these opinions, Boutmy, the French observer, concurs.[79] Hildegard Gauger commends Josiah Royce for his discernment in ascribing to their reticence the English domination over other countries. In handling subject peoples, it is through acts, not through speech, that one's superiority must be proved.[80] Carlyle, however, is the great apostle of silence. In forty books he praises its virtues. He is the eulogist of the "dumb" peoples: the Romans, the Russians, and above all, the English. In their silence lies their strength. Inarticulate in speech, the English are expressive enough in deeds—in this language their epic "is written in huge characters on the face of this planet." Beside such accomplishment, the "ever-talking, ever-gesticulating French" have little to show.[81] Hildegard Gauger believes that the talent for silence is "ein nordgermanisches Erbgut," which in England has found its fullest development and has yielded its richest rewards.[82]

Another characteristic of the Celt is his love of bright colors.[83] Again, Arnold has ample warrant for his description in Martin's account: "Les colliers, les bracelets, les anneaux d'or étincellent de toutes parts chez les guerriers de renom; l'or, l'argent et le corail ornent leurs sabres et leurs boucliers; leurs saies, de laine épaisse ou légère suivant la saison, sont bariolées de carreaux aux vives couleurs ou semées de paillettes et de fleurons éclatants."[84]

Arnold observes further that "The Celt is often called sensual; but it is not so much the vulgar satisfactions of the sense that attract him as emotion and excitement; he is truly, as I began by saying, sentimental."[85] Both the charge and the palliation of it are taken from his French source: "On a souvent accusé les Gaulois d'une tendance licencieuse; Aristote et Diodore leur imputent même un vice monstrueux trop commun dans la civilization grecque et latine . . . Les contradictions des anciens sur la moralité gauloise s'expliquent en partie par une double tendance de cette race. D'une part, l'ardeur du sang, la vivacité d'imagination, une disposition particulière à prendre la vie avec légèreté, à jouer avec elle, pour ainsi dire, poussent à la mobilité des relations; de l'autre part, une nature sympathique, passionée, généreuse, qu'exaltent des croyances dont nous parlerons tout à l'heure, enfante des attachements durables et «plus forts que la mort». Une certaine supériorité morale s'entrevoit chez les femmes, que les historiens anciens louent sans réserve quand ils accusent les hommes. C'est là un caractère important à constater chez une race où domine le sentiment, le principe essentiel de la femme."[86]

All the preceding traits of the Celts are intended by Arnold as a preliminary sketch to introduce the one characteristic for which they are chiefly distinguished, and on which he bases most of his subsequent analysis of their achievements in thought and action. "Sentimental, *always ready to react against the despotism of fact*; that is the description a great friend [Henri Martin] of the Celt gives of him; and it is not a bad description of the sentimental temperament; it lets us into the secret of its dangers and of its habitual want of success. Balance, measure, and patience, these are the eternal conditions, even supposing the happiest temperament to start with, of high success; and balance, measure and patience are just what the Celt has never had."[87] Since this is Arnold's most famous pronouncement on the Celts, and has had a notable and traceable effect not only on his own work but upon that of others in the fields of literature, economics and politics, it deserves detailed study. The account of his authority, the "great friend of the Celt", runs as follows: "leur mobilité singulière en ce qui concerne les personnes et les choses extérieures ne tient pas seulement à la vivacité de leur imagination, mais asusi à leur indomptable personnalité, toujours prête à réagir contre le despotisme du fait; cette mobilité cache une persistance opiniâtre dans les sentiments intimes et dans les directions essentielles de la vie."[88] Alfred Nutt, the Celtic scholar, in his edition of Arnold's study says that Arnold's generalization is without basis, that it can be applied with accuracy neither to the Celt of history, the Gael, the Brython, nor to the French. Celtic literature, according to Nutt, is in no way a reaction to the despotism of fact; it is filled with fancy which simply transcends fact. And of all the historic races, the French, he thinks, has least reacted against the despotism of fact. In all its manifestations, the French genius is characterized, rather, by "the recognition of fact in its bare, naked, precise reality." In this light he explains the "adultness" of the French, their impatience with the optimism and make-believe of their German and English neighbors. The French Revolution is an example in the field of politics. Further proof is to be found in their art. No people emphasizes so realistically the physical element in the passion of love. As a result, their literature is the most "naked," and "unchaste" in modern Europe.[89] Thus, he thinks, the very foundation of Arnold's analysis is shown to be questionable.

For proof of his thesis, Arnold turns to the world of spiritual creation, the world of business, and the world of politics. In each he finds that the Celt has been lamed by his rebellion against fact.

The deficiencies of the Celt—want of "balance, measure, patience"—have held him back from the highest success in all the arts. His greatest failure is evident in the plastic arts, in which, actually, he "has accomplished nothing." For music he has shown a stronger turn. "All that emotion alone can do in music the Celt has done;

the very soul of emotion breathes in the Scotch and Irish airs." But music demands more than emotion; in its higher branches it demands science also, and for this the Celt has no patience. There are, therefore, no Bachs or Beethovens among the Celts. In poetry the Celt has made his greatest contribution, has displayed, indeed, "splendid genius." Yet even here, his best work has been done in short pieces, "passages, lines and snatches of long pieces." To these a "singular beauty and power" is given. For all his passionate devotion to poetry, however, the Celt has produced no works genuinely great, such as the *Agamemnon* or the *Divine Comedy*. And the explanation is simple: he has no patience for *architectonicé* which "comes only after a steady, deep-searching survey, a firm conception of the facts of human life."[90]

If in regard to the British Celts at least—the Gaels and the Cymry—all these facts be granted, it is still not certain that they are to be attributed to race. Other influences: political, economic, social, geographic, and climatic, are important in the development of any civilization; and of these influences Arnold takes no account. In the field of poetry, his method is obviously at fault, for he compares the primitive literature of the Irish and the Welsh with that of the very highest civilizations of Greece and Italy.

It is in the application of these theories to French art, however, that Arnold lays himself open to most serious attack. One of the earliest reviewers of *On the Study of Celtic Literature*, Robert Giffen, sees this as a flaw in his argument, since it is in composition, the very quality Arnold denies them, that the French excel.[91] Arnold's editor, Alfred Nutt, takes no exception to the inadequacy of the Celts in the plastic arts; in fact, he grants that the unfavorable analysis is true enough, but becomes nonsense when applied to the French.[92] Nutt is forced to the conclusion that in speaking of the plastic arts Arnold must have forgotten that he claimed the Frenchman as a Celt, for it is in this field that the French, second only to the Italians, have attained eminence. He feels that when Arnold relies on his own critical insight and ceases to repeat current catchwords, "he recognizes, implicitly if not explicitly, that the Frenchman is not a Celt in the historic sense of the term."[93] In this extenuation, Nutt does Arnold no service. Arnold himself would have repudiated it. Five years after the publication of the Celtic studies, he still denies the French the highest eminence in the arts, still attributes their shortcomings to their Celtic nature. "More than twenty years ago we said, lovers of France as we are, and abundant and brilliant as is her work of a lower order than the very highest:

'France, famed in all great arts, *in none supreme*'—[94]

and this still seems to us to be the true criticism on her." Reviewing the long history of France, he finds no person of the stature of Goethe. Greece has given to the world Sophocles and Plato; Italy, Dante and Raphael; England, Shakespeare and Newton. There is no French pair to stand on a level with these Titans. "Probably the incapacity for seriousness in the highest sense, for what the Greeks called *τὸ σπουδαῖον*, and Virgil calls *virtus verusque labor*, is here too what keeps France back from perfection. For the Greeks and the Romans, and a truly Latin race like the Italians, have this seriousness intellectually, as the Hebrews and the Germanic races have it morally; and it may be remarked in passing that this distinction makes the conditions of the future for Latin Italy quite different from those for Celtic France. Only seriousness is constructive; Latin Gaul was a Roman construction, Old France was, as M. Renan himself says, a Germanic construction; France has been since 1789 getting rid of all the plan, cramps, and stays of her original builders, and their edifice is in ruins; but is the Celt, by himself, constructive enough to rebuild?"[95] And thirteen years later, in 1885, he repeats the indictment.[96]

As a Rhadamanthus of all the arts Arnold has some rather serious disqualifications. His knowledge of painting and music never advanced beyond that of a layman. Speaking of pictures in 1859, he confesses that he does not have, and does not wish to have, "the least of a connoisseur's spirit about them."[97] His voluminous correspondence from the Continent, so eloquent on matters social, political, religious and educational, is revealingly silent on the subject of painting. He does visit the galleries, in fact spends two hours in one at Dresden; but what he saw there he does not disclose. The galleries in Florence, he adds, "are even better."[98] There is no evidence in his published writings that he was aware of the eminent work being performed in painting by contemporary Frenchmen. For music he frankly confesses that he has not much of an ear. The choir singing at Norwich cathedral "was so good as powerfully to impress even me."[99] He goes to "*see*" Wagner's operas, *Tristram and Iseult* and *Tannhäuser*, for "of course, the music says little to me."[100] Émile Legouis with justifiable patriotism calls attention to Arnold's blindness to the French achievement in architecture. Surely, in the noble art of the Gothic cathedral, says Legouis, the French deserve a place with the very highest and greatest.[101] And in his own field, literature, Arnold's insensitivity to French poetry, as has already been shown, has aroused a chorus of protest.[102]

Turning to the world of business, Arnold discovers further evidence that the Celt is lamed by his rebellion against fact. "The skilful and resolute appliance of means to ends which is needed both to make progress in material civilization, and also to form powerful states, is just what the Celt has least turn for." Sensual, or at least sensuous, as he is, loving color, company and pleasure, in these respects resembling the Greek and Latinized races, the Celt unfortunately has not the talent of the Greeks and Latins to gratify his senses. He has failed "to reach any material civilization sound and satisfying, and not out at elbows, poor, slovenly, and half-barbarous."[103] For such a charge there was more than sufficient justification in the destitute condition of Ireland, in the migration during the middle years of the century of thousands of Irishmen to the factory towns of England. But that these conditions were due to racial incapacity was questioned by some of Arnold's contemporaries. Of these, J. S. Mill was one. T. H. Huxley questions the value of the ethnological differentiation between Englishmen of the western half of England and Irishmen of the eastern half of Ireland. Further, he sees no greater justification for applying the term Celt to the people of the western half of Ireland than to the people of Cornwall. The term Celt being as applicable to the one people as to the other, he would admit intelligence, perseverance, thrift, industry, sobriety, and respect for law to be Celtic virtues. And he deplores the tendency to attribute the absence of these qualities to Celtic blood.[104]

For Ireland's degradation, another explanation, as tenable at least as that of racial incapacity, is, of course, possible: prolonged English oppression.[105] And this view be it said in fairness, is partly Arnold's own when he gives his more considered judgment on Ireland's material civilization. In the Celtic study of 1867, the economic condition of Ireland is not his primary concern. Had it been, he would almost certainly not have been content with racial deficiency as the sole explanation. Nineteen years earlier, in 1848, he had been against shedding blood in Ireland to uphold "a body of Saxon landlords," and "a Saxon Church Establishment."[106] He does not share Carlyle's admiration for the violence of a Cromwell. When in "The Incompatibles" (1881) he again considers Irish grievances, he is convinced that the major part of the blame must be laid at England's door. By English injustice and misgovernment, by the iniquitous landlord system—based on conquest and confiscation—the Irish have been reduced to beggary and slavery. "Lord Clanricarde with his fifty thousand acres in Galway is, like Lord Lonsdale with his forty livings in the Church, an absurdity."[107] And Arnold proposes a remedy which he hopes will be as effective as it is unprecedented, "the expropriation of bad landlords."

In the field of politics, also, the Celt is disqualified. "And as in material civilization he has been ineffectual," says Arnold, "so has the Celt been ineffectual in politics.... The Celt, undisciplinable, anarchical, and turbulent by nature, but out of affection and admiration giving himself body and soul to some leader, that is not a promising political temperament."[108] That the Celt has never seemed in any epoch to display any aptitude for political life Arnold could have learned from Renan.[109] That the Celt is undisciplinable and subordinates himself completely to some admired leader he did learn from Martin. "Puissante race, mais faible société!" says Martin, "Le principe de la décadence est dans l'excès des forces qu'elle tournera contre elle-même. Le développement énorme de la personnalité, de l'indépendance individuelle, que la religion surexcite au lieu de la contenir, rend les Gaulois indisciplinables." Another cause of anarchy, with failure to recognize the law of the state, the right of the majority, and the authority of the magistrate, Martin thinks, is "le système de clientèle" with its "subordinations volontaires de l'admiration."[110] The general currency of such opinions is further indicated by Mommsen's famous remark that "the Celts have shaken all states, and have founded none."[111] American students of political economy were given the same picture in John W. Burgess' widely used text, in which the Celt was described as preferring "personal clanship" to membership in a state, as being incapable of creating any sound and durable political institution.[112] In English literature, the unruly Irishman is a stock figure from the time of Giraldus Cambrensis to the present.[113] One is not surprised, therefore, to hear from Tennyson that "The Celtic race does not easily amalgamate with other races, as those of Scandinavian origin do, as for instance Saxon and Norman, which have fused perfectly. The Teuton has no poetry in his nature like the Celt, and this makes the Celt much more dangerous in politics, for he yields more to his imagination than his common-sense. Yet his imagination does not allow of his realizing the suffering of poor dumb beasts. The Irish are difficult for us to deal with. For one thing the English do not understand their innate love of fighting, words and blows. If on either side of an Irishman's road to Paradise shillelahs grew, which automatically hit him on the head, yet he would not be satisfied. Suppose that we allowed Ireland to separate from us: owing to its factions she would soon fall a prey to some foreign power."[114]

His opinion of Celtic political capacity being what it

was, Arnold could hardly be expected to favor Ireland's independence. During the years in which Gladstone's Home Rule proposal was before the nation, Arnold vigorously opposed the measure. Ireland, he thought, should remain content, as Brittany and Wales have been, with being "a nation poetically only, not politically."[115] In his frequent discussions of the subject, in the periodicals and in the *Times*, he does not emphasize the racial issue, but bases his objections more reasonably on the ground that two islands which nature has bound together so inextricably cannot be separated politically without bringing ruin to both and particularly to Ireland.[116] The further argument is adduced that to merge Ulster, or British Ireland, with Munster and Connaught, or Celtic Ireland, is to "efface and expunge" one's friend. And finally, though it is with England's contribution to Ireland's misery that Arnold in his *Irish Essays* is chiefly concerned, he also grants that the native Irish are undoubtedly guilty of insubordination, idleness, and improvidence. In support of the accusation, he quotes again the remark of "their French kinsman," Henri Martin, that the Celts are "Always ready to react against the despotism of fact."[117]

Like most of his English contemporaries, Arnold was alarmed at France's frequent governmental upheavals in the nineteenth century. Forgetting, again like his contemporaries, England's own stormy political readjustments in the seventeenth century, he was inclined to ascribe these upheavals to French political incapacity. The French, he writes to his friend Fontanès, do not take their politics seriously enough, but prefer to make a game of it. The intrigues and agitations are what appeal to them. "This is the price you pay for the entire breach of continuity in your history made by the Revolution."[118] What this break in continuity amounted to has been shown several times in the preceding pages. It meant the dying out of the German in the modern Frenchman, the sweeping away of the Germanic construction of Old France, and the emergence of the Celt. And Arnold doubts whether "the Celt, by himself," is "constructive enough to rebuild."[119]

In closing his review of the characteristics of the Celts, Arnold compliments the race again on its sensibility. Unfortunately, the Celts have sacrificed everything else to this dominant trait, but in itself it is a "beautiful and admirable force." If it has been their weakness, it has also been their strength. Out of it, perhaps, grew chivalry and the romantic glorification of woman. For some years, Arnold had been interested in the origin of these ideals. In 1859, he had written to his sister, "Renan pushes the glorification of the Celts too far; but there is a great deal of truth in what he says, and being on the same ground in my next lecture, in which I have to examine the origin of what is called the 'romantic' sentiment about women, which the Germans quite falsely are fond of giving themselves the credit of originating, I read him with the more interest."[120] In 1867, he returns to the problem. He will not say without reservation that chivalry and romance and the glorification of woman have their origin among the Celts. But there is, he thinks, "a Celtic air" about many of the aspects of chivalry: its extravagances, its reaction against the despotism of fact, its straining human nature beyond endurance. For chivalry the Celts have an affinity, perhaps because there is a feminine element in the Celtic nature.[121] To this caution he is perhaps prompted by Renan's remark that chivalry is too complex a phenomenon to allow of a single origin. Nonetheless, Renan is convinced that in the chivalrous idealization of woman and love there is nothing of the ancient spirit, or indeed of the Teutonic. Neither the *Edda* nor the *Niebelungen* exalt pure love and devotion, which are the basis of chivalry. Rather, one must turn to the "essentially feminine race," the Celts. No other human family, he believes, has treated the ideal of woman with so much delicacy or brought so much mystery into its conception of love.[122] Henri Martin abandons even Renan's preliminary reservation: chivalry to Martin is without doubt a Celtic, and in no way a Teutonic creation. "La philosophie de l'histoire est aujourd'hui en mesure de restituer . . . au génie celtique, en général, une part plus grande encore peut-être dans le développement moral du moyen âge et de l'ère moderne. Il n'est plus possible, par exemple, de douter que l'idéal de la chivalerie ne soit tout celtique et nullement germanique dans ses origines."[123]

With Arnold's opinion that the Germans were not justified in crediting themselves with the origin of "the 'romantic' sentiment about women" Charles Kingsley would not have agreed. One of Kingsley's fondest beliefs is that "chivalrous woman-worship" is an "old Saxon" trait, "which our Gothic forefathers brought with them into the West, which shed a softening and ennobling light around the mediaeval convent life, and warded off for centuries the worst effects of monasticism."[124] Nothing, he believes, has had a nobler effect upon the human race than "the chivalrous idea of wedlock which our Teutonic race holds and which the Romance or Popish races of Europe have never to this day grasped with any firm hold."[125] And the issue is not yet settled. Boutmy, a Frenchman, considers the chivalrous attitude toward women a peculiarly French institution, chivalry having proved abortive in England where it appeared for a moment only.[126] Dibelius, a German, thinks that chivalry, whatever its origin may be, is preserved today among the English, as among no other people, in the concept of the gentleman. Nowhere, he says, does woman enjoy so much respect as in the two Anglo-Saxon lands, England and the United States.[127] In a course of public lectures in the Department of History at King's College, London, in 1925, F. S. Shears considers chivalry essentially a French institution, some of its chief features being deeply rooted in the ancient Gallic character, as the comments on the Celts by the Greek geographer Strabo attest. In the same course of lectures, H. G. Atkins grants that chivalry had its rise in France, but in that part called *Frankenreich*, Francia, peopled by the *Nordmannen*, the Normans, a Germanic race. Chivalry, then, is born from the contact of a Germanic race with Latin civilization.[128] It is, as Arnold discreetly says, "a great question."

Such, then, are the characteristics of the Celt, as Arnold sees them, largely through the spectacles of his French guides. Subsequent investigations in anthropology and ethnology have shown that some of these traits—ostentation, love of bright colors, even the love of poetry—cannot be regarded as peculiarly Celtic, since they are common to all primitive peoples.[129] The principal modern objection to the racial differentiations of Arnold and of the nineteenth-century historians, however, is that they are based almost wholly upon historical evidences and no judgments so based can be final.[130] The total effect of Arnold's portrait is not one of which the sitter can be excessively proud. It is true that he does not "make blame the chief part of what he writes, for the Celts, like other people, are to be meliorated rather by developing their gifts than by chastising their defects."[131] And even for the defects of the race he had as authority the two greatest friends of the Celts, Renan and Martin. Furthermore, the gifts he allows the Celts he praises most generously, so generously, in fact, that many of the Oxford audience before which the lectures were given probably agreed with the *Times* that the claims were extravagant. By balancing the gifts with the defects he established his position as neither a Celt-lover nor a Celt-hater, as a disinterested critic who desired only that simple justice be rendered. Through such moderation and sweet reasonableness he hoped to achieve one of the objects of the lectures: the establishment of a Celtic chair. Yet the gifts which he ascribes to the Celts, even their detractors—Froude and Mommsen, for example—allow. In the last analysis, the qualities, as Lord Lytton says in speaking of the Irish, are those "that win affection but never esteem." Of this fact G. B. Shaw is aware, and he insists that the English have deliberately encouraged these qualities in the Irishman in order to render him harmless in the field of practical affairs. In Arnold's account, the Celt is unquestionably the weaker vessel. *On the Study of Celtic Literature* was written partly for the purpose of throwing into strong outline the vulgarity, coarseness, and unintelligence of the Saxon Philistine, and this purpose was accomplished by praise of the opposite traits in the Celt. With the Celt Arnold associates "ovates and bards, and triads, and englyns," with the Saxon Philistine he associates "the sewage question, and the glories of our local self-government, and the mysterious perfections of the Metropolitan Board of Works." His final comment on the Celt is in effect the same as that sent in 1864 to Lady Rothschild, "I have a great *penchant* for the Celtic races, with their melancholy and unprogressiveness."[132]

II

Having thus established the fundamental traits of the Celt, Arnold is ready for his final task: the tracing of the Celtic strain in the Englishman and his literature. Whether or not it is possible to find the mind's, and the race's, construction in the face—the physiological test, or in such externals as habits and manners, Arnold is fairly certain that such construction can be traced in the poetry of a people. Three outstanding qualities of English poetry he would derive from a Celtic source; its turn for style, its melancholy, its natural magic—the first "with some doubt," the second "with less doubt," the third "with no doubt at all."

That the older Celtic literature does display a marked turn for style has been generally granted, but it has been pointed out that Arnold fails to take into account his earlier recognition of the defect of the style: its tendency to run off "into technic" of the most elaborate kind.[133] In commending the style, he cites but three examples, and each of these is dependent on the formal device of the triad for its effect. Since such complicated devices and elaborate machinery are not characteristic of English literature, Arnold's attempt to derive English style from a Celtic source would seem to stand discredited.[134]

No doubt at all has been expressed concerning the presence of "natural magic" in Celtic literature. Indeed, at the end of the nineteenth century, one of the main purposes of the Celtic Renaissance is the continuation of the "magical" tradition. Yet Yeats and "A. E." (George William Russell), prime movers in the Renaissance, take exception to Arnold's racial explanation. Yeats considers "natural magic" in literature to be the result of the primitive worship of nature in which all beautiful places were regarded as haunted, when the peoples of the world lived "nearer to ancient chaos, every man's desires, and had immortal models about them."[135] "A. E." finds this miraculous and imaginative quality to be dominant among modern Irishmen, not, however, because they are Celts, but because Ireland has never been subject to Latin domination and as a result has preserved to modern times "a primitive culture of the imagination."[136] Almost all commentators have praised Arnold for calling attention to the "natural magic" in Celtic poetry; in particular, they have praised him for the exquisite examples he cites in proof of its presence. But in his dealings with this same quality in English literature, he is found to be too subtle. Many readers fail to follow him, for example, in his delicate distinction between "Greek radiance" and "Celtic magic" in Keats and Shakespeare. And even if both these notes are present in English literature, why, it has been asked, should "Celtic magic" be attributed to racial influence, whereas "Greek radiance" is attributed to cultural tradition. If cultural tradition suffices to explain the one, it should suffice to explain the other.[137]

Provocative of discussion, favorable, and unfavorable, as these two qualities—the feeling for style and the feeling for "natural magic"—have been, they have aroused no heated controversy like that which has centered about "the chord of penetrating passion and melancholy." This controversy deserves an extended treatment.[138] In picturing the Celts as the most melancholy of the modern races, Arnold is continuing a tradition that was old when he took it up, a tradition which, though it has repeatedly been shown to be false to the facts, persists to the present day. James Macpherson in *The Poems of Ossian* first foisted this belief upon the world, and Arnold leans heavily upon Macpherson, as does Renan. Driven by their oppressors into the western fringes of Europe: to the bleak promontories of Brittany, to the mist-shrouded mountains of Scotland and Wales, and across the sea to Ireland, the Celts—so runs the common conception—took on the sad coloring of their surroundings. They were a beaten race, worn out with the struggle of a thousand years. For the sword which they were no longer able to wield, they substituted the harp. They were a dying race, but like the swan, they would sing a beautiful lament before they expired. Among the rocks they sat them down and wept when they remembered Innisfail. Such, in a general way, is the account as Renan gives it. His essay is an attempt to catch and describe "the divine notes" of the Celtic music before the race shall have passed away.

In like manner, Michelet closes the first book of his *History of France* with a lyric tribute to the vanishing race, "dying of sadness" on its native heath, in the solitude of its islands. Being a part of France, Brittany, of course, is more fortunate than Ireland, Wales, and Scotland. Yet the Breton language abounds in melancholy sayings. Cornwall—the Peru of England—is valued only for its mines. Its language is dead. To weep Irish has become an English proverb. In the Scottish Highlands, want and emigration have reduced the Celtic race so that the tartan and claymore are now a rarity. If the bagpipe still sounds in the deserted mountains, it is with but one plaintive strain—

> "Cha till, cha till, cha till, sin tuile."
> We return, we return, we return, no more.

Small wonder that the Celtic race is sad, since all has gone aginst it. And France, too, mourns, as she stands powerless to protect Ireland, her sister, in her sufferings; as she remembers her long neglect of her ancient allies, the Scotchmen.

This sense of racial failure and the melancholy that arises from it are best expressed in the quotation from Macpherson's *Ossian* which Arnold uses as epigraph to his book, *On the Study of Celtic Literature*: "They went forth to the war, but they always fell." The appropriateness of this quotation as an expression of the Celtic spirit has been questioned, however, by authorities on Celtic literature. J. S. Smart finds no trace of sadness in the *Mabinogion*, Arnold's other Celtic source book, and regards the emphasis on melancholy as a modern importation by Macpherson who shared the discouragement of the Scottish clansmen over the break-up of their oganization after the suppression of the rebellion of 1745.[139] According to Alfred Nutt, a similar feeling, the result of similar causes, is evident in the Irish Jacobite poetry of the late seventeenth and early eighteenth centuries. In medieval Ossianic literature, however, aside from "a note of regret for the glory of past days," he discovers no sense of failure. "The real Ossian," he says, "does not talk about falling, but about knocking the other fellow down." However admirable Macpherson's mournful reflections may be as an expression of the prevailing eighteenth century sentiment, they emphatically are not representative of the bulk of Celtic literature.[140] An even more violent objection to Arnold's quotation is raised by E. D. Snyder, who regards it as a complete misrepresentation of the genuine Celtic spirit which is characterized rather by vivacity and even humor.[141] But such scholarly warnings have had little effect. Arnold's epigraph came to be almost an epitaph on the Celts, for few indeed are the later writers on Celtic matters who do not repeat the passage. A poem by Shaemus O'Sheel represents the general view:

THEY WENT FORTH TO BATTLE, BUT THEY ALWAYS FELL

They went forth to battle, but they always fell;
  Their eyes were fixed above the sullen shields;
Nobly they fought and bravely, but not well,
And sank heart-wounded by a subtle spell.
  They knew not fear that to the foeman yields,
  They were not weak, as one who vainly wields
A futile weapon; yet the sad scrolls tell
How on the hard-fought field they always fell.

It was a secret music that they heard,
  A sad sweet plea for pity and for peace;
And that which pierced the heart was but a word,
Though the white breast was red-lipped where the sword
  Pressed a fierce cruel kiss, to put surcease
  On its hot thirst, but drank a hot increase.
Ah, they by some strange troubling doubt were stirred,
And died for hearing what no foeman heard.

They went forth to battle, but they always fell;
  Their might was not the might of lifted spears;
Over the battle-clamor came a spell
Of troubling music, and they fought not well.
  Their wreaths are willows and their tribute, tears;
  Their names are old sad stories in men's ears;
Yet they will scatter the red hordes of Hell,
Who went to battle forth and always fell.[142]

It is certain that Arnold's remarks on the nature of the Celt and his literature helped to introduce the wave of Neo-Ossianism at the close of the century. Yeats confessed that he was guided by Arnold and Renan, and more by Arnold than by Renan, to the Celtic Twilight in which he and others wandered for a decade and more. In his early works, Yeats preferred to place his settings somewhere East of the sun and West of the moon. In this dim region old Ængus wanders through the hazelwood remembering forgotten beauty. Other wraith-like figures sit by the shadowy waters thinking how Usna's children died, or about the old age of Queen Maeve or of lovely Deirdre of the sorrows. The curlews cry in the air, and all the while,

> The wind blows out of the gates of the day,
> The wind blows over the lonely of heart,
> And the lonely of heart are withered away.

In this word, dreams are substituted for reality. The interest lies in the picture, the emotion, the association, the mythology.[14] Yeats' early verse, then, would seem to be a striking illustration of that "passionate, turbulent reaction against the despotism of fact," which, according to Arnold, is the dominant trait in the Celt. At any rate, it was accepted as such by contemporary critics.[144] And Yeats himself agreed. In "The Celtic Element in Literature," written in 1897, he considered Arnold's theories at great length, particularly the idea of melancholy. Knowing something evidently of the late nineteenth century scholarly investigations in folk song and folk belief, he could not accept Arnold's racial explanation of Celtic melancholy, yet he agreed that it was characteristic of the Celts. His own explanation, he thought, was more reasonable and natural. All ancient peoples, he says, react against the despotism of fact, and from this reaction comes their delight in tales of death and separation, in contrast to the preference of modern peoples, who at the close of the tale insist on marriage bells. Among the Celts this primitive preference is still to be found, for to a degree observable in no other modern people they have kept themselves open to the stream of ancient European beliefs and passions. And that, he says, is why Irish poetry and much of Irish thought is melancholy.[145]

By 1897 the Celtic Renaissance had achieved general recognition and it was possible to bring under review the effusions of such neo-Celts as Grant Allen, George Moore, Fiona Macleod, Nora Hooper, and Mrs. Robertson Matheson. This Andrew Lang proceeded to do in a devastating article on the Celtic Renaissance in the February number of *Blackwood's Magazine*. The windiness, the wailing, and the mistiness of these Ossianized neo-Celts he takes to task. Such qualities, he maintains, are not truly Celtic. The form, the aims, and the ideas of the movement he traces directly to two men—Renan, "the Moses of the proceedings," and Arnold, "the eloquent Aaron," and Arnold is credited with the major influence. Lang finds Arnold's arguments unscientific, though they do possess "a pseudo-scientific ethnological air." They are, in fact, popular science. Arnold's Celtic theory "if not demonstrably untrue, is, at least, unproved and superfluous." The features of Celtic poetry—natural magic and the tone of defeated melancholy—which Arnold traces in English literature, are present, Lang maintains, in a form equally charming, in the epic *Kalewala* of the Finns. Since English literature and ancient Finnish literature share these qualities, why should one not infer, by Arnold's line of reasoning, that there is a Finnish component in the English blood and therefore in English literature.[146]

In spite of Lang's raillery, Dora M. Jones three years later, in 1900, could continue the Celtic theme with variations. Taking the Blue Flower of Novalis as her symbol, she applies it to the Saxon and Celtic races. Many men are bewitched by the fragrance of the Blue Flower. Their undefined desire they imagine is caused by the want of something tangible for which they are striving—"a wife or a fortune, the success of a scheme, the triumph of a cause." Such are the men of the Saxon race. But the Celts are wiser. They realize that their longing because of its very nature must remain impossible of fulfillment. Yet the unsatisfied desire is the best part of their lives. Theirs is "a wistful yet exquisite renunciation of the tangible for the intangible, the reality for the dream." This racial quality accounts for "the Celtic sadness, the Celtic longing for infinite things." The argument, as one can see at a glance, is a restatement of Arnold's thesis that "the turbulent and titanic" melancholy of the Celts is something decidedly different from the *Sehnsucht* of the Germans. The sadness of the German Werther, according to Arnold, has a definite motivation—his failure to win Lotte. Faust's discontent can also be assigned to a definite cause. But in the Celtic melancholy there is something unaccountable and defiant.[147] In like fashion, Fiona Macleod contends that the Celts have grown in spiritual outlook as the world of tangible things has slipped from their grasp, while the Teutons have lost on the spiritual side what they have gained on the moral and practical.[148]

If Renan may be considered the Moses, and Arnold

the Aaron, then Fiona Macleod, as Andrew Lang suggests, is the Miriam of the Celtic Renaissance. Like Yeats, William Sharp (i.e. Fiona Macleod) gives full credit to Arnold as a precursor of the movement. Macpherson was, of course, the primary source, but, says Fiona Macleod, his influence had waned. "Renan's essay in France and Germany, and Arnold's in this country and America, were the torches which have lit so many Celtic brands, or let us say, were the two winds which fanned the Celtic flame which is now one of the most potent influences in contemporary literature."[149] His own interpretation of the Celtic genius is derived, he says, from Renan and Arnold.[150] It is not surprising, therefore, that melancholy is a dominant mood in his works on Celtic themes. In some of these works, in fact, the Celtic Twilight deepens into darkest night.

Ovid himself records no stranger metamorphosis than that by which the burly, six-foot William Sharp, a masculine enough biographer and critic, became in his last years the delicate Fiona Macleod palpitating with feminine emotion as she surveyed the dwindling world of the Celts. From 1894 to 1905 under the pseudonym Fiona Macleod a flood of stories, plays and poems appeared, which after Sharp's death were brought together in a uniform, seven-volume edition by his wife. The prose is filled with dying falls, appropriately enough since all but a few of the tales end in death or madness. The Celts are "a doomed and passing race." They have at last reached their horizon. "There is no shore beyond" and they know it.[151] It is "Destiny, that sombre Demogorgon of the Gael, whose boding breath, whose menace, whose shadow glooms" their life upon the remote islands which they inhabit.[152] Theirs is no common grief, "it is, rather, the knowledge of the lamentations of a race, the unknowing surety of an inheritance of woe."[153] They are oppressed as no other people are oppressed "by the gloom of a strife between spiritual emotion and material facts."[154] They are filled with "vain, limitless desires."[155] And they are always remembering. Through memory they are nearer than are other peoples to "the haunted ancient shores and woods." And from this nearness "they gain spiritual exaltation, emotional intensity, troubled longing, and exquisite sadness."[156] Such being Fiona Macleod's views on the race, her seven volumes are naturally pitched in a melancholy, minor, and miserable key. By many, of course, these strains were appreciated. The *All Ireland Review*, for example, conjectured that Fiona Macleod was "a beautiful and spiritual Highland maiden, whose voice is heard from time to time

> Breaking the silence of the seas
> Among the far-off Hebrides."[157]

But even as early as 1896, *Blackwood's Magazine* had had a surfeit of her fatalism and advised the feminine Jacques to pay less attention to the theories of the pedants and ethnologists on the nature of the Celts, to cease brooding over the hopeless destiny of her people, and to prune her luxurious indulgence in melancholy.[158]

From another quarter Arnold's hypothesis received strong support. Among the Neo-Celtic writers no name carried greater weight than that of Dr. Douglas Hyde. His famous analysis of the Celtic nature in the Introduction to his *Love Songs of Connacht* (1893) did much to determine the tone of the entire Renaissance:

> Not careless and light-hearted alone is the Gaelic nature; there is also beneath the loudest mirth a melancholy spirit. The same

> man who will today be dancing, sporting, drinking, and shouting, will be soliloquising by himself tomorrow, heavy and sick and said in his lonely little hut, making a croon over departed hopes, lost life, the vanity of this world, and the coming of death.

After twenty years, however, some of these writers became weary of the attenuated dream. The twilight atmosphere had begun to pall. Yeats, as is well known, abandoned the softness of his early manner, deliberately cultivated a sharper thought and a harder diction. He even became a senator and "ranted to the knave and fool" on matters substantial enough. "A. E." also recanted. In an apostrophe to the Spirit of Beauty in the introduction to *Collected Poems* (1913), he begs forgiveness for the dark and thorny ways he has taken in his service; wonders whether he has not indulged too much in tears and sorrow. In the field of aesthetics, then, he believes that the value of excessive mournfulness and pessimism may be questioned. In the field of politics and economics, however, there is no doubt at all—the effect has been disastrous. "Ireland," he says (1912), "is a horribly melancholy and cynical country. Our literary men and poets, who ought to give us courage, have taken to writing about the Irish as people who 'went forth to battle, but always fell,' sentimentalizing over incompetence instead of invigorating us and liberating us and directing our energies."[159] As a result, the Gods and half-Gods, the hero and the saint have departed and Ireland has sunk to a petty peasant state. Life in the cities, as well as in the rural areas, is drab and mean.[160] Even Yeats had admitted that Ireland was "a nation of brilliant failures."[161] Although in earlier years "A. E." had written a great deal about Ireland as an enchanted world in which poets lay about upon the hillsides dreaming of gentle, stately figures which moved over the radiant grasses, a world which almost seemed to be "the shadow of the thought of God,"[162] he later, in 1912, rejected the conception. The Irish, he thought, had lingered too long in Druid land. A spell had been cast upon them and it was Yeats who had woven the spell. Yeats could be forgiven since at its best his poetry was the most beautiful that Ireland had produced. But in the works of a horde of followers his pastel shades had been made dimmer and paler, and the atmosphere of the Celtic fairyland had grown more and more tenuous, until one gasped for fresh air and a little sunlight.[163] Significantly, L. H. Daiken, an anthologist and a revolutionist, called his collection of Irish verse, *Goodbye, Twilight.*

G. B. Shaw, of course, never succumbed to the Celtic sadness. Yeats, Synge, and the rest, he believes, pondered too much on themselves. The themes and problems on which they sang sad songs would have resolved themselves into comedy, he says, if they had been pursued to their logical conclusions. As for himself, the clarity of his thinking made it impossible for him to become an Irish poet. He was not content to dream his life away on the Irish hills. England having conquered Ireland, no course of action remained for him except to go over and conquer England.[164] Shaw would probably agree with G. K. Chesterton's comment on the Celtic madness and sadness:

> For the great Gaels of Ireland
> Are the men that God made mad;
> For all their wars are merry
> And all their songs are sad.

In spite of its repudiation by some of the most distinguished of the "Celts" themselves, the tradition is still alive today. In many quarters, the Celts are still regarded as children of the mist. The learned German historian Wilhelm Dibelius in 1922 speaks of the Irish as visionary dreamers alternating between swift, passionate excitement on the one hand and weariness and disillusionment on the other. Ernest Barker, the English commentator, still speaks in 1927 of the "sad historic tradition," the "defeated stocks," and the melancholy landscapes of the Celts. And D. H. Lawrence in 1932, disenchanted with civilization and searching for the primitive in the far corners of the earth, has an approving word for the Irish, for "in the Celtic soul," he says, "lingers the memory of Atlantis."[165] In their theorizing on the nature of the Celtic genius, Renan and Arnold evidently struck a strain which the world cannot willingly let die.

If, as the authorities insist, the note of "passionate, penetrating" melancholy is not found in the older, authentic Celtic literature, then Arnold's subsequent labors in tracing this Celtic element in English authors are vain. Almost without exception, editors and commentators today reject this part of Arnold's thesis. But in the nineteenth century his method proved enormously attractive. Some anthropologists and ethnologists became so skilfull in analyzing the granules of the blood and in discriminating between the Celtic and Saxon strands in individual English authors, that they competed with Hudibras, who

> could distinguish and divide,
> A hair 'twixt South and South-west side.

Berkeley and Hume were claimed as Celtic metaphysicians.[166] From a study of Shakespeare's bust, J. W. Jackson, the ethnologist, decided that Shakespeare was the perfect blend of Celt and Saxon, having the Celtic fibre without its worn and wasted quality, and the Teutonic muscle without its ponderosity; the Celtic intelligence without its excitability and the Teutonic self-possession without its phlegmatic element.[167] By another ethnologist, Macaulay's shrewdness, calmness, and keen practical sense were derived from his Saxon ancestry; his eloquence, his rhetorical aptitude, and his poetic cast of mind were attributed to his Celtic blood.[168] Carlyle was inordinately proud of his Lowland Scotch, Teutonic, origin, and despised the Gaelic types of the Highlands. He would have been furious had he lived to see himself thus described by a later ethnologist: "Carlyle came of the M'Kerlies, a clan of the southwest, probably Kymric or Brythonic, and his genius, as well as his physiognomy, has traits of the first type, not to speak of the second."[169] Between them, George Moore and Fiona Macleod managed to enroll most of the major English authors under the Celtic banner. In *Lyra Celtica* and later works, Fiona Macleod claimed as Celtic, or part Celtic, Shakespeare, Milton, Keats, Byron, Burns, Scott, and Stevenson. To such extravagant lengths were these claims carried that one wonders with Andrew Lang why no Celtic genius was discovered in the House of Hanover. All competent judges agree, of course, with Arnold that English literature is distinguished for its melancholy. In England, the mists sweep in of a morning from the sea, and the poets at once repair to the cemeteries for composition; or so, at least, it seems if one may judge by the number and excellence of the threnodies, elegies, and miscellaneous plaints from the Old English *The Wanderer* to Thomas Hardy's *Winter Words*. Arnold himself, it has been remarked, is at his most eloquent when standing by a grave. To what influence are these hearse-like airs to be attributed? To the climate, to Celtic genius, to Saxon blood, or to general historical conditions? Each of these has had its ardent advocates, none of whom is wholly convincing. Or, is it possible that the elegiac strain in English literature is due to a combination of all these factors? If so, the exact proportion of the elements has thus far proved to be past all finding out.

Chapter VI

The Semitic *vs.* the Indo-European Genius

Early in the nineteenth century, the English historian John Pinkerton whimsically advocated the establishment of professorships of Celtic "to teach us to laugh at the Celts."[1] Such a proposal was still possible when the Celts were regarded as being separated from the English by an impassable gulf, or as being more alien than the Chinese. But the scientific study of the main Celtic languages by philologists like J. C. Zeuss, Francis Bopp, and Whitley Stokes effected a change in attitude so that the Celts were admitted "into the fullest and most equal right of brotherhood in the great Aryan confraternity of speech."[2] With the results of these inquiries Arnold was delighted, for they brought "Ireland into the Indo-European concert," and gave "a wholesome buffet" to those who considered the Celts aliens in speech and blood. They provided substantial proof of the unifying power of science, its tendency toward conciliation and fusion. To the evidences of a growing feeling of Indo-Europeanism he therefore devoted considerable space in the opening sections of his study of Celtic literature.

What the Celts thus gained, however, the Semites lost, for the new sciences of philology and anthropology denied the Semitic peoples a place in the charmed circle of Indo-European brotherhood. Of this fact Arnold took note. "The modern spirit," he said, "tends more and more to establish a sense of native diversity between our European bent and the Semitic bent, and to eliminate, even in our religion, certain elements as purely and excessively Semitic, and therefore, in right, not combinable with our European nature, not assimilable by it."[3] Since the distinction between the Indo-European genius and the Semitic genius plays a significant rôle in four of Arnold's major works—*On the Study of Celtic Literature*, *Culture and Anarchy*, *Literature and Dogma*, and *God and the Bible*—a brief account of the origin and development of "the modern spirit" is desirable.

The "modern spirit" had its origin, as Arnold was well aware, in the Renaissance when in the contest between Hebraism and Hellenism, Pope Leo X could openly profess a greater admiration for Plato than for Christ, and Machiavelli contrasted the pagan and Christian virtues to the disadvantage of the latter. In the same tradition several centuries later, Goethe, professing an abhorrence of representations of the anaemic and wounded Christ, said his morning prayers before a bright image of Zeus on the wall above his bed. Obviously, the pale Galilean had not conquered everywhere, and Arnold's contemporary, Swinburne, could have cited precedents for preferring the worship of the imperial Aphrodite to that of Mary with her sorrows.

Among modern spirits, one to whom Arnold listened with much respect was Wilhelm von Humboldt. Arnold spoke of him as "one of the most unwearied and successful strivers after human perfection that have ever lived,"[4] and gladly acknowledged his indebtedness to this "genuine Teuton" for some of his own ideas on government and education. What such a man had to say on religion commanded general attention and Arnold was therefore justified in citing him as an illustration of the trend of modern thought. Von Humboldt found little religious sustenance in alien Semitic works, turning by preference to Greece and India, "the Teuton's born kinsfolk of the common Indo-European family." Toward the "absorbing, tyrannous, terrorist religion" of the Semites he had a natural antipathy.[5]

In a letter to his mother, Arnold cited three other instances of the modern trend: "I have been reading this year in connection with the New Testament a good deal of Aristotle and Plato, and this has brought papa very much to my mind again. Bunsen used to say that our great business was to get rid of all that was purely Semitic in Christianity, and to make it Indo-Germanic, and Schleiermacher that in the Christianity of us Western nations there was really much more of Plato and Socrates than of Joshua and David; and, on the whole, papa worked in the direction of these ideas of Bunsen and Schleiermacher, and was perhaps the only powerful Englishman of his day who did so."[6]

As the translator and life-long disciple of Plato, as the spiritual ancestor of the psychological analysis of religion and the anthropological study of the religion of primitive peoples, and as an eminent pioneer in the rejection of the orthodox belief in a personal God and the traditional Christian faith in individual immortality, Schleiermacher helped to prepare the way for the later nineteenth century antipathy toward the Semitic elements in Christianity.[7]

The versatile Baron Christian Bunsen, historian, theologian, and diplomatist, exercised a great influence on the

Continent as well as in England, where he served as German ambassador from 1841 to 1854. In his last work, *God in History*, he attempted to trace the consciousness of divinity as it manifested itself on the one hand among the Hebrews, and on the other among the Aryans. "If the Hebrew Semites are the priests of Humanity," he said, "the Helleno-Roman Aryans are, and will ever be, its heroes," for with them the religious consciousness is evidenced in the conduct of public affairs, and in art and poetry as well as in historical and philosophical compositions.[8] The chief purpose of all his scholarly labors, according to his friend Dean A. P. Stanley, was to mark the points in human history where "the Semitic and the Japhetic (i.e., European) elements crossed each other."[9]

Like Schleiermacher, Dr. Thomas Arnold believed that the student of the Scriptures should bring to his task some acquaintance with philological and antiquarian works, as well as a knowledge of the chief philosophers and poets.[10] As Bunsen held that the deepest significance of the Bible was to be sought outside "the Jewish horizon where its scenes are laid,"[11] so Thomas Arnold maintained that Christians were not required to obey those commandments, for example, the observance of the Sabbath, which were addressed to the Jews alone.[12] Through the Jewish people, he believed, mankind had derived all its religious knowledge; through the Greeks, all its intellectual civilization—a view which anticipated in some measure Matthew Arnold's fundamental distinction between the contributions of the Semitic and the Indo-European races.[13]

It was the German philosopher Feuerbach, however, who carried the movement to its climax and earned himself a name as the anti-Christ of the nineteenth century.

In *The Essence of Christianity*, he tried to prove that only the name and some general positions of Christianity were retained in the modern world. Originally, the opposite of heathenism, Christianity, he believed, had so incorporated within itself the culture of the pagans that the result was theological incomprehensibility. He discovered contradictions in the doctrines on the nature and the revelation of God, on the Trinity, contradictions in the Sacraments, in the treatment of love and faith, irreconcilable elements in all the fundamental beliefs of Christianity.[14]

On a more strictly racial basis, Count Joseph Arthur de Gobineau, "favourably known," according to Arnold, "by his studies in ethnology,"[15] also made a distinction between the Aryans and the Semites. In his famous four-volume *Essai sur l'inégalité des races humaines* (1853–1855), he divided mankind into three main races: the white which surpassed the other two in almost all physical, mental, and moral qualities and alone had created any great civilization; the yellow which was unenergetic, practical, materialistic, and tended to mediocrity in everything; and, lowest in the scale, the black which was gifted with little intellect though it did display artistic powers. In the dominant white race, the Aryan group was supreme, but even it had suffered from degeneration through crossing with lower racial groups, notably with the Semites, who were a blend of white and negro stocks. The entire Mediterranean basin—France, Spain, Italy, Portugal—according to Gobineau, had been contaminated by intermixture with the Semites. By comparison, the Aryans of northern Europe were relatively pure, and their civilization, as a result, was superior to that of the decadent southern nations.[16]

In Ernest Renan all these elements—racial, religious, philological, and philosophical—were brought together to explain a theory basic to much of his work, the contrast between the geniuses of the Semitic and the Indo-European races. And, except for Dr. Thomas Arnold, no contemporary writer, perhaps, exercised more influence on Matthew Arnold's thinking. The affinity between Ernest Renan and Matthew Arnold is evident at a glance. Saintsbury remarked that Arnold's style, already somewhat lacking in vigor, was too much modelled on that of Renan, in which the dominant element was sweetness. But the resemblance extends beyond mere matters of style. It is evident in their deepest interests, in the opinions they held, in the very aims they pursued. The labors of the two men in the Celtic cause and in behalf of Celtic literature have already been commented upon. In the subjects to which they devoted complete essays or entire books their common interests were revealed: Spinoza, the Saint of Amsterdam, and Marcus Aurelius, whose *Meditations* served for both as a manual of the life of resignation. Arnold's *Saint Paul and Protestantism* followed hard upon the heels of Renan's *Saint Paul*. The former's *A Persian Passion Play* and the latter's *The Zeaziehs of Persia* were alike inspired by Gobineau's *The Religions and Philosophies of Central Asia* (Paris, 1865). Arnold spent ten years and Renan thirty years of his life in comment on the Bible, both believing that one of the solidest evidences of the worth of the book lay in its having survived its commentators.[17] In his works on religion Arnold's aim was essentially that which Renan claimed as his own: "La conciliation d'un esprit hautement religieux avec l'esprit critique." To this list of similarities a great deal could be added, for a kinship of spirit is apparent also in social, political and literary fields. In fact, a full discussion of Arnold's relationship to Renan could be developed into an interesting and significant essay. Such an essay, however, is aside from the purpose of the present chapter. From the correspondence, the note-books, and the published works in which the references to Renan are so frequent, it is evident that Arnold followed the distinguished Frenchman's career with great interest and read most of his essays and books. Not that he invariably agreed with him. Often he felt called upon to modify Renan's pronouncements. But even when he disagreed with his opinions, he found them brilliant, original, ingenious, and eloquently expressed. Such being Arnold's familiarity with Renan's labors, it is not surprising that he carried over into his own works Renan's underlying and often repeated contrast between the Semitic and the Indo-European races.

In an early essay, *The History of the People of Israel*, Renan gave explicit expression to the contrast. The results of modern philology, he believed, had shown a double current in the course of civilization, the product of two races wholly different in language, manners, and spirit—the Indo-European race, comprising the peoples of India, Persia, the Caucasus, and of all Europe; and the Semitic race, embracing the population of Asia, west and south as far as the Euphrates. To the Indo-European race were to be attributed all the great intellectual, political, and military movements; to the Semitic race, all the great religious movements. It was the peculiar distinction of the Semitic race that in an era in which other peoples were given up to idolatry and the pursuit of false Gods, they established monotheism, the purest religious form that humanity has ever known. This they did not by reflection or reasoning but by "primitive intuition" and from their earliest time. They had "an intuition for God."[18] Their mission was the religious and moral reform of human kind. The glory of the Hebrew genius resided in its elevated morality, in the battle centuries long which the Jewish conscience waged against the iniquities of the world.[19] Sublime devotion to monotheism and morality! Yet purchased at a price. For to the religious and ethical ideal all temporal success was sacrificed. Outside the field of religion, in which they were without parallel, the Jews barely achieved mediocrity; their qualities were mainly negative. They had neither politics, nor art, nor philosophy, nor science.[20] The very nature of their language made abstraction unknown and metaphysics impossible. From such a race with such a language no Aristotle or Kant could ever arise, though, on the other hand, the Indo-European race had never produced so exalted a disputation, at once so sensitive and so religious, as the *Book of Job*. The Semitic spirit was by its nature anti-philosophic, anti-scientific; the parables, the proverbs were all its wisdom. Rational analysis, the search into the cause of things, was to them vain and even impious. Religion itself was without dogma, without theology, without abstract speculation.[21] For the plastic arts the Jews had no appreciation. They had no architecture of their own. Quite naturally, therefore, Saint Paul was insensitive to the beauties of plastic art in Athens.[22] Furthermore, the Semitic race had been from the beginning inferior to the Indo-European peoples in the power of imagination. They were the authors of no beautiful and imaginative myths such as clothed Indo-European polytheism. They were capable only of legends.[23] And finally, the Hebrews shared with the peoples of Asia as a whole an inability to laugh. It was perhaps for this reason that they were religious. The Orient has never understood irony.[24] The crowning anomaly for Renan was the fact that Europe had adopted as the basis of her spiritual life a work least adapted to her spirit, the Bible, product of an alien race and a different soul. Only by a complete misconception of its meaning had Europe been able to accommodate herself to the sacred text. Right reason would have dictated the Vedas as the holy book, for they at least were the work of the racial ancestors of Europe.[25] Fortunately, however, modern Christianity tended to return to the Indo-European heritage, to separate itself more and more from Judaism. Eventually, he felt, it would become the religion of the heart, substituting delicacy and nuance for dogmatism, the relative for the absolute.[26] To anyone acquainted with Arnold's works most of these opinions have a familiar ring.

Before turning to Arnold's own theories, however, we must discuss one more precursor on whom he levied tribute. Émile Burnouf's *La Science des Religions* was published serially in the *Revue des deux mondes*, 1864 to 1869, and appeared in book form in 1872. Arnold probably read the articles as they appeared in his favorite magazine, but he used the book for purposes of reference in *Literature and Dogma*.[27] In Burnouf the aberrations of Gobineau and Renan united to produce an abnormal offspring. Ideas which the two more distinguished Frenchmen sometimes offered as suggestions or held tentatively were stripped of their qualifications by Burnouf and were developed into a system of inexorable law. Gobineau's distinctions among the three races of mankind, the black, the yellow, and the white were retained. On the Semites, however, Burnouf had new scientific information to offer. One illuminating passage in particular Arnold used for quotation:

> Those scholars who have studied anthropology almost all agree in placing the Semites between the Aryans and the yellow peoples: not that their distinctive traits betoken a medium condition between those of our race and those of eastern Asiatics; but notwithstanding their being far superior to the yellow races, they betray with regard to us such disparities as to prevent their being confounded with Indo-Europeans. A real Semite has smooth hair with curly ends, a strongly hooked nose, fleshy, projecting lips, massive extremities, thin calves, and flat feet. And what is more, he belongs to the occipital races; that is to say, those whose hinder part of the head is more developed than the front. His growth is very rapid, and at fifteen or sixteen it is over. At that age the divisions of his skull which contain the organs of intelligence are already joined, and in some cases even perfectly welded together. From that period the growth of the brain is arrested. In the Aryan races this phenomenon, or anything like it, never occurs, at any time of life, certainly not with the people of normal development. The internal organ is permitted to continue its evolution and transformations up till the very last day of life by means of the never-changing flexibility of the skull bones.[28]

By Burnouf religion was equated with metaphysics and for metaphysical speculation the Aryan race alone displayed any capacity. More emphatically than Renan, and on physiological as well as other grounds, he held that the Semitic race possessed no faculty for abstract thought. The best part of Christianity was its metaphysics, yet, as all the world knew, Christianity had its origin among the Jews. The reconciliation of these antinomies was worthy of the ingenuity of a true scientist, and Burnouf arose to the challenge. From Baron Bunsen he had learned of the co-existence of two races among the Jews, one black, the other of a dark color.[29] And Renan had elaborated on the difference between Jerusalem with its atrabilious Judaism, and Galilee, to the north, which produced the gentle Joseph, the Virgin Mary, and the impassioned Magdalen. According to Renan, it was Galilee, not Jerusalem, that overcame the world.[30] The one thing needful to explain this phenomenon was supplied by Burnouf: the Jews of Galilee were really Aryans. They gave to Christianity its metaphysical basis. And Christ, the Indo-European, found his natural enemies in the Semites of Judaea, who killed him.[31]

In the light of all the foregoing German and French speculations, Arnold's works remain to be interpreted. The analysis of the English people and their literature was his favorite subject and on this subject the Semitic-Indo-European contrast provided new information. "Science has now made visible to everybody," Arnold wrote, "the great and pregnant elements of difference which lie in race, and in how signal a manner they make the genius and history of an Indo-European people vary from those of a Semitic people." Hellenism was of Indo-European origin; Hebraism was of Semitic origin. As "a nation of Indo-European stock," the English should have inclined naturally towards Hellenism. Instead, they and their American descendants for two hundred years past had shown a marked affinity to the Hebrews in all matters touching conduct and morality. "Eminently Indo-European by its *humour*, by the power it shows, through this gift, of imaginatively acknowledging the multiform aspects of the problem of life, and of thus getting itself unfixed from its own over-certainty, of smiling at its own over-tenacity, our race has yet (and a great part of its strength lies here), in matters of practical life and moral conduct, a strong share of the assuredness, the tenacity, the intensity of the Hebrews."[32]

The strong resemblance between the spirit of England and the spirit of Judæa had been remarked upon earlier in France. To Renan the grave sincerity of the Protestants suggested a parallel between the English and the ancient Jews. Both races were serious and strong. And the gifts which they brought to the study of religion were essentially the same—"a great uprightness of mind, an admirable simplicity of heart, an exquisite sentiment of morality."[33] Renan's friend Taine was impressed by the fact that the grand, omnipotent Jehovah of the Bible, who in the Middle Ages had been obscured by His court and His family, had endured to the modern age in England. Only a race with the grandeur and the severity of the English could any longer rise to His high level. "More than any race in Europe, they approach, by the simplicity and energy of their conception, the old Hebraic spirit."[34] And later in the century, Boutmy, on the basis of profusion of allegory, profundity of thought, weakness of dialectic, and brusqueness of ejaculation, found the English imagination to be of the same order as the Hebraic. "There is," he said, "a congenital conformity of some sort between the two geniuses."[35]

This conformity, according to Arnold, was so marked that the average middle-class Anglo-Saxon felt himself to be much more the cousin of Ehud than of Ossian, though the latter was his Indo-European kinsman.[36] Aryan though the English were, there was a far greater chance, he thought, of bringing them to a more philosophical conception of religion "through Judaism and its phenomena, than through Hellenism and its phenomena."[37] For this curious and unnatural tendency Arnold had an explanation. Protestantism in England had taken on all the aspects of Hebraism. It was not that he followed Heinrich Heine in loving Hebraism less and Hellenism more.[38] For both forces he had a profound admiration. Each aspired after the infinite, "the true goal of poetry and all art,"—the one through beauty, the other through sublimity. The aim of each discipline was man's perfection—the one through an intelligent comprehension of one's duty, the other through the obedient practice of it. And if the world were what it ought to be, the two great spiritual disciplines would be in happy balance. Unfortunately, the world had always oscillated between the two, one force now dominating, then the other. The prevailing movement of the western world ever since the Renaissance, Arnold thought, had been toward Hellenism. England, however, had been caught in a side current, Protestantism, the "subordinate and secondary" aspect of the Renaissance.[39] As early as 1857, in his inaugural lecture as Professor of Poetry at Oxford, he had stated his belief that the crying need of the modern age was for an intellectual deliverance, rather than a moral deliverance. And for the satisfaction of this need there was no mightier agent than the literature of ancient Greece.[40] For two hundred years, as he pointed out in *Culture and Anarchy* in the late 'sixties, Englishmen had placed an excessive emphasis on Hebraism, on doing rather than knowing, on walking, to be sure, by the best light they had, but without sufficient care as to whether that light was not darkness. He therefore closed his famous chapter "Hebraism and Hellenism" with an appeal to the Indo-Europeanism of the English people, by reason of which they would "seem to belong naturally to the movement of Hellenism."

The last three chapters of *Culture and Anarchy* were devoted to a consideration of social, political and religious problems which the Hebraising of the English had failed to solve properly. On each of these problems, Arnold thought, a little Hellenizing would have been in order, but for the illumination brought by the free play of the mind upon great issues, the English "at once so resolute and so unintelligent," had never in their history displayed much sympathy. The extreme lengths to which his countrymen were carried by their adherence to "the stiff, stark notions of Hebraism" was illustrated particularly, Arnold thought, in the House of Commons, where a bill was currently being proposed which would enable a man to marry his deceased wife's sister. Such a bill violated Arnold's sense of propriety. The Book of Leviticus, to which the advocates of the bill turned for authority, was, in his opinion, no proper guide for Indo-Europeans with their delicate and sensitive perceptions. "Who, that is not manacled and hoodwinked by his Hebraism, can believe that, as to love and marriage, our reason and the necessities of our humanity have their true, sufficient, and divine law expressed for them by the voice of any Oriental and polygamous nation like the Hebrews? Who, I say, will believe, when he really considers the matter, that where the feminine nature, the feminine ideal, and our relations to them, are brought into question, the delicate and apprehensive genius of the Indo-European race, the race which invented the Muses, and chivalry, and the Madonna, is to find its last word on this question in the institutions of a Semitic people, whose wisest king had seven hundred wives and three hundred concubines?"[41] In advocating such views, Arnold was of the school of Schleiermacher and Bunsen, and finally of Renan who believed that the modern western world was indebted for all its "douceur dans l'ordre des choses de l'âme, charité, amour dans le sentiment tendre et délicat de la femme" to its Indo-European ancestors rather than to Israel.[42] Ironically, the first significant result of Arnold's plea for Indo-Europeanism was a long and laudatory article in the *Quarterly Review* on the Talmud. The author, a savant of the British Museum, credited Arnold with being the John the Baptist who prepared the way for the learned dissertation.[43]

In their literature, also, the English had paid a heavy price for their attempt to make themselves Semitic, for their failure to follow their natural Indo-European bent. Of English hymns, a considerable body of literature, Arnold had a very low opinion. What beauty and venerableness they possessed came from their association with the religious life, in which all things are transfigured. Poetical value they had little or none. The keenness of perception so evident in other departments of their literature seemed to desert the English in the composition of their hymns. "Now certainly it is a higher state of development when our fineness of perception is keen than when it is blunt. And if,—whereas the Semitic genius placed its highest spiritual life in the religious sentiment, and made that the basis of its poetry,—the Indo-European genius places its highest spiritual life in the imaginative reason, and makes that the basis of its poetry, we are none the better for wanting the perception to discern a natural law, which is, after all, like every natural law, irresistible; we are none the better for trying to make ourselves Semitic, when Nature has made us Indo-European, and to shift the basis of our poetry. We may mean well; all manner of good may happen to us on the road we go; but we are not on our real right road, the road we must in the end follow."[44] It was significant, Arnold thought, that the Indo-European masterpieces based on "the pure religious sentiment, and not the imaginative reason" were books like *De Imitatione Christi* and hymns such as the *Dies Iræ*, and the *Stabat Mater*, all of which were in medieval Latin, "the genuine voice of no Indo-European nation." Neither the genre nor the language in which it expressed itself was quite legitimate. Such noble literary monuments as the Psalms and the books of Job and Isaiah could no longer be produced. "We Indo-Europeans must feel these works without attempting to remake them," for they were based on the pure religious sentiment—a province the Hebrews had made peculiarly their own. "The one true basis for the spiritual work of an Indo-European people" was the imaginative reason.[45]

What Arnold meant exactly by "the imaginative reason" it is difficult to determine. Lionel Trilling regards the phrase as an attempt to close "the gap between head and heart, between feelings and intellect."[46] Adopting the same interpretation, H. F. Lowry believes that the expression "may well turn out to be the best of all he left us," since his work as a whole—the criticism as well as the poetry—is an endeavor to put the ideal into practice.[47] Unquestionably, both authorities are correct, though neither probably would claim that he has exhausted the possibilities of interpretation. It is evident, at any rate, from Arnold's own comments, already cited, that he denied "the imaginative reason" to the ancient Hebrews, and that he regarded it as a peculiarly Indo-European attribute. In crediting the Aryan race with greater intellectual power than the Semitic race possessed he had ample authority, as has been shown, in his German and French predecessors. No further evidence was required than that of the language itself to prove that the Hebrews were incapable of science. "The Hebrew genius," Arnold thought, "has not, like the Greek, its conscious and clear-marked division into a poetic side and a scientific side; the scientific side is almost absent; the Bible utterances have often the character of a chorus of Æschylus, but never that of a treatise of Aristotle. We, like the Greeks, possess in our speech and thought the two characters; but so far as the Bible is concerned we have generally confounded them, and have used our double possession for our bewilderment rather than turned it to good account."[48] Even in the power of imagination, according to Renan, the Semitic race was inferior to the Indo-European.[49] The modern age, Arnold thought, was faced with the necessity of interpreting a very complex present superimposed upon an equally complex past. For the comprehension of this "immense, moving, and confused spectacle," general ideas and laws were required. And in this service reason and imagination in proper balance were the prime requirements. What was demanded was "that genius, as Johnson nobly describes it, 'without which judgment is cold and knowledge is inert; that energy which collects, combines, amplifies, and animates.' "[50] To what works could Arnold turn for the best illustration of these qualities? Certainly not to the Talmud or the Apocalypse; hardly even to the book of Isaiah. It was to the works of the Greek, the Indo-European poets—Simonides, Pindar, Æschylus, and Sophocles—that he turned.[51]

The fullest and most explicit development of the contrast between the two geniuses was reserved, however, for *Literature and Dogma* (1873). In this book, Arnold tried to rescue Christianity from the theologians, who treated religion as a science, and to restore it in its simpler and grander and more practicable form to the people. The basic assumption of the book was well expressed seven years later in the opening paragraph of *The Study of Poetry* (1880). "Our religion has materialized itself in the fact, in the supposed fact; it has attached its emotion to the fact, and now the fact is failing it. But for poetry [i.e., literature] the idea is everything; the rest is a world of illustion, of divine illusion. Poetry attaches its emotion to the idea; the idea *is* the fact."[52] To the supposed facts of the prophecies, the messianic hope, and the miracles Christianity had attached itself, and the facts were now failing it, for they could not be verified. By its learned commentators the Bible was regarded chiefly as a repository of dogma, as a basis for this or that creed, and the skepticism of the modern world was shaking all creeds, showing all accredited dogmas to be questionable, and threatening to dissolve all received traditions. For a proper interpretation of the Bible, Arnold thought, its language must be understood as "fluid, passing, and literary, not rigid, fixed, and scientific."[53] Only thus and by ceasing to regard all the books of the Bible as of equal value—the Apocalypse as worthy as the book of Job—could the ideas of Christianity be revealed in their grand simplicity. And of those ideas, the grandest, the simplest, and at the same time the most difficult to practise was righteousness, or morality.

With such a project in hand, Arnold found Burnouf's *La Science des Religions* apt to his purpose. By its very title it was dedicated to the thesis that Arnold held to be inadmissible. In Burnouf's system, religion and metaphysics were one; and for this science the Aryan race displayed exceptional capacity whereas the Semitic race displayed none. The result, as Arnold expressed it, was that "Israel, therefore, instead of being a light to the Gentiles and a salvation to the ends of the earth, falls to a place in the world's religious history behind the Arya. He is dismissed as ranking anthropologically between the Aryas and the yellow men; as having frizzled hair, thick lips, small calves, flat feet, and belonging, above all, to those 'occipital races' whose brain cannot grow above the age of sixteen; whereas the brain of a theological Arya, such as one of our bishops, may go on growing all his life."[54] These scientific pronouncements were, of course, preposterous and absurd to the point of being amusing, and throughout *Literature and Dogma* Arnold treated them with a note of levity. But the distinction between the Aryan and the Semitic races he granted. "If you want to know plastic art," he said, "you go to the Greeks; if you want to know science, you go to the Aryan genius."[55] For these things, he admitted, the Israelites had no specialty. Theirs was another mission. To the world's civilization they made but one contribution—religion. And in this field, according to Arnold, metaphysics had no place. Israel's very incapacity, therefore, became its chief glory.

Instead of making religion "a synthetic explanation of the universe," Israel made of it an exhortation to righteousness. In words almost the same as those employed by Renan, Arnold paid the Jews their just tribute. "This does truly constitute for Israel a most extraordinary distinction. In spite of all which in them and in their character is unattractive, nay, repellent,—in spite of their shortcomings even in righteousness itself and their insignificance in everything else,—this petty, unsuccessful, unamiable people, without politics, without science, without art, without charm, deserve their great place in the world's regard, and are likely to have it more and more, as the world goes on, rather than less."[56]

From St. Augustine and the *Book of Soliloquies*, popularly ascribed to him, with its fantastic description of the Trinity as "superinenarrable, and superinscrutable, and superinaccessible, superincomprehensible, superintelligible, superessential, superessentially surpassing all sense," from this to the nineteenth century "athletes of logic," the Bishops of Winchester and Gloucester, with their attempt "to do something for the Godhead of the Eternal Son," the subtle Aryan doctors of the Church had attributed their own speculations to the Bible. Wild with reasoning, the Aryan race had made of Christianity one prolonged disputation. "Poor Israel! poor *ancient people!*" cried Arnold at the close of his eleventh chapter. What dreadful pangs must they have felt at seeing their "primitive intuition, simple and sublime, of the Eternal *that loveth righteousness*," so obscured and encrusted with dogma.

With its racial "intuition of God," its racial predisposition to morality,[57] Israel, Arnold thought, had been the salvation of the Indo-European race. To their "deceiving lusts" Greece and Rome had been all too prone. Down to his own time, the Latin nations, and particularly France in its worship of *l'homme sensuel moyen*, had yielded too easily to the "loose solicitations" of the senses. Without the check provided by Israel, what would have become of them? So pervasive was the worship of the *Alma Venus* that the English themselves, more moral than most Indo-Europeans, were in danger.[58] Why was it, Arnold asked, that the Hebrews, unlike other Semitic peoples, and unlike the Indo-Europeans, did not "put a feminine divinity alongside of their masculine divinity, and thus open the way to all sorts of immorality?"[59] It was because of their racial recognition of God as the God of conduct, of righteousness, of morality.

In *Literature and Dogma* Arnold had stormed "the forts of folly." That they did not at once fall caused him no surprise, for, as he knew in advance, they were manned by metaphysicians, whose trade was argument, whose special skill was dialectics. His book was described as "Amateur Theology,"[60] as "Religion in the Hands of Literary Laymen,"[61] as a robbery of the spirit, "all the more heartless because it professes to take away nothing."[62] Who so little Christian as the Doctors of the Church when roused to combat? Unless, indeed, it were Arnold himself. If his opponents were "rigorous," he said, he would be "vigorous." *God and the Bible* was his reply to his critics and he prefaced the work with the warning that "their outcry does not make us go back one inch."[63]

The main objection to *Literature and Dogma* was its definition of God as "the stream of tendency by which all things seek to fulfil the law of their being," as the "not ourselves, which makes for righteousness, or morality," conceptions which Israel arrived at by a racial intuition. Such concepts denied God as a person and rejected the supernatural inspiration of the Scriptures. As one reviewer after another pointed out, the Bible was filled with passages showing that the Jews regarded God as a person, as their Creator, their Father, their King, their leader in battle.[64] For the hosts of the orthodox, the *Dublin Review* acted as spokesman, "There is not a race of men upon earth who could believe in God as a stream of tendency. But certainly that could never have been the faith of an entire, especially a simple and unmetaphysical, race."[65] To such criticisms Arnold replied that "Israel had an intuitive faculty, a natural bent for these ideas," a natural explanation much to be preferred, he thought, to the preternatural one of the theologians, which pictured God as "a magnified and non-natural man, walking in gardens, speaking from clouds, sending dreams, commissioning angels."[66]

Not only on theological grounds, however, were Arnold's theories taken to task. From a sociological and anthropological view, also, his hypothesis was held to be untenable. A conception of God as a personal deity, according to the *Westminster Review*, was the first stage in the history of every religion, whereas the conception of morality as a part of his service was one of the most advanced. In the childhood of nations, abstract laws have no existence. Yet Arnold had attributed to Israel, a semi-barbarous people, a capacity for the most advanced and abstract thought.[67] Another objection was raised by the evolutionists, who traced moral perceptions to "two main instincts,—the reproductive instinct and the instinct of self-preservation."[68] Darwin himself was cited as an authority for the opinion that morality had its origin in "a social instinct, arising out of evolution and inheritance."[69] To all these critics Arnold gave the same sufficient answer. Their explanations might or might not be valid. In any case they were irrelevant, for they dealt with the "twilight antenatal life of humanity," with "inchoate, prehistoric man." The real history of a race began, he maintained, when such concepts as that of morality had already been formed.[70] "But, for us now, religion is, we say, morality touched with emotion, lit up and enkindled and made much more powerful by emotion. And when morality is thus touched with emotion, it is equally religion, whether it have proceeded from a magnified and non-natural man in the clouds, or arisen in the way we have supposed. And those in whom it appears thus touched with emotion most, are those whom we call endued with most bent for religion, most feeling, most apprehension; as one man and one race seem to turn out to have more gift, without any conscious intending and willing of it, for one thing, and another man and another race for another. Now such a bent, such a feeling, when it declares itself, we call an intuition. And we say that Israel had such an intuition of religion."[71]

Arnold's position as expressed in *Literature and Dogma* and in *God and the Bible* bewildered many of his contemporaries. Like the French critic Réville, they did not know what to make of a philosopher whose theodicy seemed to have the marks of pantheism, or even atheism, who doubted all the Bible miracles, who rejected the Trinity of Athanasius, and the doctrine of revelation, and yet considered himself a Christian and a member of the established church of England.[72] He was attacked as anti-Christian and anti-religious. But he never suffered the treatment accorded his contemporary, Renan. No neighbors sprinkled their chairs with holy water after Arnold had sat in them. It was never rumored that the Rothschilds had employed him at one million francs to cast aspersions on Christ and the Trinity. At worst, he suffered a rebuke like William Johnson Cory's, "I suppose he was driven to patronising Jesus Christ as the only way of earning cash. It is a mean way of getting a livelihood."[73] What Arnold called his little "vivacities" of expression were given harsher names by some of his reviewers. The vulgarity of his style was found to be in keeping with the shallowness of his criticism.[74] Certainly the ingenuity of his argument was worthy of an Aryan. And it did not escape the notice of his critics that in defining God as "the Eternal Power, not ourselves, by which all things fulfil the law of their being," the arch-enemy of metaphysics had shown himself to be pre-eminently a metaphysician.[75]

Chapter VII

Conclusion

To the "delicate and inward" task of determining racial and national characteristics Arnold addressed, as the preceding pages have shown, a considerable portion of his time and energy. In each case, his method was the same. Like his contemporary, Taine, he sought always for the dominant trait (pensée maîtresse) in the race or nation under discussion. Taine's chief difficulty as an investigator, according to his own statement, lay in the discovery of a characteristic and dominant feature around which his findings could be grouped. Once he had arrived at what he called the "formula" of his subject, the results of his researches fell naturally into place. Arnold, it would seem, followed a similar plan. "Certain races and nations," Arnold believed, "are on certain lines pre-eminent and representative."[1] Having determined the pre-eminent and representative quality, he sought for evidences of its operation in all fields of endeavor in which the race or nation was concerned. Thus, he was convinced that energy was the dominant trait of the English, energy coupled with unintelligence, or the uncritical habit of mind. "At once so resolute and so unintelligent." This was the formula which he applied to the English in his discussion of their politics, their religion, their economics, and their literature. Around this central theme much of his criticism of English life and thought was woven. For the Celts and the Teutons he discovered a formula equally simple, sentimentality being the dominant racial characteristic of the one as morality was of the other. To each of the great nations of Europe he assigned a particular "power" under which the elements of the national life could be classified, as, for example, "the power of knowledge" among the Germans, and "the power of social life and manners" among the French. Objection can be made to the method and has been made to it as it is employed by Taine and his disciple Émile Boutmy. The aspects of the national being are too many, too complex, and too varied to be comprehended in such neat categories. There was justice in the charge of Arnold's English contemporaries that he had fallen victim to the French habit of generalizing. Yet, as an English political scientist has recently insisted, there is a rock on which each nation stands and from which it is hewn.[2] If on occasion Arnold floundered in the quicksands, he not infrequently discovered the solid foundations on which the national life was established.

Some of the qualities attributed to the separate races and nations were not original with Arnold, or even with the Victorian era. Through the centuries each of the European countries had developed its peculiar characteristics. Nations like individuals, it has been remarked, have reputations and these are in the keeping of their enemies. The German lout, the Italian lecher, and the French dandy are stock figures in English literature of the Elizabethan period.[3] The "Signors of Spaygne" were pictured as braggarts, and Hans van Belch, "the swag-bellied Hollander," reeled drunkenly across the stage in many a Renaissance drama. Out of France and Italy the English traveller was said to bring but three things: an empty purse, a weak stomach, and a naughty conscience. And how were the English regarded on the Continent? They were reputed to be without manners, arrogant. Medieval report had it that they were born with tails. What the English chose to call "the French pox" was known in France as the Italian ailment, in Italy as the English disease. To this international exchange of amenities Arnold added another chapter, bringing the subject up to date. In some respects, he simply confirmed what the folk had always known.

In reference to the Celts, Arnold said that he had not made blame the chief part of what he had written since the Celts were "to be meliorated rather by developing their gifts than by chastising their defects." To judge by the outraged protests of his fellow-countrymen, he did not always display such commendable consideration in his treatment of the English. But in his comments on other races and other nations he did attempt to be dispassionate and judicial. The claims of the Celts were balanced against those of the Teutons and in the scales neither was found wholly wanting. In the Semitic genius as in the Indo-European he pointed out virtues as well as defects. In his own character he combined, as Léo Quesnel said, the seriousness of the Germanic races and the swiftness of perception usually ascribed to the Gallic spirit.[4] His very name expressed "that peculiar Semitico-Saxon mixture which makes the typical Englishman."[5] And even the *Edinburgh Review* granted that he viewed his own country with continental eyes but with an English heart.[6] On France, on Germany, and on the United States his favorable observations were many and sincere. Yet he would have been untrue to his master, Aristotle, had he failed to regard each of these nations as "a body swaying between the qualities of its mean and its excess, and on the whole, as human nature is constituted, inclining rather towards the excess than the mean."[7] Human nature being constituted as it is, however, nations seldom honor their detractors. Perhaps, therefore, the patriots of other countries which came under Arnold's scrutiny may be forgiven if, following Voltaire, they insist that no foreigner can see much beyond the façade of a nation.

It was Arnold's emphatic opinion that the English poets of the first quarter of the nineteenth century failed of their potential greatness because they did not have "sufficient materials to work with," because they "did not know enough." Life in the modern world, he felt, had become so complex that literature could no longer command much attention or respect unless it had been preceded by a great critical effort. For contemporary criticism, therefore, a high function could be claimed. Its task was "to create a current of true and fresh ideas." In turning to science for his materials Arnold was thus, by his own definition, performing the proper function of a critic. The ideas of the ethnologists were "pregnant and striking" and he put them to effective use. They provided a key to the understanding of many difficult matters, from German syntax to the political incapacity of the French, from American insensitiveness in place-names to the Hebrew intuition of God. They did not, of course, explain everything. There are whole areas of Arnold's work in which the racial theories of his day are not even mentioned. But these theories are basic in his best known books on religion, they are significant in some of his discussions of social and political issues, and they appear again and again in his analysis of literature: English,

French, German, Celtic, Semitic, and Indo-European. Unquestionably, the ideas of the ethnologists were "fresh." Whether or not they were also "true" was a question debated with much heat even in the eighteen sixties. In speaking of Christ's disciples, Arnold noted that they were men of their time and subject to its errors. In this one respect, at least, Arnold was like the disciples. He was justified, however, in employing the methods and the results of ethnology. In his day the Celtic-Teutonic and the Semitic—Indo-European controversies were part of a great intellectual current which literature could not afford to ignore. A "mere literary critic" venturing into such fields, as Arnold remarked in the disarming introduction to his Celtic studies, owed "his whole safety to his tact in choosing authorities to follow." By going to the Continent for his chief authorities—W. F. Edwards, Amédée Thierry, Henri Martin, Jules Michelet, Ernest Renan, Émile Burnouf, Heinrich Heine, and Wilhelm von Humboldt—he performed another important service for criticism. He helped to bring England into the great intellectual confederation of Europe. He struck another blow at the insularity which was a contributing factor in the severance of England and Europe, at the provinciality which

> bade betwixt their shores to be
> The unplumb'd, salt, estranging sea.

That Arnold's continental authorities were not wholly trustworthy was unfortunate. Through them he was led into some of his most questionable theorizing. For certain of his critics, like Tennyson and Sir Walter Raleigh, even the soundest of his sociological treatises had little appeal. Seeing him venture into the vast and uncharted domain of ethnology, these lovers of the poet as against the reformer might have used his own words to warn him,

> Not here, O Apollo!
> Are haunts meet for thee.

He became involved in issues beyond his competence. Had he confined his racial theories to Llandudno and the attractions of the Celtic Eisteddfod, he would have been on debatable but still partly defensible ground. When he used the same theories to explain the outcome of the Franco-Prussian war, however, he had entered into the realm of pure conjecture. Again, he was no upholder of "the torture prolonged from age to age . . . the infamy Israel's heritage." He singled out for praise the greatest virtue of the Hebrews, their bent toward righteousness. But he also granted that as a people they were "unattractive, nay, repellent," that they had no politics, no science, no art, no charm. And the weakness as well as the strength was the result of race. With the faults receiving all the stress and the virtues none, the same racial theory was invoked in France at the close of the nineteenth century as warrant for the anti-Semitism which swept the country. Alfred Dreyfus on Devil's Island and his twentieth century successors, the martyrs of Dachau and Buchenwald, were not saved from their persecutors by tributes such as Arnold's in which blame and praise were mingled. With Samson Agonistes, their kinsman, they would have been justified in crying out,

> What boots it at one gate to make defense,
> And at another to let in the foe.

To the unfounded assumptions of the racial hypothesis Arnold lent the weight of a distinguished name. His pronouncements upon the Celt, the Saxon, and the Jew have not gone unheard; they have told upon the world's practice. Shall a man be absolved of all responsibility because he would disown his fanatic disciples? Shall the advocate of culture be held blameless when his theories result in anarchy? It may be, however, that the censure implied in such questions is too harsh. After all, Arnold was merely following the *Zeitgeist*, and that, by the majority, at least, is not considered an indictable offense. Perhaps it is enough to say of him, as he said of the average Englishman, that he walked diligently by such light as he had, but took too little care that the light he had was not darkness.

FOOTNOTES TO CHAPTER I

Footnotes for pages 1–8

[1] Two excellent examples in English are: Isaac Taylor, *The Origin of the Aryans* (London, 1890); and Frank H. Hankins, *The Racial Basis of Civilization* (Revised ed., New York, 1931). In Germany and France the subject has received thorough treatment.

[2] *Edinburgh Review*, CXIV (July, 1861), 6.

[3] *Quarterly Review*, CXXV (July–Oct., 1868), 475, 489.

[4] *Athenaeum*, I (April 4, 1868), 490.

[5] *Contemporary Review*, IX (Sept., 1868), 145.

[6] "Pagan Patriotism," *Saturday Review*, XX (Sept. 9, 1865), 324.

[7] *Letters of Matthew Arnold*, ed. G. W. E. Russell (New York, 1895), I, 323.

[8] Herbert Spencer, "The Study of Sociology. IX—The Bias of Patriotism," *Contemporary Review*, XXI (March, 1873), 475–502.

[9] "Amateur Theology: Arnold's *Literature and Dogma*," *Blackwood's*, CXIII (June, 1873), 678–92.

[10] "Mr. Arnold on Lucidity," *Saturday Review*, LIV (Oct. 7, 1882), 464.

[11] *Saturday Review*, LIII (March 18, 1882), 334.

[12] A. C. Swinburne, "Arnold's *New Poems*," *Fortnightly Review*, VIII (Oct., 1867), 442.

[13] "Matthew Arnold and Insularity," *Edinburgh Review*, CC (July, 1904), 131–151.

[14] See his introduction to the reprint of the first edition of *Essays in Criticism*, 1912; or, Walter Raleigh, *Some Authors* (Oxford, 1923), p. 305.

[15] Esmé Wingfield-Stratford, *The History of English Patriotism* (New York, 1913), II, 390–99.

[16] *The Bookman*, LXIX (July, 1929), 479–484. For this reference and the one to Raleigh above, I am indebted to E. K. Brown's "The Critic as Xenophobe," *Sewanee Review*, XXXVIII (July–September, 1930), 301–309.

[17] Louis Etienne, "La Critique Contemporaine en Angleterre: Matthew Arnold," *Revue des deux mondes* LXII (1866), 755.

[18] See E. K. Brown, "The French Reputation of Matthew Arnold," *Studies in English by Members of University College Toronto* (Toronto, 1931), pp. 232–239.

[19] Hermann Levy, "Matthew Arnold und die volkscharakterologische Erkenntnis," *Zeitschrift für Völkerpsychologie und Soziologie*, V (Sept., 1929), 305.

[20] Johannes Renwanz, *Matthew Arnold und Deutschland* (Greifswald, 1927), p. 39.

Footnotes for pages 10–12

[21] A third element, the Norman, enters into the composition of the English. But this element is emphasized only in *On the Study of Celtic Literature*. Even here the point is made that the Normans, like the people they conquered in England, were mainly Germanic. In Arnold's works as a whole, it is the balance between the Celtic and Germanic parts of the English nature that receives attention.

[22] See "Democracy," the reprint of the Introduction to *Popular Education in France*, in *Mixed Essays, Irish Essays, and Others* (New York, 1883), pp. 18, 19.

FOOTNOTES TO CHAPTER II

Footnotes for pages 13–22

[1] Arnold's own comments will serve as an example: "That the French will beat the Prussians all to pieces, even far more completely and rapidly than they are beating the Austrians, there cannot be a moment's doubt; and they know it themselves. I had a long and very interesting conversation with Lord Cowley . . . . He entirely shared my conviction as to the French always beating any number of Germans who come into the field against them" (*Letters of Matthew Arnold*, ed. G. W. E. Russell [New York, 1895], I, 96). The date of this comment is June 25, 1859.

[2] Arnold's term. See *Ibid.*, p. 119.

[3] See Wilhelm Vollrath, *Th. Carlyle und H. St. Chamberlain, zwei Freunde Deutschlands* (München, 1935), pp. 41–43, 50–53; Theodor Deimel, *Carlyle und der Nationalsozialismus: Eine Würdigung des englischen Denkers im Lichte der deutschen Gegenwart* (Würzburg, 1937), pp. 121–129.

[4] *The Life and Works of Charles Kingsley* (London, 1901–1903), III, 209.

[5] R. W. Emerson, *English Traits* (centenary ed.; Boston, 1903), p. 54.

[6] "Not a Briton remained as subject or slave on English ground. Sullenly, inch by inch, the beaten men drew back from the land which their conquerors had won; and eastward of the border-line which the English sword had drawn, all was now purely English." As a result of the disappearance of the Briton from the greater part of the territory he had called his own, "the tongue, the religion, the laws of his English conquerors reigned without a break from Essex to Staffordshire, and from the British Channel to the Firth of Forth" (John Richard Green, *History of the English People* [New York, 1879], I, 28, 31).

[7] *On the Study of Celtic Literature* ("Everyman" ed.; London, 1932), p. 132. Except when indicated otherwise, all references to the text hereafter will be made to the "Everyman" edition.

[8] *Ibid.*, pp. 88, 89.

[9] Frank H. Hankins, *The Racial Basis of Civilization* (revised ed.; New York, 1931), pp. 275–281.

[10] Carleton Stanley, *Matthew Arnold* (Toronto, 1938), p. 69.

[11] *Letters*, ed. Russell, II, 134.

[12] See C. F. Tinker and H. F. Lowry, *The Poetry of Matthew Arnold: A Commentary* (London, 1940), p. 109.

[13] *Ibid.*, pp. 222, 223.

[14] The exact date on which Arnold read the essay cannot be determined. It appeared in the *Revue des deux mondes* in 1854, and was printed again in 1859 as the concluding essay in *Essais de morale et de critique*, the volume which Arnold desired his sister to read. See *Letters*, ed. Russell, I, 111, 112.

Footnotes for pages 23–24

[15] *Popular Education in France* (London, 1861), pp. 172, 173.

[16] *A French Eton: Or Middle-Class Education and the State* (London, 1864), pp. 87–89. See Amédée Thierry, *Histoire des Gaulois depuis les temps les plus reculés jusqu'à l'entière soumission de la Gaule à la domination Romaine* (dixième éd.; Paris, 1877), p. 4.

[17] For a good, though incomplete, account of this series of engagements, see M. M. Bevington, *The Saturday Review, 1855–1868: Representative Educated Opinion in Victorian England* (New York, 1941), pp. 136–152.

[18] On the violent Teutonic bias of the *Times* Arnold commented at great length, the major portion of his "Introduction" to *On the Study of Celtic Literature* being devoted to answering "the inhuman attacks" (*Letters*, ed. Russell, I, 338) made by the *Times* on the "arrant nonsense" of his remarks concerning the Welsh Eisteddfod of 1866. Because of the interest in Celtic matters displayed in his Oxford lectures, he had been invited by the Welshman Hugh Owen to address the Eisteddfod gathering. Arnold declined the honor in a letter (quoted almost in full in the "Introduction" [*On the Study of Celtic Literature*, pp. 4, 5]), expressing admiration for the cultural interests of the Welsh and commenting on "the greater delicacy and spirituality of the Celtic peoples" as contrasted with the English. In an article on the opening of the National Eisteddfod, the *Times* (Sept. 5, 1866; p. 5) quoted the letter in the form in which it had appeared in the *Pall Mall Gazette*. Three days later, the *Times* (Sept. 8; p. 8) in a leading article satirized the barbarism of such Celtic celebrations and took Arnold severely to task for encouraging the absurd "Cambrian proceedings." On the complaint of "Talhaiarn," one of the participants in the Eisteddfod, at such unfairness to his "national institution," the *Times* (Sept. 14; p. 6) returned again to the charge in an article more insulting than the first, again involving Arnold to disadvantage. In the "Introduction" (*On the Study of Celtic Literature*, pp. 6, 7), Arnold quoted representative passages from the two articles: "The Welsh language is the curse of Wales. Its prevalence, and the ignorance of English have excluded, and even now exclude the Welsh people from the civilization of their English neighbours. An Eisteddfod is one of the most mischievous and selfish pieces of sentimentalism which could possibly be perpetrated. It is simply a foolish interference with the natural progress of civilization and prosperity [*Times*, Sept. 8; p. 8]. If it is desirable that the Welsh should talk English, it is monstrous folly to encourage them in a loving fondness for their old language. Not only the energy and power, but the intelligence and music of Europe have come mainly from Teutonic sources, and this glorification of everything Celtic, if it were not pedantry, would be sheer ignorance. The sooner all Welsh specialities disappear from the face of the earth the better" [*Times*, Sept. 14; p. 6].

[19] *Saturday Review*, VIII (Aug. 13, 1859), 188, 189. See Bevington, *op. cit.*, p. 137.

Footnotes for pages 24–28

[20] *Saturday Review*, XVIII (Dec. 3, 1864), 683. These remarks are early examples of what Arnold has in mind twenty years later when he says: "People in England often accuse me of liking France and things French too well" (*Discourses in America* [London, 1885], p. 38).

[21] *Essays in Criticism* (ed. of 1865), pp. xiii, xiv. This passage is omitted in later editions.

[22] *On the Study of Celtic Literature*, p. 65. This statement is allowed to stand unaltered in the text, although a note by Lord Strangford is appended to the effect that the term Scythian cannot safely be connected with anything as yet, since it is "used to comprehend nomads and barbarians of all sorts and races north and east of the Black and Caspian seas" (*Ibid.*, p. 66).

[23] *Ibid.*, p. 133. Because of his advocacy of the Revised Code of 1862, which Arnold disapproved, and because of his narrow utilitarian views on elementary education, Mr. Lowe is a frequent object of Arnold's attack. See H. W. Paul, *Matthew Arnold* (New York, 1902), p. 67.

[24] *Essays in Criticism, First Series* (London, 1889), p. 68. The critic who "disliked the French Emperor" is evidently Fitzjames Stephen, who in his article on Arnold's *England and the Italian Question* cannot adduce a single instance "of the Emperor's having promoted either religious, or political, or social freedom in any particular" (*Saturday Review*, VIII [Aug. 13, 1859], 188, 189).

[25] "Savoy," *Saturday Review*, IX (Feb. 11, 1860), 175.

[26] "Gesta Regum Britanniae," *Saturday Review*, XVI (Sept. 26, 1863), 435.

[27] "Why Empires Fail," *Saturday Review*, XII (Oct. 5, 1861), 347. None of these three articles is listed by Bevington in his catalogue of Freeman's contributions (*op. cit.*, pp. 342–346), but the vehemence of the statements and his frequent objection in his longer historical works to this insult to the memory of Charles the Great mark the articles as probably his.

[28] "Britain and Her Language," *Saturday Review*, XX (Nov. 18, 1865), 649.

[29] *Ibid.*, pp. 649, 650.

[30] M. M. Bevington, *op. cit.*, pp. 251, 261, 262.

[31] "Primeval Antiquities," *Saturday Review*, XV (Jan. 24, 1863), 107.

[32] "Craniology," *Saturday Review*, V (Feb. 6, 1858), 142.

[33] "M. de Montalembert on English Instruction," *Saturday Review* I (Jan. 5, 1856), 177.

[34] "The French Triumph," *Saturday Review*, VIII (Aug. 20, 1859), 209.

[35] "Indigenous Races," *Saturday Review*, IV (Jan. 4, 1857), 20.

[36] "A Frenchman in Norway," *Saturday Review*, III (June 6, 1857), 527.

[37] *Saturday Review*, VI (Aug. 28, 1858), 213; IV (Oct. 17, 1857), 348; XIII (March 29, 1862), 343; XXI (June 23, 1866), 760; XXVI (Nov. 28, 1868), 725.

Footnotes for pages 28–30

[38] "Morgan's *British Kymry*," *Saturday Review*, VIII (Sept. 24, 1859), 371.

[39] "Hook's Lives of the Archbishops of Canterbury, Vol. III," *Saturday Review*, XIX (Mar. 4, 1865), 259; "Nicholas' *Pedigree of the English People*," *Saturday Review*, XXV (June 6, 1868), 757. See *On the Study of Celtic Literature*, pp. 67, 88.

[40] "Stubbs's book [*The Constitutional History of England*] is a sound and substantial one, but rather overpraised by a certain school here, the school of Freeman, of whom Stubbs is a disciple. This school has done much to explore our early history and to throw light on the beginnings of our system of government and of our liberty; but they have not a single man of genius, with the *étincelle* and the instinctive good sense and moderation which make a guide really attaching and useful. Freeman is an ardent, learned, and honest man, but he is a ferocious pedant, and Stubbs, though he is not ferocious, is not without his dash of pedantry" (*Letters*, ed. Russell, II, 149; an answer, Dec. 15, 1878, to his good friend and frequent correspondent, M. Fontanès).

[41] *Essays in Criticism, First Series*, p. 355.

[42] "Falkland," *Mixed Essays, Irish Essays and Others* (New York, 1883), p. 177. Although Arnold reacted unfavorably to Freeman's ferocity, pedantry and Teutonism, he did recognize his authority in historical matters, as is indicated in the advice he gave to Arthur Galton concerning his book on Thomas Cromwell, "men like Stubbs, and S. Gardiner, and Freeman are the men whose judgement on the book it is important to have." See Arthur Galton, *Two Essays upon Matthew Arnold, with some of his Letters to the Author* (London, 1897), p. 115. Among the Oxford historians, J. R. Green alone received an unqualified approval, unqualified perhaps because Arnold had not read the work, *The Making of England*, which he recommends. To his friend, Fontanès, Arnold wrote on February 9, 1882, "By all means get Green's book; it is sure to be well done, and I believe that it deals with that early history which is so very dull in all the received authorities such as Hume, and of which the importance and interest were never brought out till within the past thirty or forty years" (*Letters*, ed. Russell, II, 199). In "Falkland," Arnold notes that the assumption, highly questionable in spite of its being so plausible and so current, that English seriousness and political liberty are to be attributed to the Puritan influence and the Puritan triumph, pervades even "Mr. Green's fascinating History" (*Mixed Essays, Irish Essays and Others*, p. 171).

[43] *The Origin of the English Nation* (New York, 1879), p. 38.

[44] *Outlines of History* (New York, 1872), p. 80.

[45] *The Chief Periods of European History* (New York, 1886), p. 43.

[46] *Historical Essays, Third Series* (London, 1879), p. 122.

[47] *Comparative Politics* (New York. 1874), p. 364.

Footnotes for pages 30–37

[48] *Historical Essays, First Series* (New York, 1886), pp. 178, 179.

[49] *The Chief Periods of European History*, p. 64.

[50] *The History of the Norman Conquest of England* (Oxford, 1873–1879), II, 52.

[51] *The Origin of the English Nation*, p. 92.

[52] *The History of the Norman Conquest of England*, I, 363.

[53] *Ibid.*, IV, 13; *Old English History for Children* (London, n.d.), pp. 43, 44.

[54] *Historical Essays, First Series*, p. 51.

[55] *The Growth of the English Constitution* (third ed.; London, 1898), pp. 73, 74.

[56] *The History of the Norman Conquest of England*, I, 120.

[57] *On the Origin of the English Nation*, pp. 35, 57, 58.

[58] *Ibid.*, pp. 133, 134.

[59] *Comparative Politics*, pp. 144, 179.

[60] *The History of the Norman Conquest of England*, V, 226.

[61] "Freeman's *Norman Conquest*, Vol. III," *Saturday Review*, XXVIII (Sept. 4, 1869), 322.

[62] "The Teuto-Celtic and Slavo-Sarmatian Races," *Anthropological Review and Journal*, IV (1866), 64. This journal will hereafter be referred to as *ARJ*.

[63] J. W. Jackson, "The Race Question in Ireland," *ARJ*, VII (1869), 75.

[64] *ARJ*, *loc. cit.*; "The Roman and the Teuton," *ARJ*, IV (1866), 22.

[65] "Race in History," *ARJ*, V (1867), 129–141.

[66] *ARJ*, VIII (1870), 1–14.

[67] For an account of the awards, see "The Origin of the English: Pike *vs.* Nicholas, *ARJ*, VII (1869), 279–306; also, the *Times*, Aug. 23, 1866, p. 7.

[68] See also, Owen Luke Pike, "On the Psychical Characteristics of the English People," *Memoirs Read Before the Anthropological Society of London*, II (1865–66), 153.

[69] Joseph Fisher, "The Migrations of Mankind," *ARJ*, V (1867), cciv.

[70] T. Nicholas, "On the Influence of the Norman Conquest on the Ethnology of Britain," *Journal of the Ethnological Society of London, New Series*, II (1870–71), 389, 390.

[71] W. F. Edwards, *Des Caractères Physiologiques des Races Humaines considéres dans leurs rapports avec l'histoire; lettre à M. Amédée Thierry, auteur de l'histoire des Gaulois* (Paris, 1829), p. 60. Arnold has 1839 for the date of the publication, an error that remains uncorrected in Nutt's 1910 edition of *The Study of Celtic Literature*.

[72] *Ibid.*, p. 86.

[73] *Ibid.*, p. 31.

[74] "Après de long voyages et de nombreuses observations faites avec toute la rigueur de méthode qu'exigent les sciences physiques, avec toute la sagacité

Footnotes for pages 37–40

qui distinguait particulièrement l'esprit de M. Edwards, le savant naturaliste est arrivé à des conséquences identiques à celles de cette histoire" (Amédée Thierry, *op. cit.*, p. 117).

[75] T. K. Penniman, *A Hundred Years of Anthropology* (London, 1935), pp. 117, 118.

[76] *On the Study of Celtic Literature*, p. 77.

[77] "Renan," *Essays in Criticism, Third Series*, ed. E. J. O'Brien (Boston, 1910), pp. 167, 168.

[78] Grant Allen, "Are We Englishmen?" *Fortnightly Review, New Series*, XXVIII (Oct., 1880), 472–487.

[79] *Letters of George Meredith*, Collected and ed. by his Son (New York, 1912), I, 323.

[80] John Beddoe, *The Races of Britain: A Contribution to the Anthropology of Western Europe* (London, 1885), p. 269, note.

FOOTNOTES TO CHAPTER III

Footnotes for pages 41–43

[1] "Mr. Arnold on Celtic Literature," *Pall Mall Gazette*, No. 346 (March 19, 1866), p. 4. Lord Strangford's important review, along with his second paper, "Celtic at Oxford," is reprinted as Appendix A in the Everyman edition of *On the Study of Celtic Literature and Other Essays* (London, 1932). See p. 223.

[2] *Essays in Criticism, Second Series*, (London, 1888), p. 56.

[3] *On the Study of Celtic Literature*, p. 87. For a brief, informative history of the use of the work by Goethe, Heine, Carlyle, Thackeray, Arnold, and Leslie Stephen, see Lewis E. Gates, *Selections from the Prose Writings of Matthew Arnold* (New York, 1897), p. 318.

[4] *On the Study of Celtic Literature*, pp. 93, 98, 100, 104.

[5] *The Works of Thomas Carlyle* (centenary ed.; London, 1899), XXVII, 343.

[6] *One of Our Conquerors, The Works of George Meredith* (memorial ed.; New York, 1909–1912), XVII, 91. Meredith is also aware of the rising Pan-Germanism at the turn of the century. He knows also the support which such a movement gains from the belief in racial purity and unity. Prince Hermann in *The Adventures of Harry Richmond* thus outlines the future of Germany: "Then he talked of the littleness of Europe and the greatness of Germany; logical postulates fell in collapse before him . . . .Mistress of the Baltic, of the North Sea and the East, as eventually she must be, Germany would claim to take India as a matter of course, and find an outlet for the energies of the most prolific and the toughest of the races of mankind,—the purest, in fact, the only true race, properly so called, out of India, to which it would return as to its source, and there create an empire magnificent in force and solidity, the actual wedding of East and West; an empire firm on the ground and in the blood of the people, instead of an empire as with the English of aliens" (*The Works of George Meredith* [memorial ed.; New York, 1909–1912], X, 31).

[7] *Letters of Matthew Arnold*, ed. G. W. E. Russell (New York, 1895), I, 304.

[8] Les traits saillants de la famille gauloise, ceux qui la différencient le plus, à mon avis, des autres familles humaines, peuvent se résumer ainsi; une bravoure personnelle que rien n'égale chez les peuples anciens; un esprit franc, impétueux, ouvert à toutes les impressions, éminemment intelligent; mais à côté de cela, une mobilité extrême, point de constance, une répugnance marquée aux idées de discipline et d'ordre, si puissantes chez les races germaniques, beaucoup d'ostentation, enfin une désunion perpétuelle, fruit de l'excessive vanité. Si l'on voulait comparer sommairement la famille gauloise à cette famille germanique que nous venons de nommer, on pourrait dire que le sentiment personnel, le *moi* individuel

Footnotes for pages 43–45

est trop développé chez la première, et que, chez l'autre, il ne l'est pas assez; aussi trouvons-nous, à chaque page de l'histoire des Gaulois, des personnages originaux qui excitent vivement et concentrent sur eux notre sympathie; en nous faisant oublier les masses, tandis que, dans l'histoire des Germains, c'est ordinairement des masses que ressort tout l'effet" (*Histoire des Gaulois* [Dixième Edition, Paris, 1887], p. 4).

[9] *A French Eton* (London, 1864), pp. 87–89.

[10] J. Michelet, *History of France*, tr. G. H. Smith (New York, 1880), I, 78, 79.

[11] Henri Martin, *Histoire de France depuis les temps les plus reculés jusqu'en 1789* (4th ed.; Paris, 1855), I, 209.

[12] D. Mackintosh, "Results of Ethnological Observations Made During the Last Ten Years in England and Wales," *Transactions of the Ethnological Society of London, New Series*, I (1861), 213.

[13] An excerpt from his article "The Fabulous Saxon" quoted in "On the Saxon Race," *Anthropological Review and Journal* [cited hereafter as *ARJ*], VI (1868), 260. Nothing if not comparative, Maccall likens the Saxon conquest of the Celt to the Norwegian rat's almost complete extermination of the black rat of England, the Saxon being a dull, heavy, voracious rat who has conquered a more valiant, more gifted race, not by courage, scarcely even by strength, but by sheer ponderosity.

[14] *On the Study of Celtic Literature*, p. 79.

[15] For building, the noble Jews are found,
And for truly fierce envy;
For size, the guileless Armenians,
And for firmness, the Saracens;
For acuteness and valour, the Greeks;
For excessive pride, the Romans;
For dulness, the creeping Saxons;
For haughtiness, the Spaniards;
For covetousness and revenge, the French;
And for anger, the true Britons.—
Such is the true knowledge of the trees.—
For gluttony, the Danes, and for commerce;
For high spirits the Picts are not unknown;
And for beauty and amourousness, the Gaedhils;—
As *Giolla-na-naemh* says in verse,
A fair and pleasing composition.

This translation, along with the Irish original from Mac Firbis's *Book of Genealogies*, Arnold found in the 1861 edition of Eugene O'Curry's *Lectures*. See the

Footnotes for pages 45–49

re-issue, *Lectures on the Manuscript Materials of Ancient Irish History* (Dublin, 1878), pp. 224, 580. Arnold found O'Curry's work extremely informative and drew heavily upon it for illustrations in *On the Study of Celtic Literature.*

[16] *On the Study of Celtic Literature*, p. 5.

[17] *Ibid.*, p. 79; *Letters*, ed. Russell, I, 288.

[18] "Amiel," *Essays in Criticism, Second Series*, pp. 323, 324.

[19] *Letters*, ed. Russell, II, 314.

[20] *Letters*, ed. Russell, I, 288; II, 176, 177.

[21] *On the Study of Celtic Literature*, pp. 104, 105.

[22] *Ibid.*, pp. 107, 108.

[23] "A French Critic on Goethe," *Mixed Essays, Irish Essays and Others* (New York, 1883), p. 231.

[24] *On the Study of Celtic Literature*, p. 93.

[25] *On the Study of Celtic Literature and on Translating Homer* (New York, 1924), p. 147.

[26] *On the Study of Celtic Literature*, p. 87.

[27] *Letters*, ed. Russell, I, 92.

[28] "Friendship's Garland," *Culture and Anarchy and Friendship's Garland* (New York, 1883), p. 302. *On the Study of Celtic Literature*, pp. 81 and 87.

[29] Henri Martin, *op. cit.*, I, 13, note 1. Arnold employs the complete contrast, including the greater development of the respiratory organs in the French. The full account of Arnold's dependence on Martin is reserved for the section on the Celts.

English anthropologists and ethnologists make similar observations. The Saxon has "more or less tendency to obesity, especially in the epigastric region" (D. Mackintosh, *op. cit.*, p. 213). And after the age of thirty-five, he is always a heavy, fat man, with a style of walk that is heavy and important (A. C. Murray, "Temperaments," *ARJ*, VIII [1870], 18).

[30] See Jacques Barzun, *Race, A Study in Modern Superstition* (New York, 1937), pp. 239, 240.

[31] *On the Study of Celtic Literature*, p. 81.

[32] *Letters*, ed. Russell, I, 300. The comments on the deficiencies of the German race and civilization thus far cited are representative of Arnold's attitude; they are not exhaustive, for he found the subject a fertile one. For a fuller list, see Johannes Renwanz (*Matthew Arnold und Deutschland* [Greifswald, 1927], pp. 26–38), who with something of "the steady humdrum habit of the creeping Saxon" has culled most of Arnold's aspersions on the German Volk.

[33] *On the Study of Celtic Literature*, p. 131.

[34] *Culture and Anarchy*, pp. 49, 50.

[35] "The Function of Criticism at the Present Time," *Essays in Criticism First Series* (London, 1889), pp. 21–24.

Footnotes for pages 49–52

[36] *Letters*, ed. Russell, I, 238.

[37] *On The Study of Celtic Literature*, p. 121. Emerson, too, was impressed by the Celts who "gave to the seas and mountains names which are poems and imitate the pure voices of nature" (*English Traits* [centenary ed.; Boston, 1903], p. 55).

[38] *Civilization in the United States* (Boston, 1900), pp. 7 and 175. The cleverness but at the same time the monstrous unfairness of Arnold's use of names is commented upon by Sir Walter Raleigh, *Some Authors* (Oxford, 1923), p. 308. That the argument from nomenclature will not support such ethnological implications is pointed out by Alfred Nutt in his annotated edition of *The Study of Celtic Literature* (1910), p. 134, note.

[39] *Culture and Anarchy and Friendship's Garland*, pp. 221, 236.

[40] *Letters*, ed. Russell, II, 60.

[41] *Letters*, ed. Russell, I, 95.

[42] *God and the Bible* (New York, 1883), pp. 208, 209.

[43] "State of German Literature," *The Works of Thomas Carlyle* (centenary ed.; London, 1899), XXVI, 37 ff.

[44] *On the Study of Celtic Literature*, pp. 89–91.

[45] *On the Study of Celtic Literature*, p. 10; "Equality," *Mixed Essays, Irish Essays and Others*, p. 74; "Renan," *Essays in Criticism, Third Series*, ed. E. J. O'Brien (Boston, 1910), p. 173. France's untroubled rule over Brittany is another favorite example with Arnold. Alfred Nutt (*The Study of Celtic Literature*, 1910, p. xxxix, note) points out that the religious differences between England and Ireland were not present in Arnold's time between France and Brittany, but that later such differences did enter into *la question Bretonne* and were met with a severity which even the English might envy.

[46] "The Incompatibles," *Mixed Essays, Irish Essays and Others*, p. 323.

[47] *Ibid.*, p. 322.

[48] *Ibid.*, pp. 322–324.

[49] *Ibid.*, p. 315. Cardinal Newman provides a confirmation of this view: "In this world no one rules by mere love; if you are amiable, you are no hero; to be powerful, you must be strong, and to have dominion you must have a genius for organizing" (*Historical Sketches*, III [London, 1872], p. 85).

[50] "Falkland," *Mixed Essays, Irish Essays and Others*, p. 154.

[51] *Letters*, ed. Russell, II, 378.

[52] See, for example, Émile Boutmy, *The English People, A Study of their Political Psychology*, tr. by E. English (London, 1904), p. 91.

[53] *History of English Literature*, tr. by H. Van Laun (New York, 1875), I, 65, 66.

[54] Meredith was interested in the general problem of race, but was concerned particularly, as was Arnold, with the racial composition of the English people

Footnotes for pages 52–56

His posthumous *Celt and Saxon* is the culmination of a theme which is touched upon in many of his other works. In *Beauchamp's Career*, for example, he remarks: "With Germans we are supercilious Celts; with Frenchmen we are sneering Teutons" (*The Works of George Meredith* [memorial ed.; New York, 1909–1912], XII, 213). The English ability in practical affairs and in government was derived, he believed, from their Saxon ancestors. By their perseverance and a certain lordliness the English dominate the world. The lighter, but no less essential, virtues—imagination, wit, sociability, grace—are Celtic contributions. To his son he writes: "I fancy still that you are in danger of overlooking a large admixture of Celtic blood in the English race. . . .As far as I observe them, the heart of the nation is Teuton and moral, and therewith intellectually obtuse, next to speechless. It has, however, a shifty element and a poetic . . . the poetic, seeming to spring from our Celtic blood, flies at once to the well-springs of the tongue whenever it is in need of vital imagery" (*Letters of George Meredith*, Collected and ed. by his Son [New York, 1912], I, 322). And speaking of the English in *One of Our Conquerors* he has the following comment: "Without the Welsh, Irish, Scot, in their composition, there would not be much of the yeasty ferment; but it should not be forgotten that Welsh, Irish, Scot are now largely of their numbers; and the taste for elegance, and for spiritual utterance, for song, nay, for ideas, is there among them, though it does not everywhere cover a rocky surface to bewitch the eyes of aliens" (*The Works of George Meredith* [memorial ed.; New York, 1909–1912], XVII, 235).

[55] The opening lines of "The Bishop and the Philosopher," *Macmillan's Magazine*, VII (Jan., 1863), 241. For an even fuller definition, see "Ecce, Convertimur ad Gentes," *Mixed Essays, Irish Essays and Others*, pp. 359, 360.

[56] *Letters*, ed. Russell, I, 111.

[57] See pp. 43 and 44.

[58] "Lorsque je commençai, un livre de génie existait, celui de Thierry. Sagace et pénétrant, délicat interprète, grand ciseleur, admirable ouvrier, mais trop asservi à un maître. Ce maître, ce tyran, c'est le point de vue exclusif, systématique, de la perpétuité des races" (*Œuvres Complètes de J. Michelet* [Édition Définitive, Revue et Corrigée; Paris, Ernest Flammarion, Éditeur], p. vi).

[59] *Letters of Matthew Arnold to Arthur Hugh Clough*, ed. H. F. Lowry (London, 1932), p. 66; *Civilization in the United States* (Boston, 1900), pp. 91, 92, and 189.

[60] *Culture and Anarchy*, p. xxii.

[61] *Popular Education in France* (London, 1861), p. 159.

[62] "Porro Unum Est Necessarium," *Mixed Essays, Irish Essays and Others*, p. 126.

[63] *On the Study of Celtic Literature*, pp. 78, 79.

[64] *Literature and Dogma* (New York, 1883), pp. xxi, xxii.

Footnotes for pages 56–66

[65] *Letters of M. A. to A. H. C.*, p. 139.

[66] *On the Study of Celtic Literature and On Translating Homer* (New York, 1924), p. 236.

[67] *Culture and Anarchy*, pp. 54, 55.

[68] "A Speech at Eton," *Mixed Essays, Irish Essays and Others*, p. 414.

[69] *On the Study of Celtic Literature*, p. 107.

[70] *Ibid*,. pp. 109, 110.

[71] *Letters*, ed. Russell, I, 203.

[72] *On the Study of Celtic Literature*, p. 113. This attitude Arnold does not inherit from his father, who liked German hymns, translated some of them, and complimented his friend Bunsen on his collection of the best hymns from the German treasury of 36,000 (A. P. Stanley, *The Life and Correspondence of Thomas Arnold* [Boston, 1855], I, 352; II, 340).

[73] Charles H. Harvey, *Matthew Arnold; A Critic of the Victorian Period* (London, 1931), p. 38.

[74] "Eugénie de Guérin," *Essays in Criticism, First Series*, p. 142.

[75] *Culture and Anarchy*, p. xvi.

[76] *Literature and Dogma* (popular edition; London, 1897), p. 230.

[77] *Literature and Dogma* (New York, 1883), pp. xxi, xxii; see also on the mechanical nature of German Biblical criticism, *God and the Bible*, p. 96.

[78] "On the Modern Element in Literature," *Essays in Criticism, Third Series*, pp. 48, 49.

[79] See p. 34.

[80] For this defense of the working class against Arnold's blanket condemnation, see Lionel Trilling, *Matthew Arnold* (New York, 1939), pp. 277, 278. Arnold did recognize in the workers, however, a lack of that blind hatred of central control which characterized the middle classes.

[81] *Culture and Anarchy and Friendship's Garland*, p. 225.

[82] *Ibid.*, p. 346.

[83] *Mixed Essays, Irish Essays and Others*, p. 414.

[84] *Letters*, ed. Russell, II, 149.

[85] *Letters*, ed. Russell, I, 309, 310.

[86] "The Bishop and the Philosopher," *Macmillan's Magazine*, VII (Jan., 1863), p. 241.

[87] "Dr. Stanley's Lectures on the Jewish Church," *Macmillan's Magazine*, VII (Feb., 1863), 333. Or, more conveniently, in *On the Study of Celtic Literature and Other Essays* ("Everyman Library" ed.; London, 1932), p. 157.

[88] "The Future of Liberalism," *Mixed Essays, Irish Essays and Others*, p. 400. This summing-up of the deficiencies of the middle class is a favorite with Arnold, and he repeats it again and again in other essays.

Footnotes for pages 66–71

[89] For an excellent review of Arnold's opinions on English writers, see E. K. Brown's two articles, "Matthew Arnold and the Elizabethans," *University of Toronto Quarterly*, I (1932), 333–51, and "Matthew Arnold and the Eighteenth Century," *University of Toronto Quarterly*, IX (1940), 202–13.

[90] "Preface to First Edition of Poems (1853)," *Mixed Essays, Irish Essays and Others*, pp. 498–500.

[91] "Equality," *Mixed Essays, Irish Essays ana Others*, p. 60.

[92] "The Modern Element in Literature," *Essays in Criticism, Third Series*, p. 52.

[93] "Byron," *Essays in Criticism, Second Series*, p. 185.

[94] "The Function of Criticism at the Present Time," *Essays in Criticism, First Series*, pp. 6–8.

[95] *Letters*, ed. Russell, I, 239.

[96] *Letters of M. A. to A. H. C.*, p. 97.

[97] *Ibid.*, p. 136.

[98] "Preface to First Edition of Poems (1853)," *Mixed Essays, Irish Essays and Others*, pp. 494–97.

[99] From a letter to his brother Tom, in which Arnold says specifically that the *Preface (1853)* is directed against the "sins and offenses" of these young gentlemen. See Mrs. Humphry Ward, *A Writer's Recollections* (London, 1919), p. 53.

[100] *Letters*, ed. Russell, I, 200.

[101] *Letters of M. A. to A. H. C.*, p. 47.

[102] *Letters*, ed. Russell, II, 191.

[103] "In dieser Begründung und Verankerung einer Kritik der englischen Intelligenz und Geistesrichtung liegt unsres Ermessens der tiefste Wert der Lebensarbeit Matthew Arnolds" (Hermann Levy, "Matthew Arnold und die volkscharakterologische Erkenntnis," *Zeitschrift für Völkerpsychologie und Soziologie*, V [1929], 319).

[104] *Higher Schools and Universities in Germany* (London, 1874), p. 229; E. K. Brown, *Studies in the Text of Matthew Arnold's Prose Works* (Paris, 1935), p. 15.

[105] E. K. Brown, *op. cit.*, p. 15

[106] Quoted by Herbert Spencer, "The Study of Sociology. IX. The Bias of Patriotism," *Contemporary Review*, XXI (March, 1873), 485.

[107] "Matthew Arnold and Insularity," *Edinburgh Review*, CC (July, 1904), 136.

[108] *On England and Other Addresses* (New York, 1926), p. 2.

[109] See p. 24.

[110] "The Study of Sociology. IX. The Bias of Patriotism," *Contemporary view*, XXI (March, 1873), 495.

Footnotes for pages 71–75

[111] "Matthew Arnold and Insularity," *Edinburgh Review*, CC (July, 1904), 138, 139.

[112] *Literature and Dogma* (New York, 1883), p. 190.

[113] For the fullest discussion of the part which the 'imaginative reason' plays in Arnold's scheme, see H. F. Lowry, *Matthew Arnold and the Modern Spirit*, an inaugural lecture delivered at Princeton University, April 15, 1941.

[114] "Mr. Arnold's Essays," *Spectator*, XXXVIII (Feb. 25, 1865), 214; for similar charges, see also *Spectator*, XXXV (March 22, 1862), 328, 329, and *Edinburgh Review*, CXXIX (April, 1869), 251.

[115] B. Oakeshott, "Arnold, Political and Social Critic," *Westminster Review*, CXLIX (Feb., 1898), 161–76. See also Sir Walter Raleigh, *Some Authors* (Oxford, 1923), p. 305.

[116] Robert Knox, *The Races of Men: A Fragment* (London, 1850), pp. 10, 53, 54, 57, and 58.

[117] "The Incompatibles," *Mixed Essays, Irish Essays and Others*, p. 301.

FOOTNOTES TO CHAPTER IV

Footnotes for pages 77–83

[1] *Culture and Anarchy and Friendship's Garland* (New York, 1883), p. 109; *Essays in Criticism, First Series* (London, 1889), p. 49; *On the Study of Celtic Literature* ("Everyman" ed.; London, 1932), p. 78.

[2] *On the Study of Celtic Literature*, p. 94.

[3] *Ibid.*, p. 78. Drawing a distinction in which it is difficult to detect a difference, an anonymous ethnologist says that "in England, you have Teutonic power put into action by Celtic force" ("The Roman and the Celt," *Anthropological Review and Journal* [cited hereafter as *ARJ*], V [1867], 160). According to J. W. Jackson, in the Englishman "the activity and impulsiveness of the Celt are so well controlled by the Teutonic self-command as to eventuate only in a sustained and well-directed energy" ("Ethnology and Phrenology as an Aid to the Historian," *ARJ*, I [1863], 128).

[4] *On the Study of Celtic Literature*, p. 78.

[5] *Culture and Anarchy*, pp. 109, 110.

[6] *Essays in Criticism, First Series*, pp. 50, 51.

[7] *On the Study of Celtic Literature*, pp. 79, 131.

[8] *Essays in Criticism, First Series*, p. 51. In the schedule of the Oxford lectures, "The Literary Influence of Academies" had been advertised (*Times*, May 31, 1864) as "The Influence of Academies on National Spirit and Literature," a title which indicated more clearly the relationship between literature and the national character. See E. K. Brown, *Matthew Arnold* (Chicago, 1948), p. 198.

[9] *Ibid.*, p. 55.

[10] *Ibid.*, pp. 52, 53.

[11] In fact, Arnold contradicts himself, for in the Preface to *Six Selected Lives from Johnson's Lives of the English Poets* (London, 1878), he grants that Dryden, Swift, and Addison had found "the true law of prose," that they wrote in a style essentially modern, a style "plain, direct, intelligible, and serviceable" (*Essays in Criticism, Third Series* [Boston, 1910], pp. 203–209); see also, E. K. Brown, *Matthew Arnold* (Chicago, 1948), pp. 101, and 205.

[12] *Défense de la poésie française à l'usage des lecteurs anglais* (Paris, 1912).

[13] *Matthew Arnold*, pp. 377, 378.

[14] "The French Reputation of Matthew Arnold," *Studies in English by Members of University College Toronto* (Toronto, 1931), pp. 251, 252. In "Matthew Arnold and the Eighteeth Century," *University of Toronto Quarterly*,- IX (1940), 202–13, E. K. Brown treats the subject more fully and sympathetically.

Footnotes for pages 84–90

[15] For all these quotations I am indebted to John Charpentier, "La Poésie Britannique et Baudelaire," *Mercure de France*, CXLVII (No. 3; April, 1921), 290, 291, and 321. Charpentier uses them to support Baudelaire's views.

[16] *Essais de morale et de critique* (Paris, 1929), pp. 344, 345.

[17] H. A. Taine, *History of English Literature*, tr. by H. Van Laun (New York, 1875), I, 74.

[18] John Charpentier, *op. cit.*, pp. 319, 320.

[19] *On the Study of Celtic Literature*, p. 78.

[20] *Ibid.*, pp. 79, 86, 95, 96.

[21] On the ambiguity and confusion of his general use of the word, science—now in the sense of thorough and systematic study, and again, in reference to a particular branch, such as physics or biology, see Fred A. Dudley, "Matthew Arnold and Science," *PMLA*, LVII (March, 1942), 276–286.

[22] "Spinoza and the Bible," *Essays in Criticism, First Series*, p. 333.

[23] *Literature and Dogma* (New York, 1883), "Preface," pp. xxi, xxii.

[24] *Higher Schools and Universities in Germany* (London, 1874), p. viii.

[25] *Culture and Anarchy*, pp. 96, 97.

[26] *Higher Schools and Universities in Germany*, pp. viii-xviii.

[27] *Ibid.*, pp. 165, 166.

[28] *Ibid.*, pp. 212, 216, 217.

[29] See preceding chapter, "The Saxon Philistine."

[30] *On the Study of Celtic Literature*, pp. 87, 103.

[31] "The Literary Influence of Academies," *Essays in Criticism, First Series*, p. 56.

[32] D. Mackintosh, "Comparative Anthropology," *ARJ*, IV (1866), 10; Henry Hudson, "On the Irish Celt," *ARJ*, VIII (1870), 78–81.

[33] "Chartism," *The Works of Thomas Carlyle* (centenary ed.; London, 1899), XXIX, 137, 140.

[34] *English Traits*, (centenary ed.; Boston, 1903), p. 116.

[35] *The Social and Political Ideas of Some Representative Thinkers of the Age of Reaction and Reconstruction, 1815–1865*, ed. F. J. C. Hearnshaw (London, 1932), p. 128.

[36] J. B. Brebner and A. Nevins, *The Making of Modern Britain, A Short History* (New York, 1943), pp. 34, 35.

[37] These are the reasonable explanations given by Ernest Barker, *National Character and the Factors in Its Formation* (2nd ed.; London, 1928), pp. 60, 80.

[38] See, for examples, Wilhelm Dibelius, *England*, tr. by Mary Agnes Hamilton (New York, 1930), p. 166, and Émile Boutmy, *The English People, A Study of their Political Psychology*, tr. by E. English (London, 1904), p. 80.

[39] *Literature and Dogma*, p. 345.

Footnotes for pages 90–97

[40] *Nineteenth Century*, XII (Nov., 1882), 718.

[41] *Culture and Anarchy*, p. 120.

[42] "Numbers," *Discourses in America* (London, 1885), pp. 69, 70.

[43] *Civilization in the United States* (Boston, 1900), pp. 71, 72.

[44] *The Correspondence of Thomas Carlyle and Ralph Waldo Emerson, 1834–1872*, ed. C. E. Norton (Boston, 1886), I, 260.

[45] *Greater Greece and Greater Britain, and George Washington, the Expander of England. Two Lectures with an Appendix* (London, 1886), p. 38.

[46] *Ibid.*, pp. 90, 91. In a speech in the United States in 1883, John Duke Lord Coleridge, Arnold's friend, remarks that "we are one in blood, we are one in language, we are one in law, we are one in hatred of oppression and love of liberty" (*Letters of James Russell Lowell*, ed. C. E. Norton [New York, 1893], II, 68). And another distinguished English lecturer, Frederic William Farrar, stresses the same relationship: "England and America are one in language, one in manner, one in desires and habits and aspirations, one in worship and birth and blood" (*Sermons and Addresses Delivered in America* [New York, 1886], p. 342).

[47] *Emerson's Journals*, ed. E. W. Emerson (Boston, 1909–1914) VIII, 283.

[48] These four are cited by Frank H. Hankins, *The Racial Basis of Civilization* (New York, 1931), pp. 163–165. A rather full analysis of Burgess' work is given, pp. 165–174.

[49] *The American Commonwealth* (1891), II, 725, note.

[50] "We are always saying that at least we are all Anglo-Saxons, when we are descended from Romans, and Normans and Britons and Danes, and they are descended from Irishmen and Italians and Slavs and Germans. . . . We tell a continent crowded with Irishmen to thank God that the Saxon can always rule the Celt" (*What I Saw in America* [London, 1922], p. 143).

[51] "Numbers," *Discourses in America*, pp. 43, 44.

[52] "Renan," *Essays in Criticism, Third Series*, p. 175.

[53] "Numbers," *Discourses in America*, p. 49.

[54] See Jacques Barzun, *The French Race: Theories of its Origins and their Social and Political Implications Prior to the Revolution* (New York, 1932), p. 256.

[55] Quoted by William Curt Buthman in *The Rise of Integral Nationalism in France, with Special Reference to the Ideas and Activities of Charles Maurras* (New York, 1939), p. 155.

[56] See pp. 30–33.

[57] *Memoirs of the Life and Writings of Thomas Carlyle*, ed. Richard Herne Shepherd, assisted by Charles N. Williamson (London, 1881), I, 174.

[58] Thomas Arnold, *Introductory Lectures in Modern History*, ed. Henry Reed (New York, 1842), pp. 44–46.

Footnotes for pages 98–104

[59] *The Passing of the Great Race, or the Racial Basis of European History* (New York, 1916), p. 177.

[60] "Numbers," *Discourses in America*, pp. 69, 70. See also *Matthew Arnold's Notebooks*, with a Preface by the Hon. Mrs. Wodehouse (New York, 1902), p. 120. The passage is taken from one of Thomas Arnold's letters from Germany; see Arthur Penrhyn Stanley, *The Life and Correspondence of Thomas Arnold, D. D.* (Boston, 1860), II, 328.

[61] *On the Study of Celtic Literature*, pp. 128–130.

[62] *Culture and Anarchy*, pp. 20, 21.

[63] "A Liverpool Address," *Nineteenth Century*, XII (Nov., 1882), 720.

[64] *Culture and Anarchy*, p. 21.

[65] *Ibid.*, p. 27.

[66] *A French Eton* (London, 1864), pp. 27, 108, 109.

[67] "Numbers," *Discourses in America*, pp. 69–71.

[68] "Renan," *Essays in Criticism, Third Series*, pp. 166, 167.

[69] *Literature and Dogma*, p. 323.

[70] Lionel Trilling, *Matthew Arnold* (New York, 1939), pp. 344–346. Trilling thinks that the explanation for the obsession with sex must be sought in Arnold's biography.

[71] From a letter to M. Fontanès. See *Letters of Matthew Arnold*, ed. G. W. E. Russell (New York, 1895), II, 105. See also "Numbers," *Discourses in America*, p. 43.

[72] *Letters*, ed. Russell, II, 47, 48.

[73] "Italian Art and Literature Before Giotto and Dante," *Macmillan's Magazine*, XXXIII (Jan., 1876), 228.

[74] *God and the Bible* (New York, 1883), p. 107.

[75] *Hereward the Wake* (New York, 1902), I, 198.

[76] *Two Years Ago* (New York, 1887), p. xv.

[77] *Health and Education* (New York, 1874), p. 379.

[78] *Life and Works of Charles Kingsley* (London, 1901–1903), I, 263.

[79] "Irish Catholicism and British Liberalism," *Mixed Essays, Irish Essays, and Others* (New York, 1883), p. 86.

[80] *Culture and Anarchy*, p. 123.

[81] "Eugénie de Guérin," *Essays in Criticism, First Series*, p. 141.

[82] "Irish Catholicism and British Liberalism," p. 90.

[83] "Eugénie de Guérin," p. 141.

[84] *St. Paul and Protestantism; with an Introduction on Puritanism and the Church of England* (London, 1870), p. 45.

[85] *Ibid.*, p. 48; "The Function of Criticism at the Present Time," *Essays in Criticism, First Series*, p. 35.

[86] *Literature and Dogma* (popular ed.; London, 1897), pp. viii, ix.

Footnotes for pages 104–108

[87] "Numbers," *Discourses in America*, p. 45.

[88] "Renan," *Essays in Criticism, Third Series*, p. 165.

[89] *God and the Bible*, pp. xxviii, xxix.

[90] Isaac Taylor, *The Origin of the Aryans* (New York, n. d.), pp. 143, 144.

[91] *The works of Thomas Carlyle* (centenary ed.; London, 1899), IV, 3; J. A. Froude, *Thomas Carlyle, A History of his Life in London* (New York, 1884), I, 77.

[92] *The Works of Thomas Carlyle* (centenary ed.; London, 1889), XVII, 325.

[93] J. A. Froude, *Thomas Carlyle, A History of the First Forty Years of his Life, 1795–1835* (New York, 1882), I, 201.

[94] *The Letters of Robert Browning and Elizabeth Barrett Browning, 1845–1846* (New York, 1898), II, 276.

[95] *History of the Roman Empire from the Time of Julius Caesar to that of Vitellius*, ed. E. Pococke (London, 1853), pp. 417, 427; *History of the Roman Republic from the Earliest Records till the Time of Scylla*, ed. E. Pococke (London, 1852), p. 4730. *History of the Roman Empire from the Time of Vespasian to the Extinction of the Western Empire*, ed. E. Pococke (London, 1853), p. 96.

[96] *Letters*, ed. Russell, I, 280.

[97] A. P. Stanley, *op. cit.*, II, 360.

[98] A. P. Stanley, *op. cit.*, I, 260.

[99] *The Roman and the Teuton* (London, 1891), p. 2. Even E. A. Freeman, confirmed Teuton that he was, could not stomach this "silly" parable. By these "ignorant" and "frantic" lectures, he thought, Kingsley had won for himself "a sort of privilege." "It is clear that he can never write anything worse, and if he writes anything which is in the least degree better, we are inclined to welcome it perhaps beyond its due." Thus, Kingsley's lectures on the *Ancien Régime* which in another man would be regarded as a sign of lunancy, in Kingsley may be hailed as a symptom of returning sanity. See *The Saturday Review* XXIII (June 22, 1867), 792. Lord Strangford, the philologist, ridiculed Cambridge's practice of "taking an ardent novelist and making a history professor of him. It may be sport for him, but it is death to the undergraduates." See *Original Letters and Papers of the Late Viscount Strangford upon Philological and Kindred Subjects*. Edited by Viscountess Strangford (London, 1878), pp. 185, 186.

[100] *Hypatia* (London, 1927), p. xi.

[101] *The Roman and the Teuton*, p. 19, note.

[102] *The Life and Letters of The Right Honourable Friedrich Max Müller*, edited by his wife (London, 1902), II, 449.

[103] See Dora Neill Raymond, *British Policy and Opinion During the Franco-Prussian War* (New York, 1921), pp. 145, 373.

[104] H. A. Taine, *History of English Literature*, I, 65, 66; II, 5–7.

Footnotes for pages 108–110

[105] *Op. cit.*, II, 277.

[106] *The Non-Religion of the Future: A Sociological Study*, tr. from the French of M. Guyau (New York, 1897), pp. 256–271.

[107] Hamilton Fyfe, "Matthew Arnold and the Fall of France," *Hibbert Journal*, XL (January, 1942), 125–131.

[108] "France. A Reply to Mr. Hamilton Fyfe and Matthew Arnold," *Hibbert Journal*, XL (July, 1942), 355–360.

[109] See Robert H. Lowie, "Morality and Race," *Intellectual and Cultural Achievements of Human Races* in *Scientific Aspects of the Race Problem*, by H. S. Jennings, C. A. Berger, D. T. V. Moore, A. Hrdlicka, R. H. Lowie, O. Klineberg (Washington, D. C., 1941), pp. 233–235.

[110] "Wordsworth," *Essays in Criticism, Second Series* (London, 1888), p. 144.

FOOTNOTES TO CHAPTER V

Footnotes for pages 111–118

[1] "This Oxonian Gallomaniac," as Swinburne calls him. See Clyde K. Hyder, "Swinburne: *Changes of Aspect* and *Short Notes*," *PMLA*, LVIII (March, 1943), 235.

[2] *Letters of Matthew Arnold*, ed. G. W. E. Russell, (New York, 1895), I, 332.

[3] *Ibid.*, p. 328.

[4] *Letters*, ed. Russell, I, 338; *On the Study of Celtic Literature* ("Everyman" ed.; London, 1932), p. 7.

[5] George Saintsbury, *Matthew Arnold* (New York, 1899), p. 107.

[6] Herbert W. Paul, *Matthew Arnold* (New York, 1902), p. 96.

[7] Andrew Lang, "The Celtic Renaissance," *Blackwood's*, CLXI (Feb., 1897), 181–184.

[8] John Munro, *The Story of the British Race* (New York, 1899), p. 223.

[9] Wyndham Lewis, *The Lion and the Fox: the Role of the Hero in the Plays of Shakespeare* (New York, 1927), p. 306.

[10] Roland M. Smith, "The Irish Background of Spenser's *View*," *Journal of English and Germanic Philology*, XLII (Oct. 1943), 499.

[11] Carleton Stanley, *Matthew Arnold* (Toronto, 1938), pp. 137–139.

[12] Lionel Trilling, *Matthew Arnold* (New York, 1939), pp. 232–243.

[13] Stuart P. Sherman, *Matthew Arnold* (New York, 1932), p. 17.

[14] *Letters*, ed. Russell, I, 319.

[15] *Ibid.*, p. 350.

[16] *Ibid.*, p. 367.

[17] *The Study of Celtic Literature*, ed. Alfred Nutt (London, 1910), p. vi.

[18] *Letters*, ed. Russell, I, 329.

[19] *Ibid.*, p. 240.

[20] *Ibid.*, p. 85.

[21] Mrs. Humphry Ward, *A Writer's Recollections* (London, 1918), pp. 40–42.

[22] Justin McCarthy, *A History of Our Own Times* (1879–1880), IV, 277.

[23] *On the Study of Celtic Literature*, pp. 23, 24.

[24] *Letters*, ed. Russell, I, 320.

[25] Thomas Arnold, *History of Rome* (New York, 1866), p. 189.

[26] A. P. Stanley, *The Life and Correspondence of Thomas Arnold* (Boston, 1860), I, 77. In spite of his views on the Irish people, Thomas Arnold thought the English had no right to wrest their country from them. The Irish were to be allowed their own ideas, and their own institutions, including the Catholic church (A. P. Stanley, *op. cit.*, II, 44).

Footnotes for pages 118–121

[27] "Folk-Lore: Myths and Tales of Various Peoples," *London Quarterly Review*, XXXI (1868–69), 48.

[28] *On the Study of Celtic Literature*, p. 24. Lord Lyndhurst, John Singleton Copley, was accused of making the statement in the Parliamentary debates of 1836. He insisted that he did not use the phrase (Sir Theodore Martin, *Lord Lyndhurst* [London, 1883], p. 346).

[29] "Chartism," *The Works of Thomas Carlyle* (centenary ed.; London, 1899), XXIX, 135–144.

[30] Clyde K. Hyder, "Swinburne: *Changes of Aspect* and *Short Notes*," *PMLA*, LVIII (March, 1943) 234, 235. Professor Hyder suggests that Swinburne may have resented Arnold's criticism of Lord Ashburnham for withholding Celtic manuscripts from students, since the third Earl of Ashburnham was Swinburne's grandfather; and the fourth Earl, his uncle.

[31] *Ibid.*, p. 239.

[32] J. A. Froude, *The English in Ireland in the Eighteenth Century*. 3 Vols. (London, 1872–1874), I, 21, 22, 395; II, 127.

[33] *On the Study of Celtic Literature*, pp. 21, 22.

[34] *Letters*, ed. Russell, I, 130.

[35] See pp. 21, 22.

[36] *On the Study of Celtic Literature*, p. 80.

[37] *Letters*, ed. Russell, I, 332. See also, E. K. Brown, *Matthew Arnold* (Chicago, 1948), p. 206, note 74.

[38] Renan believes, and Arnold after him, that the function of a university chair should be not popular instruction but the advancement of science. The occupant should promote original research and bring the university into contact with the intellectual culture of Europe as a whole. Since Arnold's possible dependence on Renan for this section of his lecture has thus far gone undetected, the statements of both men are worth giving in full.

In Renan's opinion, instruction on the highest level should be "sans aucune vue d'application immédiate, sans autre but que la culture désintéressée de l'esprit." One of the chief weaknesses of French higher education is a tendency toward superficiality, a professor's success being judged by the number of students he attracts. In consequence, rhetoric and oratory are the methods relied upon, rather than investigation and research. After showing the desirability of a chair in Celtic, he continues: "Il n'est nullement nécessaire que les chaires du Collége de France représentent le cadre encyclopédique de l'enseignement. Ce qui est essentiel, c'est qu'il représente l'état présent du mouvement scientifique. Le but du Collége de France étant moins de fournir une série complète de cours que de maintenir la grande tradition des recherches de première main, les leçons du professeur, pour un grand nombre d'enseigne-

Footnote Continuation for page 121

ments, ne devraient constituer qu'une partie de ses devoirs. Le Collége de France n'a jamais été plus florissant qu'à l'époque où il n'avait pas de bâtiment à lui, et où chaque professeur réunissait à son domicile les disciples désireux de l'entendre. Il importe en effet d'observer que l'ancien «lecteur royal» était uniquement pensionné pour répandre et perfectionner de la façon qu'il jugeait la meilleure les études qu'il représentait. Le collége n'a commencé à avoir un local que sous Louis XIII." The professor should not be restricted by national boundaries, but should range abroad, if necessary, for his models and examples. "La culture intellectuelle de l'Europe est un vaste échange où chacun donne et reçoit à son tour, où l'écolier d'hier devient le maître d'aujourd'hui. C'est un arbre où chaque branche participe à la vie des autres, où les seuls rameaux inféconds sont ceux qui s'isolent et se privent de la communion avec le tout" (Ernest Renan, "L'Instruction supérieure en France, son histoire et son avenir," *Revue des deux mondes*, LI [May, 1864], 81, 92–95).

Arnold's general argument and his terminology follow Renan's closely; the very illustrations—the College of France, and the *Lecteur Royal*—are the same. "The whole system of our university chairs evidently wants re-casting, and adapting to the needs of modern science. I say, *of modern science*; and it is important to insist on these words. Circumstances at Oxford and Cambridge give special prominence to their function as finishing schools to carry young men of the upper classes of society through a certain limited course of study. But a university is something more and higher than a great finishing school for young gentlemen, however distinguished. A university is a member of a European confraternity for continually enlarging the domain of human knowledge and pushing back in all directions its boundaries. The statutes of the College of France, drawn up at the best moment of the Renaissance and informed with the true spirit of that generous time, admirably fix for a university professor, or representative of the higher studies of Europe, his aim and duty. The *Lecteur Royal* is left with the amplest possible liberty: only one obligation is imposed on him,—to promote and develop to the highest possible pitch the branch of knowledge with which he is charged. In this spirit a university should organize its professorships; in this spirit a professor should use his chair. So that if the Celtic languages are an important object of science, it is no objection to giving them a chair at Oxford or Cambridge, that young men preparing for their degree have no call to study them. The relation of a university chair is with the higher studies of Europe, and not with the young men preparing for their degree. If its occupant has had but five young men at his lectures, or but one young man, or no young man at all, he has done his duty if he has served the higher studies of Europe; or, not to leave out America,

Footnotes for pages 121–126

let us say, the higher studies of the world. If he has not served these, he has not done his duty, though he had at his lectures five hundred young men" (*Cornhill Magazine*, XIV [July, 1866], 127, 128. This entire section on the function of a university chair was suppressed in the book, *On the Study of Celtic Literature*, 1867. The passage is given in full by E. K. Brown, *Studies in the Text of Matthew Arnold's Prose Works* [Paris, 1935], pp. 14–16).

[39] For a detailed account of Arnold's indebtedness see Lewis F. Mott, "Renan and Matthew Arnold," *Modern Language Notes*, XXXIII (1918), 65–73; Joseph W. Angell, "Matthew Arnold's Indebtedness to Renan's 'Essais de morale et de critique,'" *Revue de Littérature Comparée*, XIV (1934), 714–733. Arnold sent a copy of his Celtic lectures to Renan and received in reply a note which gave him great pleasure (*Letters*, ed. Russell, I, 380). One cannot assume, however, that Renan read the work with any care. E. K. Brown, examining presentation copies of Arnold's religious works in the Renan Collection of the Bibliothèque Nationale, found that "neither Renan nor anyone else had cared to cut more than a few pages of any one volume." See E. K. Brown, "The French Reputation of Matthew Arnold," *Studies in English by Members of University College Toronto* (Toronto, 1931), p. 237.

[40] *The Poetry of the Celtic Races, and Other Studies by Ernest Renan* translated, with Introduction and Notes by William G. Hutchison (London, n. d.), p. 4, note 1.

[41] *Selections from the Prose Writings of Matthew Arnold*, ed. Lewis E. Gates (New York, 1897), p. 310, note 88.

[42] *The Poetry of the Celtic Races*, p. 15.

[43] See p. 23.

[44] Henri Martin, *Histoire de France Depuis les Temps les plus Reculés Jusqu'en 1789* (Fourth ed.; Paris, 1855), I, 209.

[45] *On the Study of Celtic Literature*, p. 82, note 1.

[46] *Ibid.*, p. 74.

[47] *Ibid.*, p. 89.

[48] *Ibid.*, p. 89.

[49] Henri Martin, *op. cit.*, p. 1.

[50] *Ibid.*, p. xvii.

[51] *Ibid.*, p. 204, note 1.

[52] *On the Study of Celtic Literature*, p. 15.

[53] Lord Strangford, "Mr. Arnold on Celtic Literature," *Pall Mall Gazette*, No. 346 (March 19, 1866), pp. 3, 4, reprinted in Appendix A in the Everyman edition of *On the Study of Celtic Literature* (London, 1932). See p. 227.

[54] Henri Martin, *op. cit.*, p. 2, note 1. All the existing languages of Europe, with the exception of Basque, Finnic, Magyar, and Turkish, were in the nine-

Footnotes for pages 126–131

teenth century grouped together by some scholars under the term Japhetic, a name which assumed a common descent from Japhet, the son of Noah. See Isaac Taylor *The Origin of the Aryans* (New York, n. d.), pp. 1, 2.

[55] Henri Martin, *op. cit.*, p. 12.

[56] See Isaac Taylor, *op. cil.*, pp. 2, 6, 8.

[57] *Matthew Arnold's Notebooks*, with a Preface by the Hon. Mrs. Wodehouse (New York, 1902), p. 44.

[58] *God and the Bible* (New York, 1883), p. 65; see also, *Literature and Dogma* (New York, 1883), p. 109 for "our Aryan forefathers in the valley of the Oxus."

[59] "Alton Locke," *The Works of Charles Kingsley* (de luxe ed.; Philadelphia, 1898), II, 272, 273.

[60] Frank Edgar Farley, *Scandinavian Influences in the English Romantic Movement* (Boston, 1903), pp. 190–203.

[61] *On Heroes and Hero-Worship and the Heroic in History*, (centenary ed., V; London, 1901), p. 23.

[62] *On the Study of Celtic Literature*, pp. 80, 81.

[63] Henri Martin, *op. cit.*, pp. 4, 32, 33.

[64] See p. 47. An anonymous reviewer ("The Roman and the Celt," *Anthropological Review and Journal* [cited hereafter as ARJ], V (1867), 160) perhaps echoing Arnold, speaks of the Celt in contrast with the Saxon as having more developed organs of respiration, a higher nervous system and therefore more intense cerebral action.

[65] See the *Notebooks*:

La destination de l'homme est d'accroître le sentiment de la joie, de féconder l'énergie expansive, et de combattre, dans tout ce qui sent, le principe de l'avilissement et des douleurs (p. 76).

La gaieté clarifie l'esprit, surtout la gaieté littéraire. L'ennui l'embrouille (p. 108).

Recherchons tout ce qui peut donner de la grâce, de la gaieté, du bonheur dans la vie! (p. 108).

[66] *On the Study of Celtic Literature*, p. 81.

[67] Henri Martin, *op. cit.*, p. 208.

[68] *Ibid.*, p. 36.

[69] *Ibid.*, pp. 32, 33.

[70] For this kinship between the two nations, see "The Incompatibles," *Mixed Essays, Irish Essays and Others* (New York, 1883), p. 282.

[71] *Ibid.*, pp. 323–330.

[72] "Equality," *Mixed Essays, Irish Essays and Others*, p. 48.

[73] *Ibid.*, pp. 50–52, 64, 65.

[74] Robert Knox, *The Races of Men: a Fragment* (London, 1850), p. 40.

Footnotes for pages 131–138

[75] *The Works of Thomas Carlyle* (centenary ed.; London, 1898), III, 42.

[76] *Ibid.*, pp. 109, 110.

[77] R. W. Emerson, *English Traits* (centenery ed., V; Boston, 1903), pp. 105, 106.

[78] *Autobiography of John Stuart Mill*, with a preface by John Jacob Coss, (New York, 1924), pp. 42, 106.

[79] Émile Boutmy, *The English People, a Study of their Political Psychology* tr. E. English (London, 1904), pp. 115, 116.

[80] Hildegard Gauger, *Die Psychologie des Schweigens in England* (Heidelberg, 1937), p. 19.

[81] *Past and Present* (centenary ed., V; London, 1899), p. 158.

[82] Hildegard Gauger, *op. cit.*, p. 1.

[83] *On the Study of Celtic Literature*, p. 81.

[84] Henri Martin, *op. cit.*, pp. 32, 33.

[85] *On the Study of Celtic Literature*, p. 81.

[86] Henri Martin, *op. cit.*, pp. 39, 40.

[87] *On the Study of Celtic Literature*, p. 82.

[88] Henri Martin, *op. cit.*, p. 36.

[89] Alfred Nutt, *the Study of Celtic Literature*, 1910, pp. xxi–xxiii, 85, 86.

[90] *On the Study of Celtic Literature*, pp. 82, 83.

[91] Robert Giffen, "Critical Notes," *Fortnightly Review*, VIII (July, 1867), 126; see also H. S. Fagan, "Notices of Books," *Contemporary Review*, VI (September–December, 1867), 264.

[92] Alfred Nutt, *op. cit.*, p. 87, note.

[93] *Ibid.*, p. 103, note.

[94] From "To a Republican Friend, 1848," first published 1849.

[95] See Arnold's review of Ernest Renan's *Réforme intellectuelle et morale de la France* (1871) in *Every Saturday, New Series*, I (March 23, 1872), 318; *Essays in Criticism, Third Series*, ed. E. J. O'Brien (Boston, 1910), pp. 174, 175. For a fuller account of the decay of the older racial elements, and the emergence in the modern Frenchman of the Gaulish elements, see pp. 94, 95.

[96] "Numbers," *Discourses in America*, (London, 1885), p. 50.

[97] *Letters*, ed. Russell, I, 91.

[98] *Letters*, ed. Russell, II, 305.

[99] *Letters*, ed. Russell, I, 141, 155.

[100] *Letters*, ed. Russell, II, 321, 324. These candid confessions of deficiency in music, and the amusing use of the word *see* are pointed out by H. F. Lowry, *Letters of Matthew Arnold to Arthur Hugh Clough* (London, 1932), p. 25, note 2.

[101] Émile Legouis, *op. cit.* In this connection, however, one should not forget Arnold's glowing, if vague, tribute to Carcassone. "I saw the old *city* of Car-

Footnotes for pages 138–141

cassone. . . .Let everybody see the *cité Carcassone*. It is, indeed, as the antiquarians call it, the Middle Age Herculaneum. When you first get sight of the old city, which is behind the modern town—when you have got clear of the modern town, and come out upon the bridge over the Aude, and see the walled *cité* upon its hill before you—you rub your eyes and think that you are looking at a vignette in *Ivanhoe*" (*A French Eton* [London, 1864], pp. 35, 36).

[102] See pp. 83–85.

[103] *On the Study of Celtic Literature*, pp. 83, 84.

[104] T. H. Huxley, "*The Forefathers and Forerunners of the English People*," *ARJ*, VIII (1870), 197–215. For a discussion of these opinions, see W. B. Babington, *Fallacies of Race Theories* (London, 1895), pp. 245, 246.

[105] James Joyce's Irish patriot gives eloquent expression to this view: "Where are our missing twenty millions of Irish should be here today instead of four, our lost tribes? And our potteries and textiles, the finest in the whole world! And our wool that was sold in Rome in the time of Juvenal and our flax and our damask from the looms of Antrim and our Limerick lace, our tanneries and our white flint glass down there by Ballybough and our Huguenot poplin that we have since Jacquard de Lyon and our woven silk and our Foxford tweeds and ivory raised point from the Carmelite convent in New Ross, nothing like it in the whole wide world! Where are the Greek merchants that came through the pillars of Hercules, the Gibraltar now grabbed by the foe of mankind, with gold and Tyrian purple to sell in Wexford at the fair of Carmen? Read Tacitus and Ptolemy, even Giraldus Cambrensis. Wine, peltries, Connemara marble, silver from Tipperary, second to none, our farfamed horses even today, the Irish hobbies, with king Philip of Spain offering to pay customs duties for the right to fish in our waters. What do the yellowjohns of Anglia owe us for our ruined trade and our ruined hearths?" (*Ulysses* [New York, 1934], p. 320).

[106] *Letters of Matthew Arnold to Arthur Hugh Clough*, ed. H. F. Lowry (London, 1932), p. 78.

[107] "The Zenith of Conservatism," *The Nineteenth Century*, XXI (Jan., 1887), 161.

[108] *On the Study of Celtic Literature*, pp. 84–87.

[109] *The Poetry of the Celtic Races*, p. 7.

[110] For all these statements see H. Martin, *op. cit.*, pp. 88, 89, 93. Similar views on the undisciplinable nature of the Celts are held by Amédée Thierry, *Histoire des Gaulois depuis les temps les plus reculés jusqu'à l'entière soumission de la Gaule à la domination Romaine* (10th ed.; Paris, 1877), p. 4; and J. Michelet, *Histoire de France moyen âge* (éd. définitive, revue et corrigée; Paris, n. d.), I, 102. With both these historians, as has been shown earlier, Arnold was familiar.

Footnotes for pages 141–145

[111] See also Thomas Arnold, *History of Rome*, 3 vols. in one (New York, 1866), p. 189.

[112] John W. Burgess, *Political Science and Comparative Constitutional Law* (Boston, 1890), I, 33.

[113] See E. Snyder, "The Wild Irish," *Modern Philology*, XVII (April, 1920), 147–185. Professor Snyder traces the tradition from the twelfth century to the close of the eighteenth century.

[114] *Alfred Lord Tennyson*: *A Memoir* by his Son (New York, 1897), II, 338.

[115] "From Easter to August," *Nineteenth Century*, XXII (Sept., 1887), 321.

[116] "The Nadir of Liberalism," *Nineteenth Century*, XIX (May, 1886), 655.

[117] "The Incompatibles," *Mixed Essays, Irish Essays and Others*, pp. 281, 282.

[118] *Letters*, ed. Russell, II, 115.

[119] See "Numbers," *Discourses in America*, pp. 43, 44, 49; "Renan," *Essays in Criticism, Thira Series*, pp. 174, 175.

[120] *Letters*, ed. Russell, I, 112. The "next lecture" referred to may be "The Claim of the Celtic Race and the Claim of the Christian Religion To Have Originated Chivalrous Sentiment" which the *Times* (May 29) lists as scheduled for delivery on June 8, 1861 (see E. K. Brown, *Matthew Arnold* [Chicago, 1948], p. 198).

[121] *On the Study of Celtic Literature*, pp. 85, 86.

[122] Ernest Renan, *The Poetry of the Celtic Races, and Other Studies*, pp. 8, 30.

[123] Henri Martin, *op. cit.*, p. xvii; see also p. 81 note.

[124] See for examples, *Yeast* (Everyman's Library, 1912), p. 39; *Alexandria and Her Schools* (London, 1854), p. 140.

[125] *His Letters and Memoirs of His Life* (London, 1901), III, 99.

[126] Émile Boutmy, *op. cit.*, p. 106.

[127] Wilhelm Dibelius, *England*, tr. Mary Agnes Hamilton (New York, 1930), pp. 155, 156.

[128] F. S. Shears, "The Chivalry of France," and H. G. Atkins, "The Chivalry of Germany." In *Chivalry, A Series of Studies to Illustrate its Historical Significance and Civilizing Influence*, by Members of King's College, London, ed. by Edgar Prestage (London, 1928), pp. 57 and 82.

[129] The most famous of all catalogues of the qualities of the Celts is perhaps Mommsen's (see *The History of Rome*, translated by William P. Dickson [New York, 1898], IV, 286, 287). The list closes with a terse summary: "It is, and remains at all times and all places, the same indolent and poetical, irresolute and fervid, inquisitive, credulous, amiable, clever, but, in a political point of view, thoroughly useless nation, and therefore its fate has been always every-

Footnotes for pages 145–149

where the same." W. B. Babington in *Fallacies of Race Theories* devotes an entire chapter (pp. 191–230) to an item by item refutation of Mommsen's charge that these qualities are peculiarly Celtic.

[130] See F. H. Hankins, *The Racial Basis of Civilization* (New York, 1931), p. 148.

[131] *On the Study of Celtic Literature*, p. 6.

[132] *Letters*, ed. Russell, I, 240.

[133] *On the Study of Celtic Literature*, p. 83.

[134] Alfred Nutt, *op. cit.*, pp. xxiv ff.

[135] W. B. Yeats, "The Celtic Element in Literature," *Ideas of Good and Evil* in *Essays* (New York, 1924), pp. 217, 220.

[136] See Frank O'Connor, *The Wild Bird's Nest* (Dublin, 1932), "Preface," p. 1.

[137] Andrew Lang, "The Celtic Renaissance," *Blackwood's* CLXI (Feb., 1897), 183.

[138] The section which follows in the text, dealing with Arnold's conception of Celtic melancholy and the influence of this conception upon the writers of the Celtic Twilight at the close of the nineteenth century, was read in November, 1949, before the Modern Language Club of Northwestern University and in April, 1950, before the Caxton Club of Chicago. I have made no changes in the text as read before these groups though John V. Kelleher in his essay "Matthew Arnold and the Celtic Revival" (*Perspectives of Criticism*, pp. 197–221), which appeared in the summer of 1950, has anticipated a part of my argument. Mr. Kelleher's spirited and informative essay leaves little to be desired in so far as it deals with the Celtic Revival rather than with Arnold. On the after-history of Arnold's Celtic study, on the reception given it by the critics, however, Mr. Kelleher's statements are strangely at variance with the facts, as the numerous citations in this present chapter on the Celts indicate. According to Mr. Kelleher (pp. 197–199), "Arnold's commentary has gone virtually uncontradicted since it was made, in 1866." Again, "apart from a polite footnote of Whitley Stokes's modifying one of Arnold's statements and Alfred Nutt's mild strictures in his critical edition of the essay in 1910, no one seems to have called Arnold to question for anything he said on the subject." To Mr. Kelleher "this long immunity from criticism is one of the strangest things about the essay." The facts are, however, that the essay met with repeated criticism, often enough of the most severe and violent kind, from 1866 on. A large part of Arnold's Introduction to the book is devoted to answering "the inhuman attacks" by the *Times* and the *Daily Telegraph* on "the arrant nonsense" of the studies (*On the Study of Celtic Literature*, p. 7; *Letters*, ed. Russell, I, 338; *Times* [Sept. 8, 1866], p. 8 and [Sept. 14, 1866], p. 6). The *Satur-*

Footnotes for pages 149–155

day Review bluntly stated that Arnold knew nothing of Celtic poetry (*Letters*, ed. Russell, I, 328). Each of the three early reviews of the work (Lord Strangford, "Mr. Matthew Arnold on Celtic Literature," *Pall Mall Gazette*, no. 346 [March 19, 1866], pp. 3, 4; Robert Giffen, "Critical Notes," *Fortnightly Review*, VIII [July, 1867], 126; and H. S. Fagan, "Notices of Books," *Contemporary Review*, VI [Sept.–Dec., 1867], 264) took exception to certain of Arnold's positions. Swinburne made a slashing attack on the central thesis of the book (Clyde, K. Hyder, "Swinburne: *Changes of Aspect* and *Short Notes*," *PMLA*, LVIII [March, 1943], 234, 235]. And, most important of all, at the very height of the Celtic Revival, Andrew Lang reduced to absurdity some of Arnold's main contentions and much of the work of the Celtic Revival itself ("The Celtic Renaissance," *Blackwood's*, CLXI]Feb., 1897], 181 f.). George Saintsbury (*Matthew Arnold*, p. 107) and Herbert W. Paul (*Matthew Arnold*, p. 96) pointed out flaws. And in the nineteen twenties two vigorous refutations of Arnold's leading ideas were published (E. D. Snyder, *The Celtic Revival in English Literature, 1760–1800* [Cambridge, Mass., 1923], pp. 89 f.; Wyndham Lewis, *The Lion and the Fox: the Role of the Hero in the Plays of Shakespeare*]New York, 1927], pp. 306 f.).

[139] J. S. Smart, *James Macpherson: An Episode in Literature* (London, 1905), pp. 26–29.

[140] Alfred Nutt, *op. cit.*, pp. xxi ff., 1, 90.

[141] E. D. Snyder, *The Celtic Revival in English Literature, 1760–1800* (Cambridge, Mass., 1923), pp. 89 f.

[142] *Jealous of Dead Leaves* (New York, 1928).

[143] W. B. Yeats, *Autobiographies* (London, 1926), p. 262.

[144] Dora M. Jones, "The Celtic Twilight," *London Quarterly Review*, XCIV (1900), 61.

[145] W. B. Yeats, "The Celtic Element in Literature," *Ideas of Good and Evil* in *Essays* (New York, 1924), pp. 213–231.

[146] Andrew Lang, "The Celtic Renaissance," *Blackwood's*, CLXI (February, 1897), 181–192.

[147] Dora M. Jones, *op. cit.*, p. 61; *On the Study of Celtic Literature*, p. 117.

[148] Fiona Macleod, "A Group of Celtic Writers," *Fortnightly Review*, LXXI (Jan., 1899), 36.

[149] *The Strayed Reveller, Empedocles on Etna, and Other Poems, by Matthew Arnold*, ed. William Sharp (London, 1896), pp. xiii f.

[150] *The Poems of Ossian*, ed. William Sharp (Edinburgh, 1896), pp. xlvii–li; see also the Introduction to *Lyra Celtica*, ed. E. A. Sharp and J. Matthay, with Introduction and Notes by William Sharp (Edinburgh, 1926). Further indication of Arnold's influence is shown in "The Celtic Renaissance, Ossian,

Footnotes for pages 155–157

Matthew Arnold, the Ancient Celtic Writers," a lecture which William Sharp prepared but because of a heart attack was unable to deliver (Elizabeth A. Sharp, *William Sharp: A Memoir* [New York, 1910], p. 256].

[151] "The Divine Adventure—Iona—Studies in Spiritual History," *The Writings of Fiona Macleod*, arranged by Mrs. William Sharp (Uniform ed.; New York, 1909–10), IV, 246. See also *Lyra Celtica*, p. li.

[152] "The Sin-Eater—The Washer of the Ford and Other Legendary Moralities," *op. cit.*, III, 14.

[153] *Ibid.*, p. 5.

[154] "The Divine Adventure—Iona—Studies in Spiritual History," p. 371.

[155] "The Dominion of Dreams—Under the Dark Star," *op. cit.*, II, 165.

[156] Fiona Macleod, "A Group of Celtic Writers," *Fortnightly Review*, LXXI (January, 1899), 36. The ethnologist, Hector MacLean, also believes that the dolichocephalic Celt is "disposed to melancholy from a strong love of that which is past and gone" ("On Comparative Anthropology of Scotland," *ARJ*, IV (1866), 210–216). The idea is a fixed one, also, with George Meredith, for whose views on the matter, the following passage is representative: "Now, to the Cymry, and to the pure Kelt, the past is at their elbows continually. The past of their lives has lost neither face nor voice behind the shroud; nor are the passions of the flesh, nor is the animate soul, wanting to it. Other races forfeit infancy, forfeit youth and manhood with their progression to wisdom age may bestow. These have each stage always alive, quick at a word, a scent, a sound, to conjure up scenes, in spirit and in flame. Historically, they still march with Cadwallader, with Llewellyn, with Glendower; sing with Aneurin, Taliesin, old Llywarch; individually, they are in the heart of the injury done them thirty years back or thrilling to the glorious deed which strikes an empty buckler for most of the sons of time. An old sea rises in them, rolling no phantom billows to break to spray against existing rocks of the shore. That is why, and even if they have a dose of the Teuton in them, they have often to feel themselves exiles when still in amicable community among preponderating Saxon English" ("The Amazing Marriage," *The Works of George Meredith* [memorial ed.; New York, 1909–1912], XIX, 296).

[157] *All Ireland Review*, I (No. 32; August 11, 1900), 6.

[158] "Recent Celtic Experiments in English Literature," *Blackwood's*, CLIX (May, 1896), 729.

[159] *Co-operation and Nationality* (Dublin, 1912), p. 83.

[160] *The National Being* (New York, 1937), p. 13. The first edition of this book appeared in 1916.

[161] *Letters to the New Island*, ed. H. Reynolds (Cambridge, Mass., 1934, rptd. from *Boston Pilot* and *Providence Journal*, 1889–91,) p. 130.

Footnotes for pages 158–160

[162] *Some Irish Essays* (Dublin, 1906), pp. 14 f.

[163] See the essay of 1912, "The Poetry of James Stephens," in *Imaginations and Reveries* (Dublin, n. d.), p. 34.

[164] Hesketh Pearson, *G. B. S. A Full-Length Portrait* (New York, 1942), p. 208 f. Shaw's fullest treatment of the problem occurs in *John Bull's Other Island* in which the central theme is a contrast between Larry Doyle, an Irishman, and his business partner, Tom Broadbent, an Englishman. Accused by Broadbent of possessing the melancholy of the Celtic race, Doyle savagely replies that there is no Irish race just as there is no English race and no Yankee race. There is, however, an Irish climate which produces an indelible effect upon all inhabitants of the island. And Doyle runs off into a rhapsody on the "soft, moist air," the "white, springy roads," the "misty rushes and brown bogs" of Ireland; on the "colors in the sky," the "lure of the distances," and the "sadness in the evenings." It is these, he says, that cause the passionate dreaming of the Irishman. In Doyle's opinion, all talk about the Celtic race is nonsense. To anyone familiar with conditions in Ireland, he believes, it should be apparent that a man would not have to be a Celt to feel melancholy in Rosscullen. See *John Bull's Other Island* (New York, 1916), pp. xi, 17–19.

[165] Wilhelm Dibelius, *England*, p. 155; the original German edition appeared in 1922; Ernest Barker, *National Character and the Factors in Its Formations* (Second ed.; London, 1928), p. 34; D. H. Lawrence, *The Plumed Serpent* (London, 1932), pp. 443 f.; the passage is cited by W. Y. Tindall, *D. H. Lawrence and Susan his Cow* (New York, 1939), p. 145.

[166] "Ethnology and Phrenology," *ARJ*, I (1863), 126.

[167] J. W. Jackson, "Ethnology and Phrenology As an Aid to the Biographer," *ARJ*, II (1864), 133; and "Ethnology and Phrenology As an Aid to the Historian," *ARJ*, I (1863), 132 f.

[168] Hector MacLean, "Race in History," *ARJ*, V (1867), 132.

[169] John Munro, *The Story of the British Race* (New York, 1899), p. 135.

FOOTNOTES TO CHAPTER VI

Footnotes for pages 162–164

[1] J. Michelet, *The History of France*, tr. G. H. Smith, (New York, 1880), I, 65.

[2] *Original Letters and Papers of the Late Viscount Strangford Upon Philological and Kindred Subjects*, ed. Viscountess Strangford (London, 1878), pp. 228, 229.

[3] *On the Study of Celtic Literature* ("Everyman" ed.; London, 1932), p. 26.

[4] *A French Eton* (London, 1864), p. 99.

[5] *On the Study of Celtic Literature*, pp. 25, 26. In the passage cited, Arnold says simply that he had read that von Humboldt held these opinions. His authority is the French critic Challemel-Lacour, as is revealed a decade later: "Challemel-Lacour is, or was, one of the best, gravest, most deeply interesting and instructive of French writers. His admirable series of articles on Wilhelm von Humboldt, which I read a good many years ago in the *Revue des Deux Mondes*, still live as fresh in my memory as if I had read them yesterday" (*Last Essays on Church and Religion* [London, 1877], p. ix). It is from the following paragraph that Arnold draws his extracts: "La langue que, dans cet ordre d'idées et de sentiments, Humboldt parlait le plus volontiers, était celle du paganisme et des livres religieux de l'Inde. L'effort de la Grèce pour tout intellectualiser, pour absorber l'art dans la morale, la religion, l'État, la vie privée et la nature, lui semblait une œuvre divine par excellence. Le beau avait, à un haut degré, la puissance d'élever sa pensée audessus de la réalité passagère et incomplète; et qu'est-ce que la religion, même la plus haute, sinon le détachement du fini? Les livres de l'Inde le séduisaient par une raison toute semblable. Il était trop bon paien pour approuver l'excessif dédain de la terre que ces livres inspirèrent; il était éloigné de tout écart mystique, et gardait, jusque dans ses dispositions les plus métaphysiques, un certain scepticisme de bon aloi. Mais s'il n'avait pas pour l'Inde l'admiration démesurée de plusieurs de ses contemporains; s'il avait soin d'en denoncer les extravagances poétiques et religieuses, il était cependant indulgent pour elle: il aimait dans sa langue sacrée ce mélange de méditation et de sentiment poétique qui tourne l'âme vers l'absolu, l'attache à la pensée et au monde intellectuel, la délivre du monde terrestre de l'action. Mais il avait bien moins de goût, ou plutôt il sentait comme une vague répulsion pour le sémitisme; cette précision sèche et matérielle dans les dogmes, cet esprit qui, avec des expressions poétiques, est incapable de tout vraie poésie, cette religion terroriste qui traite l'homme à coups de verges et plonge sa nature dans le néant, lui étaient au fond antipathiques" (P, Challemel-

Footnotes for pages 164–169

Lacour, *La Philosophie Individualiste, Étude sur Guillaume de Humboldt* [Paris, 1864], pp. 190–192). Arnold's memory evidently was not as reliable as he thought it to be, for Challemel-Lacour says explicitly (*ibid.*, p. iii) that the work appeared first as articles in the *Revue germanique et française.*

[6] *Letters of Matthew Arnold*, ed. G. W. E. Russell (New York, 1895), I, 381.

[7] Richard B. Brandt, *The Philosophy of Schleiermacher, the Development of His Theory of Scientific and Religious Knowledge* (New York, 1941), pp. 34, 83, 84, and 94.

[8] C. C. J. Bunsen, *God in History, or the Progress of Man's Faith in the Moral Order of the World*, tr. Susanna Winkworth (London, 1868), I, 210, 211.

[9] *Ibid.*, p. x. In a letter to his mother, June 13, 1868, Arnold wrote, "I shall read every word of Bunsen some time that I am quiet at Fox How" (*Letters*, ed. Russell, I, 392).

[10] A. P. Stanley, *The Life and Correspondence of Thomas Arnold* (Boston, 1860), I, 344, 345.

[11] C. C. J. Bunsen, *op. cit.*, I, 210, 211.

[12] Thomas Arnold, *Sermons* (5th ed.; London, 1851), II, 180; (3rd ed.; London, 1845), III, 251 ff. See also, A. P. Stanley, *op. cit.*, I, 315, 316.

[13] A. P. Stanley, *op. cit.*, I, 359. Arnold credited his father with an awareness of the influence of Hellenism on Christianity, although he realized that his father would not have given Hellenism the prominence which he himself gave it (*Letters*, ed. Russell, I, 392).

[14] Ludwig Feuerbach, *The Essence of Christianity*, tr. from 2nd German ed., Marian Evans (2nd ed.; London, 1893), pp. 65–73, 151, 197 ff., 204 ff., 213 ff., 232 ff., 236 ff., 247 ff.

[15] *Essays in Criticism, First Series* (London, 1889), p. 226. Arnold makes no reference to Gobineau's best known work, *The Inequality of Human Races.* It is his *The Religions and Philosophies of Central Asia* (Paris, 1865) that serves as a text for Arnold's "A Persian Passion Play."

[16] Arthur de Gobineau, *The Inequality of Human Races*, tr. Adrian Collins (New York, 1915), pp. 122, 206–208. See also Frank H. Hankins, *The Racial Basis of Civilization, a Critique of the Nordic Doctrine* (New York, 1931), p. 82; Jacques Barzun, *Race, a Study in Modern Superstition* (New York, 1937), p. 78.

[17] "Le livre sacré est admirable; mais rien de plus sot que le commentaire du livre sacré" (Henri Tronchon, *Ernest Renan et L'Étranger* [Paris, 1928], p. 151).

[18] *Studies in Religious History* (London, 1893), pp. 59, 60.

[19] Henri Tronchon, *op. cit.*, 128–130.

[20] Ernest Renan, "The Religions of Antiquity," *Studies of Religious History*

Footnotes for pages 169–174

(London, 1893), pp. 47, 62, and 71. L. F. Mott, *Ernest Renan* (New York, 1921), p. 219.

[21] Ernest Renan, *De l'origine du langage* (6th ed.; Paris, 1883), pp. 190–193. Henri Tronchon, *op. cit.*, p. 133.

[22] Ernest Renan, *Vie de Jesus* (33rd ed.; Paris, n. d.), p. 140; *Saint Paul* (16th ed.; Paris, n. d.), p. 172.

[23] Ernest Renan, "The Critical Historians of Jesus," *Studies of Religious History*, pp. 115, 116. Henri Tronchon, *op. cit.*, p. 107.

[24] Ernest Renan, *The Future of Science* (Boston, 1893), p. 269; *Saint Paul*, p. 16.

[25] Ernest Renan, *The Future of Science*, p. 480, note 124.

[26] Ernest Renan, *Vie de Jesus*, pp. 471, 472. L. F. Mott, *op. cit.*, p. 220.

[27] *Revue des deux mondes*, LIV (1864), 521 ff., 989 ff.; LXXIV (1868), 995 ff.; LXXVI (1868), 864 ff.; LXXVII (1868), 679 ff.; LXXXII (1869), 85 ff.

[28] Émile Burnouf, *The Science of Religions*, tr. Julie Liebe (London, 1888), pp. 190, 191. See *Literature and Dogma* (London, 1883), pp. 106–109.

[29] Émile Burnouf, *op. cit.*, p. 192.

[30] Ernest Renan, *Vie de Jesus* (33rd ed.; Paris, n. d.), pp. 66, 67.

[31] Émile Burnouf, *op. cit.*, p. 196.

[32] *Culture and Anarchy and Friendship's Garland* (London, 1883), pp. 124, 125.

[33] Ernest Renan, "Channing and the Unitarian Movement in the United States," *Studies of Religious History*, p. 252. Henri Tronchon, *op. cit.*, pp. 317, 318. The English themselves, as Arnold was aware, had noted the similarity between the Puritans and the Jews of the Old Testament (*Literature and Dogma* [1883], p. 87).

[34] H. Taine, *History of English Literature*, tr. H. Van Laun, (New York, 1875), I, 52.

[35] Émile Boutmy, *The English People, a Study of their Political Psychology*, tr. E. English (London, 1904), p. 34, note 1.

[36] *On the Study of Celtic Literature*, p. 25.

[37] *Letters*, ed. Russell, I, 373.

[38] *Culture and Anarchy*, p. 111. The terms *Hebraism* and *Hellenism* Arnold probably took over from Heine's *Über Ludwig Börne* (Hamburg, 1840), pp. 27, 28. "Jewish and Christian are with me entirely synonymous terms, as contrasted with the word Hellenic, with which word I signify no definite people, but a certain direction of spirit and manner of intuition, the result of birth as well as of education. In this relation I may say all men are either Jews or Hellenes, men with tendencies to asceticism, hatred of the plastic and excessive spiritualisation, or men with natures of cheerful views of life, endowed with pride in development,

Footnotes for pages 174–177

and love of realities" (William Stigand, *The Life, Work and Opinions of Heinrich Heine* [London, 1875], II, 126). Or, again, in *The Gods in Exile*: "The question was whether the gloomy, gaunt, anti-sensual, over-spiritual Judaism of the Nazarenes should rule the world, or Hellenic gaiety, love of beauty, and thriving zest for life" (Heinrich Heine, *Works of Prose*, ed. Hermann Kesten, tr. E. B. Ashton [New York, 1943], p. 130). On a different basis, Moses Hess in 1862 contrasted the two races. According to his conception, society was made up of organs or races, each with its own peculiar function, in the performance of which each race realized its purpose in the world. Thus, the Greeks represented multiplicity; the Hebrews represented unity. For the former, life was an eternal *being*; for the latter life was an eternal *becoming*. The Greeks were concerned with the space dimension, and were therefore interested in nature and the plastic arts; the Hebrews were concerned with the time dimension, and were therefore interested in historical development, in ethics, and the harmonizing of social forces (Moses Hess, *Rome and Jerusalem, a Study in Jewish Nationalism*, tr. Meyer Waxman [2nd ed.; New York, 1943], pp. 30, 183–185).

[39] *Culture and Anarchy*, pp. 110, 122. "Heinrich Heine," *Essays in Criticism, First Series*, pp. 185, 186.

[40] "On the Modern Element in Literature," *Essays in Criticism , Third Series*, collected by E. J. O'Brien (Boston, 1910), pp. 35–38.

[41] "Our Liberal Practitioners," *Culture and Anarchy*, pp. 175, 176.

[42] H. Tronchon, *op. cit.*, p. 127.

[43] "1. Talmud Babylonicum. Venice, 1520–23. Folio. 12 vols.; 2. Talmud Hierosolymitanum. Venice (1523). Folio. 1 vol.," *Quarterly Review*, CXXIII (Oct., 1867), 417–464. Arnold read the essay (*Letters*, ed. Russell, I, 373), and later met the author: "I met Mr. Deutsch the other day, and had a long talk with him about Hebraism and Hellenism. I was greatly interested in seeing him, and any diffidence I felt in talking about my crude speculations to such a *savant* was set at rest by his telling me that he was distinctly conscious, while writing his article on the Talmud, that if it had not been for what I had done he could not have written that article in the *Quarterly*, and the British public could not have read it. I have had no such tribute to my powers of relaxing and dissolving yet paid" (*Letters*, ed. Russell, I, 395). The article on the Talmud was published almost a year before "Hebraism and Hellenism," but Arnold had written earlier on the contrast between the two disciplines in "Heinrich Heine" (1863), "A Word More About Spinoza" (1863), and "On the Study of Celtic Literature," which appeared in the *Cornhill Magazine* (1866).

[44] *On the Study of Celtic Literature*, p. 114. See also, *Literature and Dogma*, p. 349.

Footnotes for pages 177–182

[45] *On the Study of Celtic Literature*, pp. 114, 115.

[46] Lionel Trilling, *Matthew Arnold* (New York, 1939), p. 194.

[47] H. F. Lowry, *Matthew Arnold and the Modern Spirit* (Princeton, N. J., 1941), p. 9.

[48] *Saint Paul and Protestantism* (London, 1870), pp. 92, 93.

[49] H. Tronchon, *op. cit.*, pp. 107, 108.

[50] "On the Modern Element in Literature," *Essays in Criticism, Third Series*, pp. 45, 46; *Life of Pope* in *Works of Samuel Johnson, LL.D.* (Oxford, 1825), VIII, 324. Arnold may have derived his concept of the "imaginative reason" from Johnson in whose works genius is often defined as a fusion of reason and imagination (See J. H. Hagstrum, "The Nature of Dr. Johnson's Rationalism," *Journal of English Literary History*, XVII [Sept., 1950], 202–204).

[51] "Pagan and Mediæval Religious Sentiment," *Essays in Criticism, First Series*, pp. 221, 222.

[52] *Essays in Criticism, Second Series* (London, 1888), pp. 1, 2.

[53] *Literature and Dogma*, p. xiii.

[54] *Ibid.*, pp. 108, 109.

[55] *Ibid.*, p. 293.

[56] *Ibid.*, p. 51. Ernest Renan, *Studies of Religious History*, pp. 47, 62, 71.

[57] "But long before the first beginnings of recorded history, long before the oldest word of Bible literature, these ideas must have been at work. . . .In Israel's earliest history and earliest utterances, under the name of Eloah, Elohim, *The Mighty*, there may have lain and matured, there did lie and mature, ideas of God more as a moral power, more as a power connected, above everything, with conduct and righteousness, than were entertained by other races" (*Literature and Dogma*, p. 28). See also, *ibid.*, p. 73.

[58] *Ibid.*, pp. 32, 33, 320–324. *Culture and Anarchy*, p. 119.

[59] *Literature and Dogma*, p. 297. Renan also was struck by the absence of sex in the Semitic conception of God and remarked that the feminine of the word "God" in Hebrew would be the strangest of barbarisms. See *The Future of Science*, p. 250.

[60] "Amateur Theology: Arnold's *Literature and Dogma*, a Review," *Blackwood's*, CXIII (June, 1873) 678–692.

[61] "Religion in the Hands of Literary Laymen," *The Theological Review*, X (July, 1873), 377–405.

[62] "*Literature and Dogma*, a Review," *The London Quarterly Review*, XL (July, 1873), 399.

[63] *God and the Bible, a Review of Objections to "Literature and Dogma"* (New York, 1883), pp. 3, 4.

Footnotes for pages 183–185

[64] *The Lutheran Quarterly*, III (Oct., 1873), 550 ff.; *Old and New*, VIII (Oct., 1873), 501. *The Dublin Review*, *New Series* XX (April, 1873), 365; *Athenaeum*, No. 2511 (Dec. 11, 1875), p. 781; *Blackwood's*, CXIII (June, 1873), 686.

[65] "*Literature and Dogma*, a Review," *The Dublin Review*, New Series, XX (April, 1873), 365.

[66] *God and the Bible*, p. 121.

[67] "The Bible as Interpreted by Mr. Arnold," *The Westminster Review*, CI (April, 1874), 150.

[68] *God and the Bible*, p. 126. *Literature and Dogma*, p. 15.

[69] *The Quarterly Review*, CXXXVII (Oct., 1874), 397; *God and the Bible*, p. 124.

[70] *God and the Bible*, pp. 102, 127, 128.

[71] *Ibid.*, pp. 131, 132.

[72] A. Réville, "*God and the Bible*, a Review," *The Academy*, VIII (Dec. 18, 1875), 618.

[73] *Extracts from the Letters and Journals of William Johnson Cory*, p. 532. Quoted by Lionel Trilling, *Matthew Arnold* (New York, 1939), p. 337.

[74] "*Literature and Dogma*, a Review," *London Quarterly Review*, XL (July, 1873), 399.

[75] F. W. Newman, "*Literature and Dogma*, a Review," *Frazer's Magazine*, *New Series*, VIII (July, 1873), 115; Edith Simcox, "Critical Notices," *Fortnightly Review*, *New Series*, XIII (April, 1873), 543.

FOOTNOTES TO CHAPTER VII

Footnotes for pages 186–189

[1] "Equality," *Mixed Essays, Irish Essays and Others* (New York, 1883), p. 48.

[2] Ernest Barker, *National Character and the Factors in Its Formation* (2nd. ed.; London, 1928), p. 270.

[3] For a thorough treatment of this subject, see Professor Z. S. Fink's unpublished doctoral dissertation, *Anti-Foreign Sentiment in Tudor and Early Stuart Literature* (Northwestern University, 1931).

[4] See E. K. Brown, "The French Reputation of Matthew Arnold," *Studies in English by Members of University College Toronto* (Toronto, 1931), p. 243.

[5] *On the Study of Celtic Literature* ("Everyman" ed.; London, 1932), p. 70.

[6] "Matthew Arnold and Insularity," *Edinburgh Review*, CC (July, 1904), 132.

[7] "Doing as One Likes," *Culture and Anarchy and Friendship's Garland* (New York, 1883), p. 63.

INDEX

NORTHWESTERN UNIVERSITY

The Graduate School

1951

From time to time, The Graduate School of Northwestern Univerity authorizes through the Editorial Board of *Northwestern University Studies* the publication of monographs in various fields of learning. A list of these publications appears below. Orders and inquiries are to be addressed to The Graduate School, Northwestern University, Evanston, Illinois.

Northwestern University Studies in the Humanities

No. 1. *Tales from the French Folk Lore of Missouri*, by Joseph Médard Carrière $4.00

No. 2. *Kant's Pre-Critical Ethics*, by Paul Arthur Schilpp $2.50

No. 3. *Luise Hensel als Dichterin*, by Frank Spiecker $1.50

No. 4. *The Labors of the Months in Antique and Mediaeval Art*, by James Carson Webster (Out of print)

No. 5. *Forgotten Danteiana*, by J. G. Fucilla (Out of print)

No. 6. *Speech Development of a Bilingual Child, Volume I*, by Werner F. Leopold (Out of print)

No. 7. *L'Histoire de Gille de Chyn*, edited by Edwin B. Place $2.50

No. 8. *The Aesthetic Process*, by Bertram Morris $2.25

No. 9. *The Classical Republicans*, by Zera S. Fink $4.00

No. 10. *An Historical and Analytical Bibliography of the Literature of Cryptology*, by Joseph S. Galland $5.00

No. 11. *Speech Development of a Bilingual Child, Volume II*, by Werner F. Leopold $5.50

No. 12. *Writings of John Stuart Mill*, by Ney MacMinn and others $2.50

No. 13. *Political Forgiveness in Old Athens*, by Alfred P. Dorjahn $2.50

No. 14. *Education for Journalism in the United States from Its Beginning to 1940*, by Albert Alton Sutton $2.00

No. 15. *Analytical Syllogistics*, by Delton Thomas Howard $4.00

No. 16. *Fair Rosamond*, by Virgil B. Heltzel $3.00

No. 17. *The Nonsense of Common Sense* (Lady Mary Wortley Montagu), edited by Robert Halsband $3.00

No. 18. *Speech Development of a Bilingual Child, Volume III*, by Werner F. Leopold $5.00

No. 19. *Speech Development of a Bilingual Child, Volume IV*, by Werner F. Leopold $5.00

No. 20. *Critical Prefaces of the French Renaissance*, by Bernard Weinberg $5.00

No. 21. *A Critical Bibliography of the Published Writings of Romain Rolland*, by William Thomas Starr $3.50

No. 22. *Le Panorama Littéraire de l'Europe* (1833-1834), by Thomas R. Palfrey $3.00

No. 23. *Juan de Segura: Processo de Cartas de Amores*, edited with introduction, translation, and commentary by Edwin B. Place $3.00

No. 24. *The Poems of Aimeric de Peguilhan*, edited and translated with introduction and commentary by William P. Shepard and Frank M. Chambers $4.50

No. 25. *Thackeray: The Sentimental Cynic*, by Lambert Ennis $5.00

No. 26. *William Warner's Syrinx, or A Sevenfold History*, edited with introduction and notes by Wallace A. Bacon $5.00

No. 27. *Matthew Arnold: The Ethnologist*, by Frederic E. Faverty $5.00

Northwestern University Studies in the Social Sciences

No. 1. *Predicting Criminality*, by Feris F. Laune $1.50

No. 2. *Shamanism in Western North America*, by Willard Z. Park (Out of print)

No. 3. *Seventy Years of Real Estate Subdividing in the Region of Chicago*, by Helen Corbin Monchow (Out of print)

No. 4. *The First Scientific Exploration of Russian America and the Purchase of Alaska*, by James Alton James $2.00

No. 5. *Compulsory Health Insurance in the United States*, by Herbert D. Simpson (Out of print)

No. 6. *The Neapolitan Revolution: 1820-1821*, by George T. Romani $4.00

Northwestern University Studies in Mathematics and the Physical Sciences

No. 1. *Mathematical Monographs*, by D. R. Curtiss, H. T. Davis, H. L. Garabedian, H. S. Wall, E. D. Hellinger $2.25

No. 2. *A Catalog of Illinois Algae*, by Max E. Britton $3.00

Northwestern University Studies in the Biological Sciences and Medicine

No. 1. *A Study in Neotropical Pselaphidæ*, by Orlando Park $7.50

Not in series

Galileo, Two New Sciences, translated by Henry Crew and Alfonso de Salvio $3.50

Remittances should be made payable to Northwestern University, and should be sent with orders to The Graduate School, Northwestern University, Evanston, Illinois

Prices include postage